Vision and Verse in William Blake

ALICIA OSTRIKER

Vision and Verse in William Blake

MADISON AND MILWAUKEE

THE UNIVERSITY OF WISCONSIN PRESS

1965

Published by
The University of Wisconsin Press
Madison and Milwaukee
P. O. Box 1379, Madison, Wisconsin 53701

Printed in
the United States of America
by Kingsport Press, Inc.
Kingsport, Tennessee

Library of Congress Catalog
Card Number 65–16363

I know my Execution is not like Any Body Else. I do not intend it should be so; none but Blockheads Copy one another. My Conception & Invention are on all hands allow'd to be Superior. My Execution will be found so too.

BLAKE, *Public Address*

You tell me I am wrong.
Who are you, who is anybody to tell me I am wrong?
I am not wrong.

D. H. LAWRENCE

Preface

If you write about Blake, you cannot expect to please everyone. If you write about metrics, you cannot expect to please anyone. Since I am laboring under both these handicaps, I should warn the reader of my prejudices.

I am interested in Blake the poet. Herbert Read wrote: "The poetry of William Blake descended on me like an apocalypse. . . . there is no poet with whom to-day I would more readily identify the poetic essence. For me, Blake is absolute. Shakespeare is richer, Milton is more sonorous, Hopkins is more sensuous . . . but Blake has no need of qualifying epithets: he is simply poetic, in imagination and in expression." What does this mean analytically? By studying Blake's technique, concentrating on the connection between "imagination" and "expression," I have tried to understand what his "poetic essence" was, and by what laws it developed.

I am interested in prosody for what it can show about poetry. The approach is pragmatic rather than scientific; but the status of prosody as a science is in any case questionable, since no full consensus on a body of prosodic rules, either prescriptive or descriptive, has ever prevailed for more than a small group of writers or a short time in the history of English letters. Only a few general principles seem to apply: I assume that the structural basis of verse is the sense of regular recurrence in time; that in English this recurrence is usually one of "accent"; that by an "accented syllable" we mean a syllable which if spoken would be distinguished from those surrounding it by volume or pitch or both. ("Length," except for some sixteenth-century experiments, has been a decorative rather than a structural element in English verse. Number of syllables per line, however, was structurally important in the verse against which Blake rebelled, and shall be considered as such.) Beyond these points, whatever system will yield most information about a particular poet or movement is the system to use in analysis. The one I use for Blake is basically Saintsbury's foot-scansion, which although it is not a perfect system, or absolute for everyone's poetry, does adequately represent the verse Blake began with, and from which he ultimately deviated; it has the intrinsic merit of being flexible and inclusive; and it is the most familiar form of metrical analysis today.

I have modified Saintsbury's terminology on a few points. First, I distinguish between the *meter* of a poem and its *rhythm.* By meter I mean that abstract pattern of feet which comes closest to fitting how the poem would sound as prose. By rhythm I mean the way it actually does sound to me: always a compromise between the way I would speak the words if I followed the meter precisely, and the way I would speak them if they were prose. The readings I mark are, unless otherwise noted, those of the rhythm. Thus the following lines are rhythmically different, although all are, metrically, iambic pentameters:

> The labour of an age in piled stones.
>
> And never lifted up a single stone.
>
> Howl, howl, howl, howl! O, you are men of stones.

When I say that a poem or a line is iambic, trochaic, or whatever, I mean that it is predominantly so. In ambiguous cases I use my judgment, taking into consideration both the line's own sound, and its context.

Finally, throughout most of this book I note only two degrees of accent. This of course does not reproduce the actual intonations of speech, but no notation can do that. One must choose between a normative, minimal notation with its drawback of crudity, and a more refined one with its danger of idiosyncrasy, and I have chosen the minimal. On the few occasions where a finer notation seems enlightening, I employ the signs of the structural linguists, ó, ô, ò, ŏ, respectively denoting primary, secondary, tertiary, and no stress. *I do not intend these to represent some new or separate system, but only a finer calibration of the old.*

Besides Saintsbury's work, the books which have taught me most about the nature of rhythm and meter are the classic studies of prose rhythm by William M. Patterson, André Classe, and Paull Franklin Baum; the studies of meter in Baum's *Principles of English Versification* and Henry Lanz' *The Physical Basis of Rime;* and Paul Fussell's work on the meaning of eighteenth century prosody. Among studies of Blake's metrics, Damon's chapter in *William Blake: His Philosophy and Symbols* was invaluable, as was his whole book.

The main text of Blake followed here was Keynes' 1957 one-volume edition of the *Complete Writings,* to which page, plate, and line citations refer. To reproduce Blake's own punctuation of his poetry, however, I took the engraved copies of books available in the Morgan Library, the New York Public Library, the Fitzwilliam Museum, and the British Museum; the manuscripts of *Tiriel,* the *Notebook,* and *The Four Zoas* in the British Museum; and the facsimile of *The Book of Los* available in the Ellis and Yeats edition of Blake's works. The texts of the early books given in Gleckner's *The Piper and the Bard,* and the facsimile and transcription of *The Four Zoas* recently published by G. E. Bentley, Jr., were useful checks. Unfortunately I was unable to obtain the original punctuation of poems appearing in the Pickering manuscript, which therefore are given here as in Keynes. Blake's punctuation is at best erratic, at worst chaotic. For example, he frequently etches a period in the apparent middle of a sentence or where we would expect a comma. This can be disconcerting. Nevertheless, it is safer to keep Blake's own punctuation and emend it mentally, if necessary, than to accept a finished correction, however rational.

I would like to thank Professor Helen White for her guidance throughout the research and writing of this book; Professors Alvin Whitley and John Enck for reading the first version of the manuscript and making disturbing suggestions; staff members of the libraries I have used, for their patience and helpfulness; and my husband for his advice in every phase of the writing. My gratitude is also due to the University of Wisconsin and the American Association of University Women for fellowships which enabled me to devote full time to this work.

ALICIA OSTRIKER

November, 1963

Contents

List of Abbreviations

Am	*America, a Prophecy*
BA	*The Book of Ahania*
BL	*The Book of Los*
BU	*The First Book of Urizen*
EG	*The Everlasting Gospel*
Eur	*Europe, a Prophecy*
FR	*The French Revolution*
FZ	*The Four Zoas*
J	*Jerusalem*
M	*Milton*
MHH	*The Marriage of Heaven and Hell*
PA	*Public Address*
PS	*Poetical Sketches*
SL	*The Song of Los*
VDA	*Visions of the Daughters of Albion*
VLJ	*A Vision of the Last Judgment*

Vision and Verse in William Blake

Introduction

"Execution is the Chariot of Genius." [1] Thus William Blake, in a skirmish of his unilateral war against Sir Joshua Reynolds, annotated his copy of Reynolds' *Discourses on Art.*

The President of the Royal Academy was warning young men against the "frivolous ambition of being thought masters of execution." He thought, like a good classicist, that the ideal, or generalized, beauty a painting should represent was distinguishable from and more important than its detail, ornament, execution. Blake, who believed that Reynolds was "Hired to Depress Art," disagreed. All "living" forms or ideas possessed beauty to him, and no idea or conception could be represented without its proper, "minutely appropriate" mechanics. These were the twin cornerstones of what I will call an expressivist poetic creed. The meaning of this term will become clear in what follows.

For Blake, all things existed in their own truth. "One Law for the Lion & Ox is Oppression," he wrote. "The apple tree never asks the beech how he shall grow; nor the lion, the horse, how he shall take his prey" (*MHH*, pp. 158, 152). Then, it was absurd to speak of an imperfectly realized idea. An idea could not exist at all until it took shape; and then it was that shape. "Invention depends Altogether upon Execution or Organization; as that is right or wrong so is the Invention perfect or imperfect." [2] Elsewhere he complained, "I have heard many People say, 'Give me the Ideas. It is no matter what Words you put them into,' & others say, 'Give

[1] *The Complete Writings of William Blake,* ed. Geoffrey Keynes (London and New York, 1957), *Annotations to Reynolds,* p. 454.

[2] *Ibid.*, p. 446.

me the Design, it is no matter for the Execution.' These people know Enough of Artifice, but Nothing of Art. Ideas cannot be Given but in their minutely Appropriate Words, nor Can a Design be made without its minutely Appropriate Execution" (*PA*, p. 596).

Blake evidently intended men to judge his art by its Execution as well as its Conception. This has not been done. Early studies of the poet occupied themselves with "placing" this "strange poetical and psychological phenomenon."[3] First there was the teapot-tempest about his madness. Then, perhaps because Blake tends to become all things to all men, there was the problem of enthusiasts transforming him to a mirror of themselves and their own ideas, with consequent distortion. Most Victorians who paid attention to Blake found an unworldly mystic who could write charming lyrics by miracle, but whose philosophy had best be discreetly ignored. Swinburne found romantic agony and a social rebel, but not a religious and political thinker. Ellis and Yeats found an Irishman, and someone they could use to substantiate certain occult doctrines. Today, Blake would not be amused by commentators who acclaim him for his radical social ideas and blame him for his impractical religious fervor. Even Northrop Frye, an outstanding Blake scholar, sometimes makes me think that he would not like Blake nearly so well if Blake were not so wonderfully archetypal. But to be called archetypal, that is to be everything in general and nothing in particular, might not have been so pleasing to the poet.

Among all these attempts to place Blake as a thinker, Blake the artist and craftsman wanders neglected. Most studies still try to explain his meaning.[4] His work has been turned inside out for its ideas on sex and psychology, on politics and history, on the nature of God and Man and the imagination. His symbolism has been

[3] Paul Berger, *William Blake, Poet and Mystic*, trans. Daniel H. Conner (London, 1914), p. 3.

[4] Northrop Frye, "William Blake," in *The English Romantic Poets and Essayists, a Review of Research and Criticism*, ed. W. H. Houtchens and C. H. Houtchens (New York, 1957), p. 4.

explored. His geography has been explained. His Animal, Vegetable, Mineral, and Spiritual correspondences have been elucidated. This is as it should be. Blake has aptly been called an "intellectual drunkard," [5] and he abundantly needs and deserves elucidation. Yet surprisingly little attention has been paid, even by fellow poets like Swinburne, Yeats, and T. S. Eliot, to his poetic technique, the chariot without which Blake, for all his amazing intellect, would never have rolled past the door of his little print-shop down to our time.

Of the various stylistic problems connected with Blake's work, the question of his prosody consistently puzzles and irritates commentators. Although only four essays in all the Blake literature treat his metrical technique at length,[6] many writers have taken pot shots at this problem from afar, before retreating. The lack of consensus only indicates that his technique is as mysterious as everything else about him.

Blake's metric needs analysis for several reasons. First, he was fascinated with it himself, and since he anticipated both Romantic innovation and the Free Verse movement, it has historical significance. This is a minor point, until we connect it with the poet's love of liberty. Second, to understand his poetry, a proper reading of his verse is as necessary as a proper comprehension of his ideas. (This unpopular truth applies to all poets, but perhaps needs special iteration with Blake.) Finally, Blake provides an ideal—because extreme—test case of his own theory of art, a theory in which form is valuable only as a vehicle of expression, never for its own sake. Thus he is a plumb line for a whole area of esthetic possibility.

[5] Lytton Strachey, *Books and Characters* (New York, 1922), p. 230.

[6] Lawrence Binyon, ed., *Poems of Blake* (London, 1931), "A Note on Blake's Metrical Experiments." S. Foster Damon, "The Chariot of Genius" In *William Blake, His Philosophy and Symbols* (Boston, 1924). Jack Lindsay, "The Metric of William Blake" in *Poetical Sketches,* ed. Eric Partridge (London, 1927). George Saintsbury, "William Blake and Robert Burns" in *A History of English Prosody* (London, 1906–10), Vol. III. See also Edith Sitwell, *The Pleasures of Poetry* (London, 1934), pp. 248–70.

Let us consider these reasons more fully. First, Blake was an inveterate experimenter, contemptuous of his century, a continual seeker after liberated modes of verse. He did not hug his achievements. Like an eighteenth-century Picasso of poetry, full of vitality and careless of perfection, he no sooner mastered one technique than he flung it aside for another, with the result that no other poet before his time, and few since, exhibits such an extraordinary range of styles. He shot off sparks in all directions. Some are blazing still. Even his less successful efforts may shine, when viewed amid the encircling gloom of his poetic environment.

His innovations, however, have more than historical interest. Blake's handling of music, and our reception of it, has done and shall do much to make or break his reputation as a poet. Until recently this reputation rested on his lyrics, lyrics which have been appropriated by countless readers of English poetry, each feeling in his heart that Blake's songs are his own private property. This is very largely because simple beauty of sound has a charm to open hearts' gates. Like children's rhymes, the songs strike our hearing and rhythmic senses pleasurably before they do anything else; their intellectual and emotional riches form an extra dividend which allows us to retain a childlike delight in them without feeling irrational or foolish as we may when we detect in ourselves a lingering affection for nursery rhymes. Often when we cannot remember the words of a Blakean lyric we keep the feel of its cadence and melody, which even alone seem tokens of perfection. To understand the success of the lyrics, we must understand their sound as well as their meaning.

If, on the other hand, Blake's Prophetic Books have not been assimilated by the reading public, a prime reason is that they are difficult to read; by which I mean not only that they are difficult to follow intelligently. We may read symbolic works as abstruse as the Revelations of St. John straight along without troubling to wonder whether we are making proper sense of the thing (which probably we are not), because Biblical prose is a strong tide which can lift and carry us, and do its work, without special effort on our part. The power of its music is of a sufficiently familiar type. The music of Blake's Prophetic Books is another matter. It is as difficult as Schoenberg to an ear accustomed to Mozart, as a late Picasso to an eye trained on Gainsboroughs. One must cultivate a taste for its dissonance, for its stretch and cramp, for its alternations between wild disorder and sawlike monotony, a taste no less necessary for comprehension of these books than the ability to tap a finger or foot is necessary for the *Songs of Innocence.*

Understanding and submitting oneself to the music may be half the battle in reading Blake properly. Among scholars, exegesis of Blake's lyrics has become a fashionable sport. But while no doubt it is useful to know from the poet's later elaborations that "oak" is associated with Druidism or "stars" with Reason, we should not let the explanations of the lyrics protrude through the poems themselves like fractured bones through skin, but should follow the dictate of the form. Similarly with the Prophetic Books, if we never proceed beyond the commentary-thumbing stage to the stage of spontaneous responsiveness, we might as well be in a dissecting laboratory; for Blake is then to us no more than an interesting specimen, not a poet.

Northrop Frye has rightly suggested that Blake's poetry is like a fascinating mystery story.[7] Yet surely, although a desire to unravel may be the beginning of wisdom with such poetry, it cannot be the end. "Knowledge," Blake said, "is not by deduction, but Immediate by Perception or Sense at once." [8] Explanations, even charts, tables, and diagrams, may be needed to clarify *Milton* or *Jerusalem;* but these should come as kindling to the reader's mind, to be consumed. The end is to read with a spirit like that of the author when he wrote; to see through his eyes and hear with his ears.

The third reason for studying Blake's verse technique is that it forces consideration of his position as an artist. Two independent

[7] Northrop Frye, *Fearful Symmetry, a Study of William Blake* (Princeton, 1947), p. 7.

[8] *Annotations to Berkeley*, p. 774.

sets of criteria have always existed for judging creative work, one requiring it to show mastery of traditional technique, the other requiring nothing of technique save that it be somehow expressive.[9] While most great artists have been able to find ways of making tradition expressive, there has always been a group which cared little or nothing for decorum. For example, Euripides at one end of Western drama, O'Neill at the other; the young Donne; Whitman; leaden-handed Dreiser: [10] all were men with something passionate to say, who did not care what tools they used provided they said it. Blake belongs here. He is an extreme example of the sect. Too isolated, too naïve, and too impatient to assimilate the forms of others, he made his Everlasting Gospel the good news of liberation from external restraints, a freedom to act as he thought Christ acted, "from impulse, not from rules" (*MHH*, p. 158). It is important to realize that much of Blake will always court condemnation by any standard definitions of art. It is also important to remember that outlaws like Blake often provide the life's blood by which the normal, the orderly, and the traditional art survive.

In exploring Blake's poetic technique, I hope to make clear the brilliance and range of his metrical innovation, and to suggest guidelines for apprehending the music in all his work as an aspect of its meaning. Part One of this book surveys conservative and

[9] "In art there are two modes by which men aim at distinction. In the one by a careful application to what others have accomplished, the artist imitates their works or selects & combines their various beauties; in the other, he seeks excellence at its primitive source—nature. In the first, he forms a style upon the study of pictures, & produces either imitative or eclectic art; in the second, by a close observation of nature, he discovers qualities existing in her which have never been portrayed before, & thus forms a style which is original. The results of the one mode, as they repeat that with which the eye is already familiar, are soon recognized and estimated, while the advance of the artist in a new path must necessarily be slow, for few are able to judge of that which deviates from the usual course, or are qualified to judge original studies." Constable; quoted by John Dewey, *Art as Experience* (N.Y., 1958, paperback), pp. 269–70.

[10] Any list of rebel writers would have many Americans on it, since America is *par excellence* the land of self-reliance, whose main tradition is to repudiate tradition.

liberal prosodic trends in the eighteenth century, and concludes with a technical résumé of Blake's *Poetical Sketches.* These juvenile experiments exhibit a broad stylistic range, as did his later work. His choice of models places him among the liberals of his generation. But his reluctance to follow exactly his models' forms adumbrates the future iconoclast.

Part Two discusses the mature lyrics. The dominant feature of *Songs of Innocence and Experience* is a drive toward simplicity and exclusion. As their major symbol is the child, so their style resembles that of children's song. Blake works, first, with a primitive basic beat, the simplicity of which is reinforced by simple and repetitive diction and structure, short lines, and jingling rhymes. This has a primarily kinetic effect, and is a main ingredient of the poet's apparent naïveté. It is modified by free rhythmical variations, which violate eighteenth-century standards not only by devices like internal inversion and foot-substitution, but also by a general use of mixed meters throughout whole poems. These irregularities help express the "minute particulars" of mood and thought.

Part Three considers the Prophetic Books. Here some attention will have to be paid to the theoretical questions of what the difference between prose and verse is, and which side Blake is on. I will deal with these controversial matters as briefly and uncontroversially as possible. From the clearly metrical septenary of *Tiriel* and *Thel,* Blake proceeds, with sidetracks and regressions along the way, to a style which almost destroys meter. Blake's late prophetic style is the analogue of his epic scope, his sense of complexity in the human psyche and the cosmos, his mistrust of conventional beauty, and his faith in liberty and energy—all these factors, making for formal chaos, crossed against a belief that the universe ultimately was ordered, was unified, was identical with God. It was this latter belief, I think, which prevented Blake from taking the logical next step into a Whitmanesque free verse. But he does not so much attain a balance between the factors of order and disorder as he exhibits a perpetual battling between them.

It is my opinion that even the last prophecies yield to analysis more profitably as verse than as prose, but I have tried not to be dogmatic about this. I hope therefore that my readings of Blake's rhythms will prove helpful even to those who do not share my assumption of a loose metrical substratum in these works. What we call a thing is less important than whether we understand it.

PART I

Background and Apprenticeship

1

The Conservative Background

Whether on Ida's shady brow,
  Or in the chambers of the East,
The chambers of the sun, that now
  From antient melody have ceas'd;

Whether in Heav'n ye wander fair,
  Or the green corners of the earth,
Or the blue regions of the air,
  Where the melodious winds have birth;

Whether on chrystal rocks ye rove,
  Beneath the bosom of the sea
Wand'ring in many a coral grove,
  Fair Nine, forsaking Poetry!

How have you left the antient love
  That bards of old enjoy'd in you!
The languid strings do scarcely move!
  The sound is forc'd, the notes are few!

(*PS*, p. 10)

It may be an exaggeration to declare, as Swinburne did, that Blake began to write "in a time when the best verses produced had merely the arid perfume of powder, the twang of dry wood and adjusted strings" [1]—but probably not a great exaggeration. In

[1] Algernon Charles Swinburne, *William Blake, a Critical Essay* (London, 1906), p. 10.

1757, when Blake was born, Pope was still, despite some underminings of the fortress, the prince of English poetry, the heroic couplet still its supreme standard, and the critic Bysshe, rule-giver and anthologist of *The Art of English Poetry*, although unknown today, was still its ubiquitous Minister of Public Affairs. In this same year, as if to prefigure the coming clash between old guard and avant-garde, Johnson completed his *Dictionary*, and Walpole established his Strawberry Hill Press.

The cautionary tale of Augustan poetry is too familiar to require great elaboration here. That seemingly impregnable structure firmly founded on the rock of Reason seemed meant, like Hitler's Reich, to last a thousand years; but the stream of "Ode, and Elegy, and Sonnet" was seeping below ground ruinously all the while, and by 1798 the whole edifice stood ready to crumble before the diminutive onslaught of the *Lyrical Ballads*.

Here we are concerned with only one battleground of the war between neoclassic and romantic, that of versification. This one issue, however, typifies a schism which began in England with the Renaissance, and has not healed today, between two ideals of poetry. According to one, poetry orders, refines, and improves experience; according to the other, poetry expresses experience.

Beginning in the sixteenth century, English literary critics had been proposing metrical rules for poetry, based less on observation and codification of what English poets wrote than on assumptions that the already extant systems of other, presumably superior, languages could be adapted to their own.[2] When early attempts to

[2] See G. Gregory Smith, ed., *Elizabethan Critical Essays* (London, 1904), pp. xlvi–lx; and especially the essays by Ascham, Gascoigne, Harvey, the Spenser-Harvey correspondence, Stanyhurst, Sidney, Webbe, Puttenham, Campion, and Daniel. The issue drawn in the sixteenth century was between the classicists who believed English should be made to scan quantitatively, and the more empirical group who recognized that the structural principle of English verse would have to be accent. Even the more descriptive prosodists, however, are limited by their selectivity. Poetry derived from the traditional, irregular, accentual English verse of the romances and ballads, in disrepute for its "Gothick" origins, could not serve as examples for learned critics. This excluded not only the ragged rout of rakehelly rimers, but most of the playwrights as well. Even *The Shepherd's Calendar*,

scan English quantitatively on a classical model failed, they were succeeded by theories based on the scansion of the Romance languages, first Italian, then French, which depended on syllabic count. Dramatic blank verse writers, sporting like black sheep outside the fold of literature proper, resisted for one brief and glorious period the idea that verse like theirs must contain precisely ten syllables per line with regular alternation of accented and unaccented syllables. The more independent lyricists followed suit. Milton was the last great poet of this period to practice the native English compromise between Romantic syllabic versification and the "barbarian" accentual verse of the Germanic tongues. In 1660 *Paradise Lost* was already anachronistic. Either the theorists were having their way with the writers of verse, or, more likely, the same desire for a sophisticated, cultured, orderly poetry, which would meet Continental standards, was now motivating the poets as well as the theorists.[3]

Among the influences favoring Restoration "new verse" was the crystalization of a conservative society about the court of Charles II. To Restoration writers, feeling themselves civilized at last after a half century of mental and moral excess, literary regularity was a point of pride and safety.[4] "Discord" endangered poet and society alike, in Dryden's "age more gallant than the last."

There was also the new respect for France. Edward Bysshe, the almost unchallenged rule-giver for most of the eighteenth century, based his prosody on a 1663 *Quatre Traitez de Poësies, Latine, Françoise, Italienne, et Espagnoles,* by Claude Lancelot, one of the Port Royal educators. The opening section of his *Art of English Poetry,* "containing Rules for making Verses," simply

---

though written by a learned poet, could not be used by the rule-makers. Thus the prosodists do not suggest the possibility of trisyllabic substitution, inversion, or mixed meters.

[3] T. S. Omond, *English Metrists* (Oxford, 1921), p. 29. See also George Saintsbury, *A History of English Prosody* (London, 1906–10), II, the chapters on prosodic theory.

[4] Paul Fussell, Jr., *Theory of Prosody in Eighteenth Century England,* Conn. Coll. Monograph, No. 5 (New London, 1954), pp. 9–10.

translates and adapts the essay on French versification, with English examples instead of French.[5] His system is syllabic: "The Structure of our Verses, whether Blank, or in Rhyme, consists in a certain Number of Syllables, not in Feet composed of long and short Syllables."[6]

Taking the heroic line as his standard, Bysshe announces that it has ten syllables, neither more nor less. Awkward extra syllables are to be apostrophized away. There are proper and improper places for pauses; proper and improper places for accents: "In all Verses of 10 Syllables, the most prevailing Accents ought to be on the 2nd, 4th, or 6th syllables; for if they are on the 3rd, 5th, or 7th, the Verses will be rough and disagreeable."[7] Bysshe enforces his conviction that all accents must fall on even syllables by emendations of lines which contain inversions, e.g., of Milton's

Void of all Succour and needful Comfort

to

Of Succour and all needful Comfort void;

or of Davenant's

And both Lovers, both thy Disciples were

to

And Lovers both, both thy Disciples were.

Most of Bysshe's rules deal with the heroic couplet. In his discussion of lines other than the decasyllable he does not mention what we would call trochaic meter at all. Meters which we would call trisyllabic (anapest and dactyl), he says "are employ'd only in Compositions for Musick, and in the lowest sort of Burlesque Poetry; the disagreeableness of their Measure having wholly ex-

[5] A. Dwight Culler, "Edward Bysshe and the Poet's Handbook," *PMLA*, LXIII (1948), 878.
[6] Edward Bysshe, *The Art of English Poetry*, 3rd ed. (London, 1708), p. 1.
[7] *Ibid.*, p. 6.

cluded them from grave and serious subjects." [8] As an example of the "disagreeable Measure" he offered Congreve's lines:

> Apart let me view then each Heavenly Fair,
> For three at a time there's no Mortal can bear.

Among his other rules are injunctions to eschew hiatus, and to contract *-ed* endings; not to use alliteration; and to avoid rhythmic run-on from line to line. All these pronouncements, of course, are made in the name of correctness and harmony.

Bysshe's handbook, first printed in 1702, went through nine editions by 1762. Credit for this popularity goes in part to the book's second section, an anthology of poetry arranged by topics so that aspiring poets might find agreeable "Allusions, Similes, Descriptions" to borrow for any purpose. The prosodic "Rules" also met an eager audience. While more liberal opposing theories appeared from time to time, the overwhelming mass of school grammars and dictionaries, popular literary essays and handbooks for poets, all using the telltale phrase "a certain number of syllables," are dominated by Bysshean precept.[9] In the second half of the century, the great impetus behind continuation of the conservative faith lay with the brief prosody prefixed to Johnson's *Dictionary*. This declared that "the feet of our verses are either iambick . . . or trochaick." In iambics, "the accents are to be placed on even syllables; and every line considered by itself is more harmonious as this rule is more strictly observed." Johnson, being a sensible man, elsewhere admits a distinction between "pure" and "mixed" heroic measure. The former occurs "when the accent rests upon every second syllable throughout the whole line," and provides "the most complete harmony of which a single verse is capable." The latter permits some variation of accent. This, "though it always injures the harmony of the line considered by itself," is required by the infirmity of human nature which, alas, cannot tolerate the unmixed blessing of a pure line for long

[8] *Ibid.*, p. 7.
[9] Culler, "Bysshe," p. 879.

without becoming wearied.[10] Johnson's adoption of foot-scansion, his allowance for "mixed" lines, and his recognition in the *Dictionary* that "the variations necessary to pleasure belong to the art of poetry, not to the rules of grammar," seem to mark him as far more liberal than Bysshe. Yet the gist of his teaching was "the purer the better." His critical writings censured many poets, from Milton to Cowper, for their impurities, and his pronouncements were accepted by the great majority of critics and grammarians.

No critical theory occurs in a philosophical vacuum. The triumph of a rigidly prescriptive prosody depended on its concurrence with certain popular philosophical assumptions, which are worth noting for the picture they evoke of everything William Blake most despised about his century.

Paul Fussell, in his excellent study of eighteenth-century prosody, has suggested that the efforts of critics and poets alike to impose "harmony," that is, order and symmetry, on verse "may be compared with those of Hobbes in ordering the commonwealth and Locke in ordering the methods of human perception." [11] Poetry, like everything else in nature and society, proceeded by rational means to effect a rational end. A perhaps extreme, yet telling example of the faith that poetic technique could be reduced to a science is the belief expressed by one theorist that "all poetry partakes of the Elements of Geometry and Musick" and that the "best Interpreters of poetical Numbers are those who apply the rules of Musick and Geometry to Poetry." [12] By "Musick" of course is understood that numerical interpretation of times and tones which reaches back to Pythagoras. Small wonder that Blake, who remarked "Bring out number, weight & measure in a year of dearth" (*MHH*, p. 151), who thought the aphorism "Grecian is Mathematic Form: Gothic is Living Form" (*On Homer's Poetry*,

[10] Samuel Johnson, *A Dictionary of the English Language . . . From the Author's Last Folio Edition* (London, 1877), p. 42; *The Rambler* (London, 1794), II, No. 86, 178–79.

[11] Fussell, *Theory of Prosody*, p. 39.

[12] Edward Manwaring, *Stichology: or, a Recovery of the Latin, Greek, and Hebrew Numbers* (London, 1737), p. 74.

p. 778) sufficed to condemn all classical art, and to whom Newton and materialism were anathema, was to rebel against such mechanical conceptions of verse.

Moreover, the positivist, moralizing eighteenth century often linked correct prosody with correct rules of conduct, presuming that regularity of stress not only reflected regularity of character in the poet, but by Lockean association tended to instill the same in the reader.[13] Johnson, praising Dryden, "from whose time it is apparent that English poetry has had no tendency to relapse to its former savageness," finds "the rectitude of [his] mind" revealed by his "rejection of unnatural thoughts and rugged numbers." [14] Elsewhere Johnson discovers among the virtues of "harmony" that it "shackles attention, and governs passions," [15] two evident desiderata in poetry. That the moral-psychological approach to art is not defunct, incidentally, may be seen by any twentieth-century tirade against the wickedness of "modern" art, poetry, fiction. Presumed ugliness and disorder of image are equated with the expression and provocation of immorality. Blake, however, came to believe that his mission was, precisely, to express and provoke what the world calls immorality. This is one reason for the "rugged numbers" of his prophecies.

One final rationale for regular verse was an esthetic one. It was assumed that the matter of vulgar reality was to be raised to the spirituality of poesy—which "pleases by exhibiting an idea more grateful to the mind than things themselves afford" [16]—by dint of form. Hence, just as poetic diction avoided common vocabulary, so it was a typical eighteenth-century idea that "the pronunciation of verse is a species very distinct from the pronunciation of prose. . . . The latter is as different from the former as the elegant step of a minuet is from the common motions of walking." [17]

[13] Fussell, *Theory of Prosody*, p. v.

[14] Samuel Johnson, *Lives of the English Poets*, ed. George Birkbeck Hill (Oxford, 1905), I, 421; III, 220.

[15] Johnson, *The Rambler*, II, No. 88, 189.

[16] Johnson, *Lives*, I, 292.

[17] John Walker, *Elements of Elocution* (Boston, 1810), p. 263.

Blake's enemy Reynolds observed in his *Discourses* that "the manner in which poetry is offered to the ear, the tone in which it is recited, should be as far removed from the tone of conversation, as the words of which that poetry is composed. . . . Whatever is familiar, or in any way reminds us of what we see and hear every day, perhaps does not belong to the higher provinces of art, either in poetry or painting." [18] In accordance with such ideas, poetry actually was declaimed with all the contractions and elisions necessary to keep each line to its requisite number of syllables, notwithstanding any damage this Chinese binding might do the skeleton of the language.[19]

Or rather, poetry was so declaimed where it was possible so to declaim it. Upon writers born too early to benefit from the establishment of fixed principles, the axe fell. One might read "Scatter thy leaves before the mellowing year" as if it were "melwing year." But what to do about the unwanted syllables in

> Ăbóm|ĭnáb|lĕ ĭnút|tĕráb|lĕ ănd wórse | (*P.L.* II.626)
>
> Shŏots ĭnví|sĭblĕ vér|tue even to the deep (*P.L.* III.586)

or the pyrrhics and trochees in

> Ŭnĭ|vérsăl | reproach, far worse to beare (*P.L.* VI.34)
>
> Ĭn thĭr | tríplĕ | Degrees, | Régĭons | to which
> (*P.L.* V. 747)

or the hundreds of other aberrant Miltonic lines? [20] Since Milton could not easily be reformed, he was taken, even by admirers, as a great but irregular genius, whose prosodic deformity must be

[18] Sir Joshua Reynolds, *Discourses on Art* (San Marino, 1959), p. 235.

[19] See Fussell, *Theory of Prosody*, pp. 71–80, 87–100. Fussell offers substantial evidence that many contractions were standard in colloquial speech as well as poetical declamation, from about the time of the Restoration until the 1730's and '40's, and decreasingly thereafter. He argues, however, that much of the influence was *from* poetic pronunciation *to* colloquial; what was felt to be genteel was adopted in common speech.

[20] Robert Bridges, *Milton's Prosody* (Oxford, 1921), argues that Milton scanned syllabically, and explains the extrasyllabic habit by a complex of rules for elision, even more painstaking than those of Bysshe. He admits, however (p. 36), that the *rhythm* as spoken aloud was intended to override and "disguise" the abstract *scansion*.

pardoned as the product of a barbaric age. The same measure applied to Shakespeare. Although Bentley's redaction of Milton was hissed, Shakespeare was ancient enough history for editors' improvements to be a matter of course.[21] Blake opposed the prettification of life by art; his admiration for Shakespeare was unconditional; and his reactions to criticisms of Milton's verse are predictable: Dryden's version of *Paradise Lost* is "Monotonous Sing Song, Sing Song from beginning to end," and "Stupidity" will prefer Dryden to Milton for just that reason (*PA*, p. 600).

In sum, whether it masqueraded as science, ethics, or esthetics, Augustan versification depended on the faith that common reality was like a beast which needed taming. The purpose of art was to take the raw material of experience, set it into prescribed pre-existent patterns, and thus render it rational, wholesome, and delightful. This is a valid philosophy of art, whose only drawback is that it does not allow for growth. The contrary possibility, that experience might be trusted to evolve entirely new forms, or that the natural disorganization of experience might itself become both subject and method of art, did not occur to the conservative theorist. Blake understood the Augustan assumption very well, and detested it. "I do not condemn Pope or Dryden because they did not understand Imagination, but because they did not understand Verse. . . . That is not either Colouring, Graving or Verse which is Unappropriate to the Subject" (*PA*, pp. 602–3). Of course Blake is not doing Pope or Dryden justice. All he saw, standing aloof in giant ignorance, was that they had set themselves some limits, and would never exceed them; and that was all he needed to see. The image he invented in *Tiriel* to describe Augustan verse was that of a "great cage" into which a silly and depraved old man walks every evening after dinner, and shuts himself in, and sings.

[21] Bentley advised, for example, changing Milton's "Created hugest that swim th'Ocean stream" (*P.L.* I, 202) to "Of all the Kinds that swim the ocean stream." A typical revision of Shakespeare, made by Nahum Tate and retained by Pope, was from "Prevent it, resist it, stop this breach in time" (*R III*, IV, i, 148) to "Prevent, resist it, stop this breach in time."

2

The Liberal Background

What is now proved was once only imagin'd.
(*MHH*, p. 151)

Bysshean and Johnsonian conceptions of versification did not command the whole field, either in theory or in practice, throughout the eighteenth century. Rebels, existing even in the first half of the century, had grown numerous enough by Blake's time to constitute a real rival school, although they were still a minority. While their innovations in doctrine and practice may have been slight, and their influence on Blake even slighter, the existence of an atmosphere which permitted any novelty at all must have made a difference to him.

As the conservative theorists took the heroic couplet for their standard, deprecated Milton's ruggedness, and glorified the virtues of "harmony," so the liberals justified themselves by the example of blank verse, praised Milton's power, and raised as their watchword the principle of "variety." These sentiments began disturbing the peace of the Augustans fairly early. The dissenting clergyman Isaac Watts criticized the couplet principle in the preface to the second edition of his *Horae Lyricae*, as early as 1709:

In the Poems of heroic measure, I have attempted in rhime the same variety of cadence, comma, and period, which blank verse glories in. . . . It degrades the excellency of the best versification when the lines run on by couplets, twenty together, just in the same pace, and with the same pauses. It spoils the noblest pleasure of the sound: the reader is tired with the tedious uniformity or charmed to sleep with the unmanly softness of the numbers, and the perpetual chime of even cadences.[1]

Watts does not suggest any new theoretical basis for scansion, however, nor are his metrical novelties very striking. Despite impatience with couplets and admiration for blank verse, the clergyman complains that Milton sometimes puts him out of breath. His own verse is not breathtaking. Probably the first real inroads into conservative prosody were made by Samuel Say, in an *Essay on the Harmony, Variety, and Power of Numbers* published in 1745. Say, who scans some of his own prose to ensure its being read correctly, associates variety with expressiveness. "The Numbers, in Every Just Composition, will be as Various as the Passions and Idéas."[2] Ignoring the assumption of syllabic uniformity, he scans by feet; and having found a number of different kinds of feet in Milton, cries with delight, "Such is the Variety in Such an Uniformity!"[3]

Unlike the conservatives, Say endorses surprise in verse; rules should be broken sometimes to wake the reader up. Unlike them too, he insists on reading poetry with a natural voice and appropriate rhetorical emphasis, and thus opposes what he considers the artifice of elision: "But what Monsters of Sound would *Ann'al* or *An-wal*, Syr'an or Am'rous be? or does anyone reälly pronounce any otherwise than annual, Syrian, amorous, in three short, but distinct Syllables?"[4] To illustrate his point, and incidentally to show how more than one kind of foot may be pleasing in a line, Say offers the following couplet:

> Ănd mānў ăn āmŏrŏus, mānў ă hūmŏrŏus Lāy,
> Whĭch mānў ă Bārd hăd chāntĕd mānў ă Dāy.

[1] Isaac Watts, *Horae Lyricae and Divine Songs* (Boston, 1854), p. cii.
[2] Samuel Say, *An Essay on the Harmony, Variety and Power of Numbers,* Augustan Reprints, No. 55 (Los Angeles, 1956), p. 126.
[3] *Ibid.*, p. 102.
[4] *Ibid.*, p. 131.

Say's couplet was used by many later writers. John Mason, expanding on Say's ideas, suggests the analogy between a metrical foot and a bar of music, and explains the admission of such trisyllables as "amorous" to iambic lines by saying that "two of these very short Times may be substituted for one . . . without any detriment to the Measure." [5] This idea of measuring verse roughly by times, instead of precisely by syllables, was to become the basis of Romantic prosody. He also allows for what he calls "mixt Iambics," to which spondees, trochees, and pyrrhics are admitted, and which, unlike Johnson, he enjoys for their own sake.

Say and Mason pointed out the lines which rebellion was to follow. Later writers, especially after 1770, continued to defend variety, correspondence between passion and rhythm, and occasional wholesome discord. Technically they pursued the bar-foot analogy until it might yield any kind of metrical substitution; and they began to read without elision even the older writers like Pope, where elision had been intended, so that they found trisyllabic feet wherever they looked.[6]

Judging by the theorists, it would seem plausible that by the time Blake started to write, at least a few poets would have thoroughly sloughed off Augustan technique. However, either because the theorists were too few and far between, or because the spirit was willing but the flesh weak, liberal practice in versification limped far behind liberal theory.

Lyric and blank verse poets are usually supposed to have contributed most to the decay of the Augustan ideal. Of the blank verse writers, it is true that many could claim some Miltonic

[5] John Mason, *Essays on Poetical and Prosaic Numbers, and Elocution*, 2nd ed. (London, 1761), p. 8.

[6] For detailed discussion of the liberal prosodists, see T. S. Omond, *English Metrists* (Oxford, 1921), ch. 3; George Saintsbury, *A History of English Prosody* (London, 1906–10), II, 542–66; and Paul Fussell, Jr., *Theory of Prosody in Eighteenth Century England*, Conn. Coll. Monograph, No. 5 (New London, 1954), chs. 4–5. Among the men who challenged the conservative prosody before 1740 are Charles Gildon and John Dennis. Around the mid-century were Charles Avison; Fortescue; Gray when dealing with pre-Restoration poetry but not when occupied with contemporaries or his

lineage, that they usually valued feeling and sensibility as well as good sense, that they indulged in descriptions of Nature, that their dominant note was more often melancholic than witty, that they often strove for an effect of sublimity through appeals to men's sense of the vast, the dangerous, or the obscure. Unfortunately, they were not great poets. As Blake complained, "He who copies does not Execute; he only Imitates what is already Executed. Execution is only the result of Invention" (*PA*, p. 596).

Thomson, with his swollen diction and Latinized construction, stolen from Milton and serving equally to embellish a winter storm or an exposition of Newtonian mechanics, kept well within the bounds of Augustan propriety. The Graveyard School of Young and Blair weights every ounce of poetry with a ton of poetic bombast. Frigid Akenside lectures on the Imagination; the Wartons cultivate wildnesses. All apply what they conceive to be the suitable styles toward their respective themes instead of drawing their poetry from the felt heart of a matter. It follows that their verse, while imitating some of the more acceptable variations in Milton or earlier poets, evinces little individual character. But character is precisely what blank verse, lacking an inherently interesting or elegant form, must possess, and does possess in all its great practitioners—Shakespeare, Milton, Wordsworth, Tennyson, Browning—none of whom can possibly be mistaken for another. Thomson's trick of internal full stops, or Blair's trick of frequent feminine endings, do not give the impression of being forced by the pressure of the thought.[7]

One genuine original in this group is Cowper, who, for all his humility of soul and diffidence of manner, possessed a good deal of artistic self-reliance. "Blank verse," Cowper wrote,

---

own verse; John Armstrong; Daniel Webb; Dr. John Brown; Shenstone; and John Rice. After 1770, William Kenrick, Thomas Warton, and Lord Monboddo contributed to the decay of conservatism in a small way; Ramsey, Thomas Sheridan, and Joshua Steele, in a great.

[7] See, however, George Saintsbury, *A History of English Prosody*, II, Book VIII, ch. 2, for more detailed and somewhat more generous estimates of the eighteenth-century blank verse writers, particularly Thomson.

is susceptible of a much greater diversification of manner than verse in rhyme: and why the modern writers of it have all thought proper to cast their numbers alike, I know not.... I flatter myself, however, that I have avoided that sameness with others, which would entitle me to nothing but a share in one common oblivion with them all.[8]

Cowper's blank verse, accordingly, does "escape from the buckram prison of eighteenth-century metre and diction." [9] At its best in *The Task*, and more consistently in *Yardley Oak*, Cowper's rhythm, quiet and unflamboyant, follows his meditation in a manner anticipating Wordsworth, but with less prosiness.

Except for Cowper, the blank verse poets of the century choked on Milton. He could not be resisted, but he was too thick a morsel for their slender throats. Happily for the period's few lyric poets, no such great prior figure stood impassably in the way of lyric verse; for although *L'Allegro* and *Il Penseroso* inspired imitations, their influence was never so all-embracing as that of *Paradise Lost*. In lyric, where the important writers include Collins and Gray, the hymnodists, Thomas Percy, and Chatterton, there thus appears a somewhat brighter scene than in blank verse.

Collins and Gray are refiners of their poetic heritage rather than innovators. Both experimented, in their odes, with novel stanza forms. Both had a delicate feeling for the music of language. Both could at times evoke images through sound, as in Collins' "Ode to Evening," or the opening of Gray's "Elegy." Gray in particular exhibits a distinct progression from the restrained periods of the "Ode on a Distant Prospect of Eton College" or the "Hymn to Adversity," to sensuous enjoyment of sound in relatively meaningless lines (as Johnson pointed out) like "Weave the warp, and weave the woof" in "The Bard." Still, "there is little positively new of the prosodic kind in either poet except their patterns and the spirit of their fingering." [10]

[8] William Cowper, *Correspondence*, ed. Thomas Wright (New York and London, 1905), II, 280.
[9] Saintsbury, *English Prosody*, II, 496.
[10] *Ibid.*, p. 514.

Blake was perhaps more affected by verse which ran outside the mainstream of poetry. The revival of English hymnody, particularly in the Low Church movement exemplified by Watts, Wesley, and Cowper, lay in its effort to bring the masses gospel truth through simple but powerful diction, uncomplex construction, and a strong repeated beat to the line. The lines are short, the stanza forms plain. These qualities undoubtedly influenced the author of *Songs of Innocence and Experience*, where they are carried much further. Wesley, the most prolific of the hymnodists, has the beginnings of some other traits which will reappear in Blake. He writes trochaic and anapestic verse as well as iambic; he has many stanza forms which combine iambic and trochaic lines; and he seems to have been careless about the correctness of his rhymes. However, there is not a trace of internal irregularity in Wesley's lines.[11] If Blake learned the techniques of substitution from any eighteenth-century source, it must have been from the redactions and imitations of older verse, where metrical irregularity was tolerated as quaint evidence of primitivism.

The forms of ballad or folk poetry, traditionally scorned by serious poets, had been acceptable to the Restoration for burlesques, jocular verse, or political broadsides. In other words, if a poem was low or comical enough, it could safely imitate ballad form. As antiquarian interest rose, literary men began admiring the ballads for their "simplicity," until, at the time of Blake's birth, quite a few poets were writing what they considered to be ballad-imitations. These, derived less from traditional ballad than from contemporary broadside verse which had itself been affected by neoclassical standards, were usually sentimental narratives of separated lovers like Mallet's "William and Margaret," Tickell's "Colin and Lucy," Shenstone's "Jemmy Dawson," or Goldsmith's "Edwin and Angelina," with the diction of broadside cleansed, the

[11] Wesley's editor Frank Baker (*Representative Verse*, London, 1962, pp. xlvii–xlix) claims that Wesley was a great reformer and varier of verse, but the only variation he mentions, and the only one I can find, is the opening inversion. This of course was standard, not a novelty.

doggerel smoothed, and the attitude pathetic and condescending.[12] Percy's *Reliques*, though not the first collection of ballads, was a turning point in the attitude toward popular poetry. It both capitalized on an already existing fondness for the nobility and simplicity of England's past, and turned that interest toward work that was genuinely antique.

Unlike the decorous ballads then being written, these were strong—even crude—in form as well as language. Their rhymes were often imperfect, their stanzas of unequal length, their lines too short, or more commonly, too long for the meter. The fact that they had originally been composed for singing accounts for this, since a given melody can accommodate crowding and stretching of syllables. The difference between fashionable ballad and Percy's versions may be seen by a brief comparison:

> God have merci on his soll, sayd Kyng Harry,
> Good lord, yf thy will it be!
> I have a hondrith captayns in Ynglonde, he sayd,
> As good as ever was hee.
>
> (*The Ancient Ballad of Chevy Chase*)

> No, never from this hour to part,
> We'll live and love so true:
> The sigh that rends thy constant heart
> Shall break thy Edwin's too.
>
> (Goldsmith, "Edwin and Angelina")

The revival of traditional ballad ultimately helped teach readers to enjoy freer movements of verse, and poets to write them. For a while after Percy there was more "ballad-and-water" imitation than ever, in poems which "represent usually the strictest periodic style." [13] A singer was found, however, to capture the spirit and style of the old poetry: Chatterton, the marvellous forger of the Rowley poems. Chatterton could write with a swing, he was bold

[12] See Albert Friedman, *The Ballad Revival* (Chicago, 1961), pp. 156 ff.

[13] *Ibid.*, p. 164; George R. Stewart, Jr., *Modern Metrical Techniques as Illustrated by Ballad Meter, 1700–1920* (New York, 1922), p. 44.

enough to introduce an occasional anapestic foot among iambic lines, and he could sometimes mix his meters, as in the "Mynstrelles Songe":

> O! synge unto mie roundelaie,
> O! droppe the brynie teare wythe mee,
> Daunce ne moe atte hallie daie,
> Lycke a ryning ryver bee;
> Mie love ys deade,
> Gon to hys deathe-bedde
> Al under the wyllowe tree.

The fact that Chatterton without Rowley is a conventional poetaster suggests that he believed with most of his contemporaries that metrical irregularity could be sanctioned only in terms of primitivism. A similar phenomenon occurs with Burns, whose dialect poems are notoriously freer than his English, and who even observed in his Commonplace-book "a certain irregularity in the old Scotch Songs, a redundancy of syllables with respect to that exactness of accent & measure which the English poetry requires, but which glides in, most melodiously with the respective tunes to which they are set." [14]

In fact, the official rejection of syllabic scansion in serious English verse, as opposed to imitations of folk-irregularity, comes only with the famous statement of Coleridge's 1816 preface to *Christabel:*

> The metre of *Christabel* is not, properly speaking, irregular, though it may seem so from its being founded on a new principle, namely, that of counting, in each line, the accents, not the syllables. Though the latter may vary from seven to twelve, yet in each line the accents will be found to be only four.[15]

This "new" doctrine, Saintsbury points out, had been anticipated by Southey as early as 1799. Having been criticized by a friend for

[14] David Daiches, *Robert Burns* (New York, 1950), p. 87.

[15] Samuel Taylor Coleridge, *Selected Poetry and Prose*, ed. Donald A. Stauffer (New York, 1951), p. 25.

such lines as "I have made candlĕs ŏf ínfants' fat" in his *Ballads,* Southey wrote back:

> I could heap up authority on authority for using two very short syllables . . . instead of one—they take up only the time of one. 'Spirit' in particular is repeatedly placed as a monosyllable in Milton; and some of his ass-editors have attempted to print it as one, not feeling that the rapid pronunciation of the two syllables does not lengthen the verse more than the dilated sound.[16]

The battle was ultimately won. But by this time we have flown far past the moment of Blake's entry into English poetry. While all these quite necessary public skirmishes were taking place, he had been alternating disyllables and trisyllables since before 1778, doing precisely what Coleridge congratulated himself for in *Christabel;* and doing it, to some tastes, less academically.[17]

Blake was born too early to be influenced or aided by Southey and Coleridge, or even Burns. Almost certainly he never read the poetic theorists who might have equipped him with sanctions for his experiments. He could not have seen the one document of the century which anticipated his later style, Smart's *Jubilate Agno.* But he did read Percy, Cowper, and Chatterton, not to mention Macpherson's *Ossian.* He did grow up in a time when some people were trying to revive old things, or produce new; and he extrapolated from what he encountered. However great his isolation in later years, the attractive legend of a Blake who sprang full blown from a one hundred percent Philistine eighteenth-century brow cannot too often be countered. Blake's sources of inspiration must be admitted, and his debts and similarities to others acknowledged, if only for the sake of isolating his actual originality.

[16] Robert Southey, *Selections from the Letters,* ed. J. W. Warter (London, 1856), I, 69. Incidentally, Southey was probably wrong; Milton very likely did pronounce "spirit" as one syllable. Southey's indignation shows how far conventions had changed by his time.

[17] S. Foster Damon, *William Blake, His Philosophy and Symbols* (Boston, 1924), p. 47.

3

Blake's Poetical Sketches

To learn the Language of Art, "Copy for Ever" is My Rule.
(*Annotations to Reynolds*, p. 446)

Of the Blake who wrote *Poetical Sketches*, T. S. Eliot has remarked, "He is very like Collins, he is very eighteenth century."[1] On the other hand, one of Blake's few early sympathizers felt that "his genius in this line assimilates more with the bold and careless freedom peculiar to our writers at the latter end of the sixteenth and former part of the seventeenth century, than with the polished phraseology, and just, but subdued thought of the eighteenth."[2] Both statements fairly characterize the young Blake, although neither would apply to the mature poet.

Like the heroine of the child's rhyme, "Whatever Miss T. eats turns into Miss T.," Blake had a capacity of transforming beyond recognition whatever he consumed; he absorbed ideas, phrases, symbols he liked, without regard to their contexts or the systems to which they belonged, and fitted them into his own system. In the *Poetical Sketches*, however, he is not yet a systematizer, he has

[1] T. S. Eliot, *The Sacred Wood* (London, 1934), p. 152.
[2] Benjamin Heath Malkin, *A Father's Memoirs of His Child*, reprinted in Arthur Symons, *William Blake* (New York, 1907), p. 317.

not yet embarked upon "the fury of my Course among the Stars of God & in the Abysses of the Accuser" (*Letters*, p. 816). He is still casting about for a style, with the marks of an apprentice on him.

Blake wrote these *Sketches* between the ages of twelve and twenty years. His constellation of stars included Shakespeare and Milton, Elizabethan lyric and the Authorized Version of the Bible, the ballad and Macpherson's *Ossian*, Thomson, Chatterton, Collins, and Gray. Except for the Elizabethan lyrics, which at that time only Chatterton was imitating successfully, these were common sources for the more liberal poets. We may only wonder in passing how an "untutored youth" of the shopkeeping middle classes, studying to be an engraver, got hold of some of them. As if to preview in miniature the poet's later broad range, the experiments Blake produced from these sources include a ballad, dramatic blank verse, lyric blank verse, "Elizabethan" lyric, a genre sketch, a Gothic narrative, and some Ossianic prose-poetry. The level of this work is uneven. If nothing in Blake's later writings surpasses the beauty of some of the lyrics, nothing surpasses the mawkishness of "Blind-Man's Buff" or "Fair Elenor." Yet all these pieces have one trait in common. Imitative as they are, not one is thoroughly imitative. For better or worse, each item in the *Poetical Sketches* reveals the impatient hand and the already active drive to innovate which were to distinguish Blake all his life.

This impatience is clearest in the two pieces whose antecedents are most obvious, the "Imitation of Spenser" and the fragment of a blank-verse historical drama entitled "King Edward the Third." The "Imitation" has the archaisms and personifications, the attempt at lush sound and imagery, which every eighteenth-century aspirer to sixteenth-century quaintness knew how to copy. It does not have the Spenserian personality, and still less does it have the Spenserian form. The lines of its six stanzas, which an early editor pronounced "all different and all wrong," [3] are stiff

[3] John Sampson, ed., *The Poetical Works of William Blake* (Oxford, 1905), p. 21.

and end-stopped, with none of the flow and swell one expects of the Spenserian stanza. The irregular stanza-lengths and the repeated nonobservance of the alexandrine and the final couplet betray the arrogance of a pupil who thinks he knows better than his teacher. One remembers the anecdote of his Royal Academy encounter with Moser, who made the mistake of trying to instruct the youth in what painters he should copy. "How I did secretly Rage!" Blake records of this incident. "I also spoke my Mind." [4]

"King Edward the Third" has *Henry V* for its spiritual father. Here, in the internal molding of the lines, balancing of the pauses, occasional substitution of anapests for iambs, and smooth, strong use of overflow for verse-paragraph effects, Blake shows himself an apt student. The following is a typical sample:

> *Sir Walter.* Sir Thomas Dagworth, I have been weeping
> Over the men that are to die to-day.
> *Dagworth.* Why, brave Sir Walter, you or I may fall.
> *Sir Walter.* I know this breathing flesh must lie and rot,
> Cover'd with silence and forgetfulness.—
> Death wons in cities' smoke, and in still night,
> When men sleep in their beds, walketh about! . . .
> Yet death is terrible, tho' borne on angels' wings!
> How terrible then is the field of death,
> Where he doth rend the vault of heaven,
> And shake the gates of hell!
> O Dagworth, France is sick! the very sky,
> Tho' sunshine light it, seems to me as pale
> As the pale fainting man on his death-bed,
> Whose face is shewn by light of sickly taper!
> It makes me sad and sick at very heart,
> Thousands must fall to-day! (*PS*, p. 30)

There is something ineffably Shakespearean about the texture of the versification throughout the fragment, comparable in impressiveness to Tennyson's youthful tour de force, *The Devil and the*

[4] *Annotations to Reynolds*, p. 449.

Lady. Yet Blake was no dramatist. His playlet exhibits types rather than characters, and never settles down to any action. Nor is this blank verse in the ordinary sense. The trick of varying line-lengths, basic as it was to the Elizabethans and Jacobeans, here becomes absurdly exaggerated. Odd-length lines ranging from dimeter to septenary, instead of being saved up for relief or dramatic effect, are cast about recklessly, and almost outnumber the pentameters. Blake shows impatience even with such slight formal restrictions as blank verse enforces, seeming to feel that if a little freedom is good, a lot must be better. The "Imitation of Spenser" and "King Edward the Third" foreshadow the Blake who was in old age to declare that "the outward Ceremony," in art and religion equally, "is Antichrist" (*The Laocoön*, p. 776).

Two other pieces, "Gwin, King of Norway" and "Blind-Man's Buff," remain formally closer to their sources, yet miss catching the right spirit. "Blind-Man's Buff," an attempt at genre painting with meter taken from *L'Allegro* and opening lines

When silver Snow decks Susan's cloaths,
And jewel hangs at th'shepherd's nose, (*PS*, p. 15)

from "When icicles hang by the wall" in *Love's Labours Lost*, attempts jollity; but despite the lively rhythm, this is a tedious and trivial tale. "Gwin, King of Norway" is a heroic-saga type poem in ballad measure, possibly taken from Percy's *Reliques*, of which Blake at some time possessed a first edition,[5] and also influenced by Chatterton's "Godred Crovan."[6] Its account of a rebellion against tyranny, Erdman has supposed, allegorizes the American revolt;[7] and its propagandistic tone ("O what have kings to answer for, / Before that awful throne!") resembles Shelley's efforts to

[5] Margaret Ruth Lowery, *Windows of the Morning, a Critical Study of William Blake's Poetical Sketches, 1783*, Yale Studies in English, No. 93 (New Haven, 1940), p. 160.

[6] Not published with Chatterton's *Poems* until 1778; *PS* presumably composed 1769–77. But Blake might have seen the piece in *Town and Country Magazine* of August, 1760. See Lowery, *Windows of the Morning*, p. 171.

[7] David V. Erdman, *Blake, Prophet Against Empire* (Princeton, 1954), ch. 2.

adapt his art to the simple understanding of the masses. Here again, Blake's rhythm has variety and vigor. But the poem misses that impact which traditional ballad makes through understatement. Its sentiment is too thick, its didactic intent too apparent, and its descriptions of gore are too laden with romantic metaphor, neither sufficiently conventional nor journalistically precise enough for ballad.

If the *Poetical Sketches* contained only these juvenile items, a reader would have no cause to expect that their author, who seems unwilling to overcome a natural clumsiness, and reluctant to obey the simplest rules of his craft, would pursue the irksome path of verse much longer. But then there are the briefer lyrics, one group in blank verse, another in rhyme, which show as great an impatience with "outward ceremony" as the longer pieces, but also show good cause for their impatience.

The songs to the Seasons, Evening Star, and Morning are Blake's first youthful triumphs in the art of sweet sound. These unrhymed lyrics claim several forebears. Their music recalls Collins; either Thomson or the Spenser of the "Mutabilitie" cantos might have suggested the "Seasons," with their rich sensuous imagery; and the inspiration for "To Morning" has been attributed to the Spenser of the "Epithalamion." Certainly the call to morning to "issue forth" as a virgin, pure yet radiant and spirited, nicely catches the Spenserian invocation of chastity. Similarly, Blake's cry to the evening star to light her "bright torch of love," an influence protective of mortal amorousness against the dangers of night and the wild beasts of the forest, recalls the close of the "Epithalamion." There are a few notes of purest Augustan, as in the balanced epithets of "Flourish down the bright cheek of modest eve" in "To Autumn." Milton, too, has touched these poems. Compare the close of *Lycidas* with that of "To Autumn":

> "The spirits of the air live on the smells
> Of fruit; and joy, with pinions light, roves round
> The gardens, or sits singing in the trees."

> Thus sang the jolly Autumn as he sat;
> Then rose, girded himself, and o'er the bleak
> Hills fled from our sight; but left his golden load.
>
> (*PS*, p. 2)

Perhaps the most interesting metrical fact about these lyrics is that they follow the letter, but not the spirit, of syllabic scansion. Blake owned, at some point in his life, Bysshe's *Art of English Poetry;*[8] and in his preface to *Jerusalem* he seems to acknowledge that his readers will expect uniformity of syllabic count and iambic regularity, for he takes the trouble to inform them that he has "produced a variety in every line, both of cadences & number of syllables" (p. 621). He would certainly have heard, even as a youth, of the decasyllabic rule. But he has cheated his preceptors; or, in his naïveté, he has imagined that he was actually doing what the Byssheans said he should, although in fact he was doing something more interesting. While careful in most places to limit himself to ten count-out-able syllables per line, his rhythms hold to regular iambics only enough to establish them as the base beat, from which he freely diverges. The lyrics are very boldly enjambed, often with a weak preposition or conjunction placed as last syllable, the hazards of such boldness being at least partially averted by sensitive handling of stress and pause:

> O thou who passest thro' our vallies in
> Thy strength, curb thy fierce steeds, allay the heat
> That flames from their large nostrils! thou, O Summer,
>
> ("Summer," p. 1)

> Let thy west wind sleep on
> The lake; speak silence with thy glimmering eyes,
> And wash the dusk with silver. ("Evening Star," p. 3)

> O radiant morning, salute the sun,
> Rouz'd like a huntsman to the chace, and, with
> Thy buskin'd feet, appear upon our hills. ("Morning," p. 3)

[8] See *Notebook*, pp. 440–41.

Note that the weak final syllable is caught up by a pause after the first following foot in two cases, and is in the third worked smoothly into a rhythm which runs / ˘ ˘ / ˘ ˘ ˘ / ˘ ˘ ˘ / from "Rouz'd" to "busk-," then straightens out again. Manipulating his internal cadences by ear instead of by iambs, Blake has the trochee opening of "Róuz'd lĭke"; the spondees of "Ó thóu," "lárge nóstrils," "spéak sílence"; and the internal stress-reversals of "cúrb thy̆," "Lét thy̆," "sléep ŏn" and "mórnĭng." The excellence of lines like "Ŏ rádĭănt mórnĭng, sălúte thĕ sún" is that this rhythm appears as a fresh opening (fitting the spirit of invocation) after five plain iambic lines; and at the same time, because the influence of the prior lines cannot immediately be dispelled, one's reading adjusts slightly to what the metrical beat was expected to be: "Ŏ rádĭánt mŏrníng, sălúte thĕ sún." The net effect includes a kind of sustaining of -ing, which is assisted by the ensuing pause, and which helps produce the lyric's effect of eager pleading.

The remaining lyrics of the *Poetical Sketches* are "Elizabethan and Caroline" in manner. As Saintsbury points out, "nobody except Chatterton had sung like that—had modulated measures like that—since the beginning of the seventeenth century."[9] Included in this group are "How sweet I roamed from field to field," "My silks and fine array," "Memory, hither come" and the "Mad Song," the last of which Saintsbury considers the opening document of modern prosody. These lyrics, at last, require no apology. They are as perfect and transparent as their models, depending on typically Elizabethan inventions of stanza patterns in slight lines of two, three, and four stresses. Often there is some variation of stress in corresponding lines of successive stanzas. The first lines of the four stanzas of "Memory," for example, read:

Mémŏry̆, híthĕr cóme,

Ĭ'll póre ŭpŏn thĕ stréam,

[9] George Saintsbury, *A History of English Prosody* (London, 1906–10), III, 11.

Ĭ'll drínk ŏf thĕ cléar stréam,

Ánd, whĕn níght cómĕs, Ĭ'll gó (*PS*, p. 8)

Blake's most radical alteration of stanza-pattern comes in the "Mad Song." The first stanza of this goes:

The wild winds weep,
  And the night is a-cold
Come hither, Sleep,
  And my griefs infold:
But lo! the morning peeps
  Over the eastern steeps,
And the rustling birds of dawn
The earth do scorn. (*PS*, pp. 8–9)

The poem's basic meter is iambic: one quatrain of dimeters, one of three trimeters and a closing dimeter. Blake keeps these line-lengths (dimeter and trimeter) throughout, but varies the iambs with inversions, spondees, and anapests, so that in the course of three stanzas every line is lifted from its pattern at least once. These variations follow the sense, swelling and contracting in intensity with it, though never to the point of puncturing the basic metrical unity. Blake's inspiration for this lyric might have come from *Lear*, or from several "mad songs" in the second volume of Percy's *Reliques*. From none of these models, however, could he have taken the principle of substitution employed as he employs it here. Here again, then, the young poet departs from precedent; but this time with success.

On the other hand, to show what Blake at the age of fourteen could do with iambs which vary no more than Pope's, we may consider the song, "How sweet I roam'd from field to field." The usual epithets, "charming," "delightful," miss half the point of this poem, whose underlying spirit is terror.[10] It is the young who discover that "one may smile and smile and be a villain"; the

[10] See, for example, the analysis of the poem's sound in Edith Sitwell, *The Pleasures of Poetry* (London, 1934), pp. 248–50, which captures all the charm, and misses all the terror.

exquisitely sweet sound of this poem is, like that of the Queen of the Night's aria in *Die Zauberflöte*, exquisitely ironic, for the beauty of the prince of love is malevolent:

> With sweet May dews my wings were wet,
>   And Phoebus fir'd my vocal rage;
> He caught me in his silken net,
>   And shut me in his golden cage.
>
> He loves to sit and hear me sing,
>   Then, laughing, sports and plays with me;
> Then stretches out my golden wing,
>   And mocks my loss of liberty. (*PS*, p. 6)

The "swéet Máy déws" convey rapture—and on second reading, pathos, when we have realized the meaning of the delicate, symmetrical emphasis of "He cáught me in his sílken nét, / And shút me in his gólden cáge." The final stanza is accented perfectly evenly, with only a hint of dying fall in the alternate lines, "sports and plays with me," "loss of liberty." The caged bird sings, the gold remains untarnished. This technique of ironic smoothness will reappear, in the period of *Songs of Experience*, in *Thel*, and occasionally in the Prophetic Books. Blake's eye for poetic decorum was not so jaundiced as to prevent him from employing it when he chose, but his attitude remains rebellious. The "outward Ceremony" appals him, and beauty, he perceives, can be a bitter thing.

In concluding our survey of Blake's early experiments, we come to the strangest and most ominous among them, his imitations of Ossian. Blake rightly recognized Macpherson's fiction as the harbinger of a style nearer his own heart than any his century had yet generated. This was enough to prove its authenticity for him. "I believe both Macpherson & Chatterton, that what they say is Ancient Is so," he wrote. "I own myself an admirer of Ossian equally with any other Poet whatsoever, Rowley & Chatterton also." [11]

[11] *Annotations to Wordsworth*, p. 783.

The *Fingal* and other poems of Ossian employ prose form, but they have a prominent iambic beat, and they can usually be broken up with fair regularity into septenaries having a strong caesura after the fourth beat (and thus approximating the ballad form), often alternating with alexandrines or other line-lengths. Blake, evidently intrigued by this marginal form, attempted similar effects with a pentameter base in several sketches with such titles as "The Couch of Death," "Contemplation," and a "Samson" taken partly from the Bible, partly from Milton. As in the "King Edward the Third" experiment, he treats his meter with extreme freedom, so that the five-stress lines often barely emerge beneath such readings as:

"Parting is hard, and death is terrible; / I seem to walk through a deep valley, / far from the light of day, alone and comfortless! / The damps of death fall thick upon me! Horrors stare me in the face! / I look behind, there is no returning; Death follows after me; / I walk in regions of Death, where no tree is; / without a lantern to direct my steps, without a staff to support me."

("The Couch of Death" [divisions mine], p. 35)

There is a hiatus of several years in this sort of radical experimentation. When Ossian returns to Blake's poetry, he appears in full battle-dress with his septenaries intact, although now lined up to look as well as read like verse. But this is not until the prophecies, of which we will postpone discussion in order to deal with what many consider the only valuable part of Blake's work, his lyrical books.

PART II

The Lyrics

4

The Discovery of Childhood

> Piper sit thee down and write
> In a book that all may read.—
>
> (Introduction to *Innocence*, p. 111)

However lovely the best songs in *Poetical Sketches* may be, they are not in Blake's own voice. With the possible exception of "How sweet I roam'd from field to field," which may be taken as something more specifically Blakean than the traditional love complaint, these songs might have been written by someone else, if not by anyone else in Blake's time. They are conventional. They belong to the world of Elizabethan artifice, where the impulse to clothe the emotion of a dirge or a lover's woe in such metrically light, fine raiment as "Fear no more the heat o' the sun" or "Come away, come away death" corresponded to an understanding of art as an imitation of Beauty. That Blake was responding to just such an impulse in those songs of the *Poetical Sketches* which blow passions about as if they were soap bubbles, is obvious. If the songs are, as C. S. Lewis would say, as "golden" as their models, it is because the alchemy is the same.

These lyrics demonstrate for the first and last time what Blake might have done, had he chosen to follow traditional paths as a poet. He did not so choose. Never again will he be caught using an artistic convention for its own, or for beauty's, sake. He will always, from *Songs of Innocence* on, let his ideas dictate his forms, so that, as the ideas grow less and less to resemble anything the world had previously encountered, the forms less and less accord with what the world calls art. Craftsmanship remains, but this is the property of a man who hammers together a chair to be sat on, not one who makes a delicate statuette to be deposited on a shelf, looked at, and not touched.

The craftsmanship in *Innocence* is so utilitarian that many early critics failed to recognize it. This accounts for much of the sentimentality surrounding these lyrics, for the fallacy of the inspired doggerelist—"Blake with his singularly pure though artless melody" [1]—and for the dangerous biographical fallacy:

> This was a time in his career when life had not begun to throw its shadows over the brightness of his youthful visions. Reality had not yet brought him any of those sufferings and disillusions that it keeps in store for all of us,[2]

which conveniently forgets that Blake was thirty-two, had written *An Island in the Moon* and possibly *Tiriel*, and had attended the deathbed of a beloved brother, when he etched *Songs of Innocence*.

For his readers, the lucky accident about the songs is not Blake's skill, but the concurrence of his inspiration with a form which happens to be widely acknowledged as beautiful, the children's song.

Some form of lyric was inevitable for him at this point. "Lyrical poetry, song," as Professor Grierson has stated it,

> took its rise . . . in union with music and dance, and even though the poet no longer writes with music and dance as conceived accompani-

[1] T. S. Omond, *English Metrists* (Oxford, 1921), p. 114.

[2] Paul Berger, *William Blake, Poet and Mystic*, trans. Donald H. Conner (London, 1914), p. 303.

ments to his words, he yet retains what was the essential motive and effect of the union, the trinity in unity. A good song, even if set to no music and read in silence, still sings and dances in the reader's brain, because it is still an expression of the mood of ecstasy, of escape from the control of reason and prudence.[3]

In *Innocence* and *Experience* Blake intended to slip behind people's "reason and prudence" in order to reach the intuition, which in an "ecstasy" either of delight or of horror would recognize his truths about the human soul. Lyric is the only form brief enough to let a poet present a vision and then run away, if he wishes, without explanations. The reader, denied any external intellectual handles, then must either enter the poet's world entirely, or remain outside. As for the implied union of music and dance in lyric, we remember that Blake was a singer of his own songs at the Mathews salon;[4] and perhaps the illustrations to his illuminated books, with their flying birds, creeping tendrils, and animated figures, attempt to supply the dimension of dance.

The approach through children's verse, which in some ways is a distillation of lyric as lyric is a distillation of common speech, came partly from the fact that "the child" was at once Blake's intended audience and his chief symbol in the *Songs*. He noted, as he wrote his dissatisfied patron the Reverend Dr. Trusler in 1799, "a Great Majority of Fellow Mortals who can Elucidate My Visions, & Particularly they have been Elucidated by Children, who have taken a greater delight in contemplating my Pictures than I even hoped" (*Letters*, p. 794). The Reverend Doctor may or may not have caught Blake's implied reference to the Gospel dictum requiring men to become as little children before entering heaven. But we, at least, can find in Blake as the original inventors of childhood and pastoral symbolism, whether religious or literary, a strong drive toward simplification, reduction, exclusion,

[3] H. J. C. Grierson, *Lyrical Poetry from Blake to Hardy* (London, 1928), p. 17.

[4] J. T. Smith, *Biographical Sketch of Blake*, reprinted in Arthur Symons, *William Blake* (New York, 1907), p. 360.

purification. This is the dominant impulse behind *Songs of Innocence and Experience.*

Blake seems first to have stumbled on his *Songs* while clambering about some ungainly escarpments of *An Island in the Moon*, in the eleventh and penultimate chapter of which shrill satire, as at the eleventh hour, three characters suddenly sing the first drafts of "Holy Thursday," the "Nurse's Song," and "The Little Boy Lost." It is difficult to conceive what these three embryo songs of innocence are doing in the Moon, amidst the thrashings of Blakean disgust at social convention, rationalist philosophy, chemistry, women, the literary world, and what not. They hardly seem to belong in the mouths of the fatuous characters who speak them. Probably they got there by accident; one burst of energy among many happened to take the form of indirect rather than direct satire, of mockery by escape.

Note the sequence of these songs. The first ("Twas on a Holy Thursday, their innocent faces clean") most resembles its lunar environment, since it take place in the city, has didactic intent, and its singer is an adult who does not participate in, but only observes, the beatification of the charity children. The second lyric ("When the voices of children are heard on the green") uses the point of view of a kindly nurse who seems half child herself, its scene is idyllic countryside, and it teaches no moral; it only discloses happiness. The third ("Father, Father, where are you going") has entirely entered the child's world. Scenery and personality have vanished equally, because the very young possess no conceptual frame for them. There is only the frightened child's self, aware for the first time of its solitary Fatherless identity. In context, this gradual exclusion of adulthood works satirically. Blake has temporarily turned off his Moon-world as certain cranky persons turn off their hearing aids, in a gesture of disgust and defiance.[5]

But in that silence, a private music appears. The elaborated

[5] See David V. Erdman, *Blake, Prophet Against Empire* (Princeton, 1954), pp. 110–12.

Songs of Innocence, etched four or five years later, make childhood the symbol of a state of joy, love, and trust, in an Eden presided over by a tender mother who, helpless herself, waits upon a gentle God. Evil, like a wild beast, is tamed by these guardians, or by the power of the child's innocence to disregard it:

> Hush Tom never mind it, for when your head's bare,
> You know that the soot cannot spoil your white hair.
>
> (*Innocence*, p. 117)

No satire seems implicit in the *Songs of Innocence*, until its publication along with *Songs of Experience* makes clear that the "two contrary states of the human soul" are parodies of each other in which "the Eye altering alters all." [6] An infant's name is not necessarily Joy; he may be a fiend in a cloud. A chimney sweeper may or may not redeem physical misery by vision. A happy nursemaid may sympathize with her charges' frolickings, but a frustrated one may grit her teeth and think nasty thoughts about infant sexuality. The human form divine is Love, or a hungry Gorge, depending on "the Organ that beholds it." [7] By publishing the two sets of songs together, Blake tried to make it impossible for anyone to react sentimentally to either set. Whoever wished to babble over the natural sweetness and happiness of childhood would be reminded by *Songs of Experience* that childhood was by no means always sweet, and that happiness was against Nature.

[6] "The Mental Traveller," *Pickering MS*, p. 426. Mark Schorer, *William Blake, the Politics of Vision* (New York, 1946), p. 245, seems to observe only half the irony: "Imitations of the 'good-Godly' songs of the newly founded Sunday schools, the *Songs of Innocence* appropriate the piety doled out to the underprivileged children of the factory and the mining districts, and then, in the same meters, the *Songs of Experience* shift from the ideal images of shepherds and lambs ... and retain only those which the children of the poor really knew, the images of poverty, despair, and death."

Cf. Northrop Frye, *Fearful Symmetry: a Study of William Blake* (Princeton, 1947), p. 237: "The *Songs of Experience* are satires, but one of the things that they satirize is the state of innocence. They show us the butcher's knife which is waiting for the unconscious lamb. Conversely, the *Songs of Innocence* satirize the state of experience, as the contrast which they present to it makes its hypocrisies more obviously shameful."

[7] *For the Sexes: the Gates of Paradise*, p. 760.

Rousseau—or at least the popular conception of him—would be answered. Wordsworth—four years before the *Lyrical Ballads* and a decade before the completion of *The Prelude*—was answered in advance. On the other hand, social reformers who might wish to use the *Songs of Experience* as a stick to beat Church and State would be reminded by *Songs of Innocence* that human perfection never arises from material well-being, but only and always from spiritual strength. The rationalist, materialist outlook was no less sentimental, because no less limited, than blind adoration of the child or the savage. Godwin would be answered. Paine would be answered.

Yet the animating spirit of *Songs of Innocence and Experience* would not be clever argument, but the presentation of simple, self-evident truths. For us, much of the poetic effectiveness of the *Songs of Experience* comes from the tension established between the simple *rhythms* of "The Tyger" (compare its opening lines with "Twinkle twinkle little star") or "A Poison Tree" and their apparently complex *sense*. But we have no reason to suppose that the meaning of "The Tyger" was any more abstruse to Blake than that of "The Lamb." If we can judge by his coupling of the two books in the same form, Blake seems to have felt the state of experience to be as essentially simple as that of innocence. In order to write *Innocence* he had to purge his mind, temporarily, of Experience; and to write *Experience*, he had to cauterize Innocence. In each set, a state of the human soul would stand pristinely pure, divested of its contrary. Popular symbolism states Blake's requirements nicely in the phrase "naked as a newborn babe." What better techniques to use for this purpose than the most primitive, those associated with infancy and childhood?

The only earlier poetic work suggested as a source for Blake's new style is Isaac Watts' *Divine Songs Attempted in Easy Language for the Use of Children*, a book immensely popular in the eighteenth century, several of whose poems in the section entitled *Moral Songs* find parallels in Blake (see Appendix A). In one sense, Blake intentionally perpetuated the eighteenth-century tradition of morally oriented children's literature. But Blake and Watts have different approaches to both children and morality.

Comparing Watts' "Cradle Hymn" and Blake's "Cradle Song," we find that the mother in Watts improves the occasion by preaching a well-organized little Addisonian sermon to her infant, explaining to it what hardships the Christ child endured to save it from eternal fire, and telling it to be grateful that "here's no ox anear thy bed." Blake's singer also mentions "thy maker." "Thou his image ever see," she says, assuming that the baby knows him well enough. The Saviour's smiles when he became an "infant small" were like an infant's and a mother's smiles, and his tears were like a mother's tears, and no sermon is required. Where Watts finds disparity, Blake finds identity. Where one lectures, the other loves.

Prosodically, too, the only value of a comparison between the two poets would be to show how Blake almost invariably overleaped the pitfalls of simplicity into which Watts, for all his good will, almost invariably stumbled. In the songs just compared, both poets use a four-accent trochaic line. Watts marches boldly along:

> Sleep, my babe; thy food and raiment,
> House and home thy friends provide;
> All without thy care or payment,
> All thy wants are well supplied.[8]

But Blake's language is as full of repetition as a chant, and his crooning, hypnotic rhythms are the rocking of the cradle:

> Sweet dreams form a shade
> O'er my lovely infants head.
> Sweet dreams of pleasant streams,
> By happy silent moony beams. (*Innocence*, p. 120)

[8] Isaac Watts, *Horae Lyricae and Divine Songs* (Boston, 1854), p. 346. See Vivian de Sola Pinto, "William Blake, Isaac Watts, and Mrs. Barbauld," in *Studies in the Poetry and Art of William Blake*, ed. Vivian de Sola Pinto (London, 1957).

Watts' technical apparatus was too limited to suggest the sleepy sensuousness of maternal love, even if such a thing had occurred to him. Internal rhyme belonged to light verse, the closeness of "happy" and "moony" would be bad taste, the careless switch from trochaic to iambic lines (which occurs twice in Blake's poem) would be outside his range, and long monosyllabic feet like "Swéet | dréams | " had in effect not been invented yet. Blake, unhampered by the harness of decorum, was able to present emotion directly in terms of meter and sound.

Much greater resemblances obtain between Blake's work and popular nursery rhymes, the first English collection of which had recently been compiled, probably by Goldsmith, under the title of *Mother Goose's Melody*.[9]

Blake had quoted "The Froggy would a-wooing ride" in *Island in the Moon*, and an echo of "Fe, fi, fo, fum" occurs, queerly enough, in *Jerusalem*. "Boys and girls come out to play, / The moon doth shine as bright as day" [10] was popular as early as Queen Anne's reign, and could have inspired Blake's "Laughing Song" or "Nurse's Song." "Who Killed Cock Robin," [11] which dates from antiquity and was widely printed in eighteenth-century chap-books, probably contributed two birds, the sparrow and robin, and a rhyme (sparrow-arrow) to Blake's "The Blossom." Blake's line "When my mother died I was very young" strikingly resembles the first line of a jingle associated with the American Revolution:

> My father died when I was young
> And left me all his riches:
> His gun and volunteering-cap
> Long sword and leather breeches.[12]

[9] *The Original Mother Goose's Melody, as issued by John Newbery of London, circa 1760...reproduced in facsimile from the first Worcester edition, circa 1785* (London, 1892), contains the preface and the often facetious morals, presumably by Goldsmith.

[10] Iona Opie and Peter Opie, eds., *The Oxford Dictionary of Nursery Rhymes* (Oxford, 1952), pp. 99–100.

[11] *Ibid.*, pp. 130–33.

[12] *Ibid.*, p. 163.

Lambs and sheep were staples of children's verse, in rhymes like "Bo-peep," "Little Boy Blue," and "Baa Baa Black Sheep," for centuries. Blake's affinities with the insular world of nursery rhyme are obvious. Nor would the oral tradition of which Mother Goose is but the skimmings have provided inspiration only for *Innocence,* as anyone will realize who recalls some of the nastier, usually unanthologized, rhymes children invent and recite to each other. George Orwell made the final couplet of that charming song "Oranges and lemons say the bells of St. Clemens" a theme of his *1984* with good reason. It runs, "Here comes a candle to light you to bed, / Here comes a chopper to chop off your head." The *Oxford Dictionary of Nursery Rhymes* notes that "because of their nonsense, or the sadistic tendencies some of the rhymes are alleged to arouse in children, there have been several attempts to suppress or alter them," [13] from the seventeenth to the twentieth century. And nursery rhymes are tame in comparison with the choppings, burnings, and drownings which quite frequently occur in the unsupervised rhymes of older children. These can be gleefully nonchalant:

> Jumbo had a baby
> All dressed in green.
> Jumbo didn't like it
> Gave it to the Queen.
> The Queen did not like it
> Because it was so fat,
> Cut it up in slices
> And gave it to the cat.[14]

It is not a great step from this to Blake's

> In the morning glad I see:
> My foe outstretchd beneath the tree.
>
> (*Experience,* p. 218)

[13] *Ibid.,* p. 2.
[14] *Ibid.,* pp. 200–201.

Even Blake's complaints about the Church may have drawn something from juvenile sources. His little vagabond thinks it would be fine

> . . . if at the Church they would give us some Ale,
> (*Experience*, p. 216)

and children have parodied a well-known hymn as follows, with similar attention to the stomach:

> Jesus, lover of my soul,
> Lead me to the sugar bowl,
> If the sugar bowl is empty,
> Lead me to my mother's pantry.[15]

Technically, Blake could find in the children's songs a flowering of clear, bright, everyday imagery comparable to that of the Bible but with more urban material. He could also find unvarnished English; and his own language in the *Songs* seems to contain as little Latin as could be managed.

Very possibly, too, Blake learned something about cadence from the short stanza-patterns, the rich parallelism and repetition of phrase, and the strong accentual rhythms of nursery rhymes, which constitute the first experience most of us have of linguistic beauty. A prosodic analyst of the Mother Goose rhymes observes that

> children like them because they are rhythmical, and the rhythm is quantitative [i.e., the accents must come at regular intervals regardless of the number of syllables separating them]. . . . The regularity of metrical accent must be maintained even at the expense of logical emphasis, as in
>
> *Pease* porridge *hot, pease* porridge *cold,*
> *Pease* porridge *in* the pot, *nine* days *old.*
>
> . . . The function of rhyme is, perhaps, not primarily to emphasize the accent, but this it does in Mother Goose because the rhymes are so

[15] Iona Opie and Peter Opie, *The Lore and Language of Schoolchildren* (Oxford, 1959), p. 87.

close together. If the lines are short, end-rhyme only is used; if long, internal rhyme is ordinarily employed.[16]

The prime effect which nursery rhymes try to get is that of jingle.

The short lines; the numerous repetitions, found in dozens of the jingles and the basis of such jingles as *There Was a Crooked Man* and *The Old Woman and the Sixpence;* the frequent recurrence of the rhyming sounds . . . all this makes the jingling more pronounced.[17]

This could easily describe many of Blake's songs. Compare the short-line couplets of

> Jack and Jill
> Went up the hill

or

> One, two
> Buckle my shoe,
> Three, four
> Close the door,

with

> Sound the Flute!
> Now it's mute.
> Birds delight
> Day and Night. (*Innocence*, p. 123)

Compare the free-wheeling anapests of

> There was an old woman went up in a basket

with

> When the voices of children are heard on the green
> (*Innocence*, p. 121; *Experience*, p. 212)

or

[16] Walter Barnes, *The Children's Poets* (New York, 1932), p. 23.
[17] *Ibid.*, p. 26.

Dear Mother, dear Mother, the Church is cold.
But the Ale-house is healthy & pleasant & warm.

(*Experience*, p. 216)

The technique Blake uses in "A Cradle Song," of beginning stanzas with monosyllabic feet in lines like | "Swéet | dréams form a shade," | "Swéet | sléep | with soft down," and | "Sléep | sléep | happy child," which have a sing-song rock, appears nowhere so commonly as in nursery rhyme. A few examples are:

Jack Sprat could eat no fat.

See-saw Margery Daw.

Baa, baa, black sheep.

Tom Tom the piper's son.

Rain, rain, go away.

It is also from this source that Blake learned to establish a beat and a mood at the same time by doubling his first word: "Merry Merry Sparrow," "Father, father, where are you going," "Tyger Tyger. burning bright." All these devices are crude, when judged by eighteenth-century standards of poetic subtlety, or even when judged by our own. Yet they constitute an important element of Blake's appeal. By being crude, Blake automatically was criticizing artifice and false complexity, and establishing his own standard of truth.

5

Metrics: Pattern and Variation

How Wide the Gulf & Unpassable!
between Simplicity & Insipidity.
(Mirror-writing, *M*, p. 518)

There is a Buddhist proverb which explains the three stages of wisdom as follows. When you are unenlightened, mountains are mountains and rivers are rivers. As you approach Enlightenment, mountains are not mountains and rivers are not rivers. When you have achieved Enlightenment, mountains are mountains and rivers are rivers.

One's reactions to Blake's *Songs* follow a similar curve. First there is the surface delight. Then we discover that every symbol in these poems has a precise philosophical meaning, and we try to explain the songs in terms of Blake's system. We call this "understanding." Finally, there is again the surface. It is the same with Blake's versification. The immediate impression his verse makes on an unprepared reader will resemble that of jingle. It will seem extremely simple and obvious, providing the same sensuous pleasure which children's rhymes provide. Then the reader will discover that the poetry contains a good deal of formal variation and irregularity, and that the variations not only keep the verse from cloying, but contribute as far as rhythm and sound can do to the establishment of precise meanings. We must analyze their deviations from rhythmic norm. Yet this sort of analysis does not complete our understanding, since we must always return at last to the physical and emotional appeal of Blake's simplicity. Swinburne believed that "the . . . faculty of being right, proper to great lyrical poets, was always an especial quality of Blake's. To go the right way and do the right thing, was in the nature of his metrical gift." [1] He did not elaborate on this feeling. But we can see that Blake's lyric rightness depends on a continual interplay between a primitive regularity which identifies Blake's world with the child's, and a functional irregularity which is the man's work.

The surface naïveté in Blake's metrics associates naturally with the same quality in his language. In diction, simplicity asserts itself through his plain Anglo-Saxon vocabulary, his uncomplicated sentence-structure, and his very heavy use of repetition. Metrically, it is revealed in the two areas of stanza-form and rhythmic beat.

First we can consider the naïveté of language. The most conspicuous stylistic feature of the *Songs* is their extraordinary use of repetition and parallel phrasing. Josephine Miles has found that in a thousand lines taken from Blake's whole poetic work some seventy or eighty nouns, adjectives, and verbs will appear more than ten times, instead of the thirty or forty common to other poets.[2] Actually, the concentration is greater than this implies, for Blake repeats some words in the *Songs* which scarcely reappear in the Prophetic Books, and, conversely, many ubiquitous prophetic favorites like "terrific" make no appearance in the *Songs*.

In *Innocence*, the following words (or variants of them) all occur over ten times: bird, child, infant, lamb, little, laugh, mother, father, sweet. Weep, sleep, and joy occur over twenty

[1] Algernon Charles Swinburne, *William Blake, a Critical Essay* (London, 1906), p. 148.

[2] Josephine Miles, *Eras and Modes in English Poetry* (Berkeley, 1957), p. 79.

times. Blake portrays the infant's and child's world by suggesting the child's limited, intense, and affective vocabulary. Some of these words are distributed evenly through the lyrics, but intensity is also heightened by clustering in single poems, by the "Piping down . . . Piping songs . . . Pipe a song . . . Piper pipe" of the "Introduction," the "Merry Merry Sparrow . . . Pretty Pretty Robin" of "The Blossom," the bare "weep weep weep weep" of "The Chimney Sweeper," the "green woods laugh . . . air does laugh . . . green hill laughs . . . meadows laugh" of "Laughing Song," the "Sweet dreams . . . Sweet sleep . . . Sweet smiles . . . Sweet moans . . . Sleep sleep" of "A Cradle Song." You cannot look anywhere in *Songs of Innocence* without finding these hypnotic repetitions. Then, reinforcing them, you find parallel structures of phrase. "So I piped . . . So I sung . . . And I made . . . And I stain'd . . . And I wrote" defines the process of creation in the "Introduction," and things are typically this simple for Blake. "By the stream & o'er the mead," "I a child & thou a lamb," "Comfort in morning joy in the noonday," "My mother died . . . and my father sold me," "I love to rise in a summer morn . . . But to go to school in a summer morn," "The child was wet . . . the child did weep." These are the beads he strings together to make the *Songs*. It is a world of plain identities, progressions, and contrasts. Only rarely does *Innocence* have a construction even so complicated as "wrath by his meekness / And by his health. sickness."

In *Experience*, which is a briefer group, only love, weep, and night appear more than ten times, although variations of self, father, hand, and fear follow close behind. *Experience* is slightly less mesmeric than *Innocence*, less restricted. As befits its broader world, where the symbols can be more diverse, fewer terms repeat from song to song. Within the poems there is still a fairly high degree of repetition, from "O Earth O Earth" and "Tyger Tyger" to "The Human Dress . . . The Human Form . . . The Human Face . . . The Human Heart." The rule of parallel phrasing also still holds.

In brevity of sentence-structure, which is almost as significant a feature of these songs as verbal repetition, the two groups are virtually identical. The typical complete sentence time and again takes only one or two lines:

> I have no name. (*Innocence*, p. 118)
>
> And now beside thee bleating lamb
> I can lie down and sleep; (*Innocence*, p. 119)
>
> O Rose thou art sick. (*Experience*, p. 213)
>
> Am not I
> A fly like thee? (*Experience*, p. 213)
>
> But a Pebble of the brook,
> Warbled out these metres meet.
> (*Experience*, p. 211)

In longer sentences the common lengtheners are "and" and "but," "if" and "when." Clauses remain brief. As a result, the single unit of the line almost becomes the unit of perception. The line is vivid, compact, complete, a moment of vision; each song composed of such lines is a chain of such moments; and each set of songs is constructed like a mosaic out of these innumerable tiny independent parts.

The metrical form of the songs both reinforces these traits of diction and structure, and is reinforced by them. In both *Innocence* and *Experience* the stanzaic patterns are extremely plain. The lines are usually short, seldom longer than a tetrameter, so that the rhymes come thick and fast. The stanzas themselves are brief units, most commonly quatrains in couplets or cross-rhyme. Only one poem of *Innocence* is in pentameter, one in septenary, and one in dimeter quatrains with a single-line pentameter refrain. In *Experience*, only the "Introduction" and "Earth's Answer," less simple than the rest in diction and more abstract in theme, use complex stanzas. Except for the pentameter refrain of "A Little Girl Lost," no line in *Experience* is longer than four beats. The lines are almost invariably end-stopped in both books, and because the line-unit is also the unit of meaning, we are not allowed to leap ahead or to suspend our thought from line to line. Blake makes us take baby steps, and we feel that each line affords a finished, if minute, esthetic satisfaction.

The use of pause in these poems adds symmetry to simplicity. Consider one of Blake's most famous quatrains:

> Tyger Tyger. / burning bright
> In the forests / of the night;
> What immortal / hand or eye
> Could frame / thy fearful symmetry.

The first two lines each split roughly in half, with the same number of beats before and after the pause. The third line can really be read without a pause, but if there were a break, it would come after "immortal," again dividing the line down the middle. Only the fourth line is asymmetrical. The remainder of "The Tyger" contains only one other asymmetrical line. This pattern is the norm for the *Songs*, as in the following typical first lines from *Innocence:*

> Piping down / the valleys wild
>
> Once a dream / did weave a shade
>
> The Sun / does arise
>
> Sweet dreams / form a shade
>
> Twas on a Holy Thursday / their innocent faces clean,

or these from *Experience:*

> Love seeketh not / itself to please
>
> A little black thing / among the snow
>
> O Rose / thou art sick
>
> Dear Mother, Dear Mother, / the Church is cold.

Lines of two or four feet either split evenly or do not split at all, with few exceptions. Only some of the more rhetorical pieces like

"The Divine Image" and "On Another's Sorrow" in *Innocence,* "The Little Vagabond," "London," and "A Little Boy Lost" in *Experience,* have more than three asymmetrical lines. The three-beat poems usually omit the pause.

These stanza forms of three and four beats, symmetrically divided, are like nursery rhymes, folk songs, and ballads. The four-stress line divided into distichs, with alliteration to help the stresses, was also the meter of *Beowulf.* Although this line may or may not be in some mysterious way "native" to English,[3] it has historically acquired an aura of naturalness, primitiveness, and artlessness, at hand to any poet who uses it. Because of all these factors, we can intone Blake's songs with the kind of regular jingle or thump which children enjoy, without severe distortion. Most poetry cannot be read in this way. We cannot let our voices thump primitively through

> Of *man's* first *disobed*ience *and* the *fruit*
>
> True *wit* is *N*ature *to* ad*van*tage *dress'd*
>
> That *time* of *year* thou *mayst* in *me* be*hold*

without feeling silly. But a primitively accented

> *Lit*tle *Lamb* who *made* thee
> *Dost* thou *know* who *made* thee

does not sound too foolish, even if, ordinarily, we might prefer to stress the "made" in each line a little less, and the first "who" more. And the primitive

> *Ty*ger *Ty*ger. *burn*ing *bright,*
> *In* the *for*ests *of* the *night*

rings in our minds even when we do not intend to stress "in" and "of." Short lines are easier to accent regularly. Alliterated words are easier to accent strongly. A central pause emphasizes the accents. Parallel constructions, brief phrases, images without sur-

[3] See Northrop Frye, *Anatomy of Criticism* (Princeton, 1957), p. 251.

face difficulty, all encourage reading with a fixed beat. This is the first form of rhythm the human ear can perceive. It remains the most accessible, since it is associated with regular organic processes like heartbeat, with semivoluntary activities like breathing and walking, and with simple exercises like foot-tapping and hand-clapping. Blake's *Songs* are so constructed that we will hear in them, with a part of our ear, the unsophisticated succession of regular beats, even while our conscious reading accents more subtly. This undercurrent of simple rhythm must be allowed to go its way, affecting us kinetically rather than mentally, or we will miss a good part of Blake's message.

Yet we cannot ignore the superstructure Blake erects on his primitive rhythmical base. The drawback of children's songs is that they all sound rather alike, lacking the "minute particulars" which induce the more refined mental and emotional satisfactions in poetry. One lullaby, one comic jingle, one counting-out rhyme, is like another. The tune counts more than the words. This is not so in Blake's *Songs*.

To help him fit his measures to his meanings, Blake began with a command of more meters than were dreamt of in the current prosodic philosophy. Iambs, of course, were standard fare. Blake could never serve them up with proper Popean flourish, although some of the notebook epigrams aim at it. Usually he does not try. About a fourth of the lyrics in *Innocence*, and a third in *Experience*, are iambic. They are the soberer pieces in each book: "The Little Black Boy," "The Divine Image," "Holy Thursday" in *Innocence*, the didactic "London," "The Clod and the Pebble," "A Little Boy Lost" and "To Tirzah" in *Experience*. His accomplishment in the pentameter quatrain rivals that of Gray's *Elegy*. From such poems as "The Little Black Boy," remarks Damon, "it would be very difficult to know that Dryden and Pope had existed." [4]

[4] S. Foster Damon, *William Blake, his Philosophy and Symbols* (Boston, 1924), p. 47.

The trochaic line, somewhat less popular in the eighteenth century, was a favorite of Blake's, from which he elicited diverse effects. Several of his best-known pieces are trochaic. One student of metrics finds this "the chief technical means by which Blake obtains his characteristic infantine effect, and gives the impression of speaking through the lips of a child," [5] as in "The Lamb," "The Blossom" or "The Little Girl Lost." This childlike effect comes from the fact that trochaic rhythms, since they start on the downbeat and are usually subject to less variation than iambs, give a more emphatic feeling. They have a quality of directness which lends itself well to Blake's "infant" style. But "Love and harmony combine" from *Poetical Sketches*, "The Tyger" and "A Poison Tree" from *Experience*, and "Never seek to tell thy love" from the Rossetti Notebook, are all different and all excellent. Between one-half and one-third of the poems in *Innocence*, including many of the longer ones, are trochaic; somewhat fewer in *Experience*.

Finally, the uses of anapestic meters, e.g., in "The Ecchoing Green," "The Chimney Sweeper," "The Shepherd," and "Laughing Song" in *Innocence* alone, were virtually his own discovery.

Discussing Blake's anapests, Damon somewhat erroneously states that the Elizabethans never used this meter except accidentally and with poor results.[6] Exceptions, for example the finale of Jonson's "Celebration of Charis," do exist. And, although this was considered a low burlesque meter in the neoclassical period, and was stigmatized as such by Bysshe,[7] Damon errs in implying that the eighteenth century continued to use anapest exclusively for "drinking songs and hunting choruses." The meter was popularized by Prior for dainty society verse and used by Shenstone for pastoral ballads and Cowper for "The Poplar Field." Watts, out of his thousand poems, has five in anapest, and Wesley has thousands of anapestic lines. Wesley, however, inclines to gallop:

[5] Enid Hamer, *The Metres of English Poetry* (London, 1930), p. 242.
[6] Damon, *Blake*, pp. 45–46.
[7] See pp. 16–17, *supra*.

I rode on the Sky
(Freely justified I!)
Nor envied *Elijah* his Seat;
My Soul mounted higher
In a Chariot of Fire,
And the Moon it was under my feet.

Thus although anapest was not unknown in Blake's time, the few serious poems in this meter never exceed prettiness, and tend to lapse into singsong.

Blake's handling of the meter avoids this hazard. We might have expected him to produce poems like the dimpling

The Sun does arise,
And make happy the skies. (*Innocence*, p. 116)

When the voices of children are heard on the green
And laughing is heard on the hill, (*Innocence*, p. 121)

for anapest is well suited to a cheerful, rapid run, in waltz or polka time. But he is not limited to such relatively obvious music. The anapest darkens, with him, to form the strangely grave beat of the first "Chimney Sweeper," the ironic spriteliness of "The Garden of Love," and the terrible, gyring "Rose thou art sick" of *Experience*, where the waltz has become a *danse macabre*.

The poet's facility with trochaic and anapestic measures permits him a greater range of expressiveness than confinement to iambs alone would allow. The iambic poems are closest to normal discursive or argumentative speech. The trochaic poems are barer, more emphatic, purer. The poems in anapest resemble music, and carry the reader along more by the swing and sway of rhythm than by any rational content. Blake had another advantage over his contemporaries: a willingness to vary his lines internally in a manner which had not been practised since the seventeenth century. These irregularities have the double function of avoiding metrical monotony, and of helping him realize his ideas and emotions with as much precision as possible.

The importance of variation in English metrics cannot be overemphasized. If a poet has established enough of a regular metric pattern to set some beat going in our heads, the next most important thing for him is to know how to ring changes on it. These changes will form a counterpoint to the steady beat underneath, and the combination of base-beat and counterpoint will create the unique rhythm of a poem, which a reader always feels whether he knows what is happening or not, and will also help create its unique mood. One of the things that hindered eighteenth-century poets from achieving as full an emotional or musical range as their seventeenth-century forebears or nineteenth-century heirs was their inhibition about metrical irregularity.

To understand the quality of Blake's counterpoint, it will be useful to consider which techniques of variation he did not use, as well as those he did; and also to note where he went beyond the established techniques even of earlier times. The following list of standard variations in English metrics may therefore be compared with Blake's practice.

1. Foot-inversion: usually iamb ◡ ′, inverted to trochee ′ ◡. Inversion of the first foot in iambic meters was a variation common enough to pass uncensured by Augustan critics. Internal inversion was uncommon and final-foot inversion was ignored or condemned by almost everyone, although Milton unquestionably uses it in several lines. A notable Romantic example is Keats' "Bright star! would I were steadfast as thóu ărt." In trochaic and other meters, inversion rarely occurs.
2. Foot-distention: use of more than one stress in a foot, as in a spondee ′ ′. Eighteenth-century writers used spondees, though they may not have called them that; e.g., Pope's "Shút, shút the door, good John!"
3. Foot-substitution: use of a trisyllabic foot for a disyllable, or vice versa. Discovery of this "new" principle, generally ignored in the eighteenth century, was Coleridge's great

announcement in the preface to *Christabel.* On the same principle is:

4. Incomplete or monosyllabic foot: a syllable is dropped, or pause takes the place of a syllable, as in music. The classic example is Tennyson's

> Break, break, break,
> On thy cold grey stones, O sea!

Not affecting the scansion as such, but also used to avoid monotonous cadence, are:

1. Enjambment: run-on or absence of pause at the close of the line.
2. Use of pause or caesura within the line: variation of its position.
3. Accentual variation: (*a*) light or omitted accent on a syllable in stress position—usually admissible anywhere but in the last foot, and sometimes occurring there also; (*b*) variations in degree of normal stress, indicated, from primary to secondary to tertiary, by ´, ^, \` , in the notation currently used in American linguistics.[8] These distinctions, although not ordinarily perceived consciously by an untrained ear, help order the meaning of sentences to us.

[8] See George C. Trager and Henry Lee Smith, Jr., *An Outline of English Structure, Studies in Linguistics,* Occasional Papers, No. 3 (Norman, Okla., 1951).

Among the articles which have applied the Trager-Smith notation to prosody are: Harold Whitehall, "From Linguistics to Criticism"; Seymour Chatman, "Robert Frost's 'Mowing': an Inquiry into Prosodic Structure"; and Chatman, "Mr. Stein on Donne," all in the symposium "English Verse and What it Sounds Like," *Kenyon Review,* XVIII (1956), 411–77. These are more significant as propaganda than as analysis, and have provoked dissenting articles such as W. K. Wimsatt and Monroe C. Beardsley, "The Concept of Meter: an Exercise in Abstraction," *PMLA,* LXXIV (1959), 585–98.

Some more recent, and more genuinely analytical, articles which employ this notation are: Martin Halpern, "On the Two Chief Metrical Modes in English," *PMLA,* LXXVII (1962), 177–86 (in which "The Tyger" is analyzed, p. 179); Joseph M. Williams, "Caliban and Ariel Meet Trager and Smith," *CE,* XXIV (1962), 121–26; and Frederic G. Cassidy, "From Stress to Rhythm—Some Analytic Considerations," Unpubl. art. (Madison, 1962).

4. Variations in tempo, produced partly by heaviness of accent and pause, partly by presence or absence of long vowels or diphthongs, liquidity or clustering of consonants.

The variations of this second group, dependent as they are on the writer's habits of syntax, sentence-structure and sound-pattern, also depend on each reader's habits of intonation, on whether he prefers more or less stress, more or less pause at a given point. Thus, individual instances of such variation, when not bluntly dictated by syntax and punctuation, are often disputable. The general principle is not. Pope, being denied access to most of the major variations, had to rely on these minor ones. They, therefore, make all the difference between the elegant Leviathan of the eighteenth century, and the smaller fish who hurried in his wake. In Blake, however, the situation almost reverses itself, for he makes rather less use of the minor variations, and more of the major.

Only one of these minor variations finds no place in the *Songs of Innocence and Experience:* enjambment, with its verse-paragraph functions. Although Blake was experimenting with run-on in *Poetical Sketches*, and was already developing a paragraph technique in several Prophetic Books composed before the etching of *Experience*, the lyrics of both *Innocence* and *Experience* depend on chains of single lines linked by the conspicuous chime of like sounds; their music gives one grain of sand at a time, rather than the prospect of a whole beach at once. Thus the lines are almost always end-stopped.

Two other variations used only slightly in the *Songs* are asymmetrical pause-placement and dropped accents. As observed above, Blake's pauses tend to split his lines in half. In addition, he tends to avoid placing light syllables in stress positions. He does have some lines like:

I was angry wĭth my friend (*Experience*, p. 218)

Gave thee clothing ŏf delight
(*Innocence*, p. 115)

Nor is it possiblĕ to Thought
A greater thăn Itself to know.

(*Experience*, p. 218)

But these are relatively rare. If there were many more, the verse would lose its steady thump.

Still, despite the sparseness of dropped accents and unbalanced pauses, the rhetoric provides enough slight variation to prevent monotony. The "Introduction" to *Innocence*, for example, remains lively despite its considerable regularity. This becomes clear if we use the notation of structural linguistics:

Píping dówn the válleys wíld
Píping sóngs of pléasant glée
Òn a clóud I sâw a chíld.
And hé láughing sáid to mê.

Pípe a sóng abôut a Lámb:
Sò I píped with mérry chéar,
Píper pípe that sóng agáin—
Sò I píped, he wépt to héar. (*Innocence*, p. 111)

The tripping quality of this measure, and of many others in Blake, is due to our skimming past one or more full accents in over half the lines. Several of the stresses I have marked might be considered optional by a still more skim-minded reader; e.g., "down," l. 1, "song," l. 7. Conversely, one might wish to accent "saw," l. 3. Note also that the internal pause, where it exists, comes mostly after the third syllable, but once clearly after the fourth (l. 4), and once after the second (l. 7).

To illustrate the importance even of slight differences in degree of stress, perhaps the clearest example is the last stanza of "Spring," where the lines could hardly be shorter, the beat more regular, or the diction more monosyllabic. Almost no room remains for any variation; yet the verse simply does not read so rigidly as a strict scansion of it,

´ ˘ ´ | ´ ˘ ´ | ´ ˘ ´ | ´ ˘ ´ |, etc.,

would imply, for the degree of stress is not quite identical everywhere. My reading is as follows:

> Líttlĕ Lámb
> Hére Ĭ ám,
> Cóme ănd lîck
> Mỳ whĭte néck.
> Lét mĕ pûll
> Yòur sŏft Wóol.
> Lét mĕ kîss
> Yòur sŏft fáce.
> Mérrĭlў Mérrĭlў, wĕ wélcŏme ín thĕ Yéar.
>
> (*Innocence*, p. 123)

The tone would be a somewhat wheedling one: "*Come* and . . . *Let* me . . . *Let* me," changing into bouncing assurance for the dactyls and iambs of the refrain. Probably, too, some account should be made of the slight difference in rhythm between the disyllable "Little" and the monosyllables "Here I"; of the slight difference in length of pronunciation between "and . . . me . . . me" and "white . . . soft . . . soft" which gives the latter words a shade more emphasis; and of the differences in strength of the pauses at the line-ends. Put together, all these variations produce even in this least complex of poetic constructions a little play of contrapuntal pattern: while the rhyme-scheme gives the pattern aa bb cc dd e, the rhetorical structure of the phrases gives a pattern 1,2 3,4 3,4 3,4 5.

Blake's control of tempo may be seen if we compare certain poems with each other. The line of "Little Lamb who made thee" is slower than "Merry Merry Sparrow," although they scan alike. A few of the lyrics also reveal some internal variation of tempo. In "London," for example, the first stanza has a moderate pace:

> I wander thro' each charter'd street,
> Near where the charter'd Thames does flow
> And mark in every face I meet
> Marks of weakness, marks of woe. (*Experience*, p. 216)

Then, in its progress of vision from the surface stigmata, "marks," of evil to the internal causes, "mind-forg'd manacles," and finally to perception of the inevitable connections between evils, "London" reads in a crescendo of volume, intensity, and sonorousness, growing slower and more damning at each stage, until the final

> But most thro' midnight streets I hear
> How the youthful Harlots curse
> Blasts the new born Infants tear,
> And blights with plagues the Marriage hearse

with its strong alliteration, the explosive consonant clusters of "*bl*asts . . . *bl*ights . . . *pl*agues" and, to cap "Harlots curse," the bitterly outflung "Marriage hearse."

"The Fly" shifts tempo in mid-course. The opening is rather rapid, rather conspicuously casual:

> Little Fly
> Thy summers play,
> My thoughtless hand
> Has brush'd away. (*Experience*, p. 213)

Succeeding stanzas keep this tone, up to the easy homiletic "For I dance / and drink and sing / Till some blind hand / Shall touch my wing." This is ancient doctrine: Blake has said nothing new yet. Then in the fourth stanza comes the change:

> If thought is life
> And strength & breath;
> And the want
> Of thought is death;

The language is suddenly impersonal, the idea striking, and the words more difficult to articulate because of the consonants. We are forced to slow up, to pronounce each key word deliberately: "if thought—is life—and strength—and breath. . . ." But in the last stanza the poem returns to its initial smiling rapidity. "Then am I / A happy fly. / If I live / or if I die." "The Fly" has been considered a hard poem to understand, among critics who try to expound Blake's meanings logically.[9] This is because the façade of logic in the poem is a joke, a trap. If we listen without ratiocination to the poem's sound, we find a dialectic of moods from tarnished cheerfulness, to solemnity, to a higher cheerfulness, which is not at all effected by logical means. The conclusion of Blake's if-then construction does not *follow* from its premise, although both premise and conclusion are assumed true. What happens instead is that the poet is momentarily lifted from the plane of moral reflection to the plane of vision. He discovers himself thinking—with sudden fervor—that "thought is life," and realizes by his own intensity of thought that he himself is alive, and therefore happy, and therefore like the fly (which of course also thinks and is happy), and that nothing else matters. It does not even matter if he will die in the future, since he has discovered himself living now. The last stanza can afford to be purely merry, because Blake's moment of vision has obliterated both his guilt about the fly and his concern for his own morrow.

In the original MS version of this poem, the final stanza came immediately after the third: "For I dance / And drink & sing / . . . Then am I / A happy fly." This makes sense, but lacks power. It leaves the poem all on one level. By inserting the crucial fourth stanza, Blake spoiled his logic and perfected his lyric. "The Fly" is an excellent example of a poem which achieves its ends through surface manipulation.

Except in "London" and "The Fly," internal tempo-variation is an insignificant part of Blake's technique. This is not surprising, since most of the songs express stasis rather than progress; they keep to one pace for the same reason that they keep their lines end-stopped.

In his use of the minor variations, Blake does no more than any competent lyricist might do. Except for small signs like the single-

[9] See the controversy in *Essays in Criticism,* XI (1961): Leo Kirschbaum, "Blake's 'The Fly,'" pp. 154–62; F. W. Bateson, "An Editorial Postscript," pp. 162–63; and John E. Grant, "Misreadings of 'The Fly,'" pp. 481–86. Robert Gleckner, *The Piper and the Bard* (Detroit, 1959), p. ix, has declared that he does not know how to read this poem.

stanza break in tone and tempo of "The Fly," which would never have been perpetrated by a Collins or Gray, it is difficult to distinguish him, technically, from other poets of his age. Only in the major variations, where formal scansion is affected and where his contemporaries feared to tread too far, does his difference become pronounced.

Inversion, the most commonly acknowledged of the major variations, figures in thirteen of the 23 songs in *Innocence*, fifteen of the 23 (counting "A Divine Image") in *Experience*. Most of the usages are initial, although internal inversion, as in

> When the painted birds láugh ĭn the shade,
>
> (*Innocence*, p. 125)

occurs occasionally in both books. Blake does not invert his iambs very heavily compared with other poets. But he does break precedent by having several inverted trochees, sometimes bearing considerable expressive weight. In "Earth's Answer," an inverted initial foot throws stress on the phrase "frée Lóve":

> Selfish! vain!
> Eternal bane!
> Thăt frée Love with bondage bound.
>
> (*Experience*, p. 211)

In "On Another's Sorrow," the repeated cry "And not" throws stress on "not"; it is a lyric of incredulity:

> Can I see anothers woe,
> Ănd nót be in sorrow too.
> Can I see anothers grief,
> Ănd nót seek for kind relief.
>
> (*Innocence*, p. 122)

In "The Tyger," two inversions in one line emphasize the mystery-denoting particle "what":

> Ănd whát shoulder, &̆ whát art,
> Could twist the sinews of thy heart?
>
> (*Experience*, p. 214)

In each case, the suggestion of a human voice, articulating its anger, wonder, or terror, is the more vivid because of the wrenched accents.

Like initial iambic inversions, spondaic feet were accepted among Blake's peers. In the *Songs*, spondees appear fairly frequently, usually for some specific rhetorical emphasis, as in "Súch súch were the joys" or "The mínd-|fórg'd mán|acles I hear." They can also help mold the entire spirit of a poem, when tellingly employed as in "The Tyger," where they pound away repeatedly, or in the two flower lyrics of *Experience*, "O Rose thou art sick" and "The Sunflower":

> Áh Sún-flower! weary of time.
> Who countest the steps of the Sun:
> (*Experience*, p. 215)

This tragically top-heavy effect in the opening, with the slender stemlike regularity of the remainder of the poem, anticipates Tennyson's

> Heavily hangs the broad sunflower
> Over its grave i' the earth so chilly.

Or there is that poised effect produced by the final spondee in a tiny Notebook lyric:

> He who binds to himself a joy [10]
> Does the winged life destroy;
> But he who kisses the joy as it flies
> Lives in eternity's sún ríse. (*Notebook*, p. 179)

Blake also, I think uniquely among English poets except Browning, sometimes slips extra stresses in among his anapests, generating quite novel rhythms. He does this a few times in the first "Chimney Sweeper," where he lets the speaker's enthusiasm overflow into extra accents for an effect of wide-eyed eagerness:

[10] Keynes' reading is "bends"; Joseph H. Wicksteed, *Blake's Innocence and Experience* (London, Toronto, and New York, 1928), p. 271 n., claims to see a dot over the vowel, and reads "binds." The latter word is more typical of Blake.

That thousands of sweepĕrs Díck Jóe, | Néd & Jáck
And by came an Angel who had ă bríght kéy
Then down a green plain léapĭng láughing, they run.
(*Innocence*, p. 117)

Quite a different effect appears at the close of "The Ecchoing Green." The first two stanzas here end with a merry refrain: "While our sports shall be seen / On the Ecchoing Green." "In our youth time were seen / On the Ecchoing Green." But the third, which tells of sunset and twilight after the day of mirth, when the children are gathered to their mothers, concludes gravely:

And sport nó móre seen
On the darkening Green. (*Innocence*, p. 116)

Monosyllabic feet are rare in Blake, as in most English verse. Two notable instances, however, occur in the swaying rhythms of "A Cradle Song," and in the powerful first line of the "Introduction" to *Experience:*

Héar | thĕ vóice | ŏf thĕ Bárd!

where the successive feet consist of one, two, and three syllables.

This brings us to the technique of substitution, which is milk to modern taste, but was bones to the critical philosophy of Blake's day. Blake had begun substituting anapests for iambs in several of the *Poetical Sketches*, most radical of which was the "Mad Song." Slightly over half the lyrics of both *Innocence* and *Experience* are sown with substitution, and the gain in flexible movement seems incalculable. Blake's use of this device marks his emancipation from the golden cage of eighteenth-century precept. He could also use his versatility to create new patterns in which a particular variation becomes the rule, and freedom is turned to the service of order. One charming instance of such patterning is the mixed-meter stanza of "Laughing Song," with its iambic catches among the anapests:

When the green woods laugh with the voice of joy
And the dimpling stream runs laughing by,
When the air does laugh with our merry wit.
And the green hill laughs with the noise of it.
(*Innocence*, p. 124)

Another is "Night," which has a stanzaic pattern consisting of a ballad quatrain followed by four lines in anapestic dimeter. In each stanza, the iambic lines are placed as it were horizontally, with independent clauses which parallel each other, while the anapests, in a soft continuous flow of one sentence, suggest the vertical:

The sun descending in the west,
The evening star does shine.
The birds are silent in their nest,
And I must seek for mine.
The moon like a flower,
In heavens high bower;
With silent delight,
Sits and smiles on the night. (*Innocence*, p. 118)

The repeated alternation from stanza to stanza produces a sensation of hovering between waking and dream.

A third instance is "The Sick Rose," which gives the impression of strictest unity where Blake is in fact being most free. In my reading, only the fourth and eighth lines scan identically:

Ó Róse thŏu ărt síck.
Thĕ ĭnvísĭblĕ wórm.
Thăt flíes ĭn thĕ níght
Ĭn thĕ hówlĭng stórm:

Hăs fóund óut thy̆ béd
Ŏf crímsŏn jóy:
Ănd hĭs dárk sécrĕt lóve
Dŏes thy̆ lífe dĕstróy. (*Experience*, p. 213)

When read without pauses, this approaches the pulse of continuous anapest. The downward, spiraling motion fits the poem's evocation of eroticism. The sound-linked spondees *Ó* R*ó*se, F*óu*nd *óu*t, dá*rk* sé*cr*et, make the motion slow, emphatic, and therefore the more cruel. The anapests, and the sound-links between accents—*sí*ck, *in*ví*s*ible; *flíe*s, n*í*ght; *in the* níght / *In the* hówling; h*ów*ling, f*óu*nd *óu*t; *l*óve / Does thy *l*ífe—give the sense of inevitability. The effect is a fierce one, which the balancing iambs and spondees on either side of the anapests punctuate without dissipating. Nor was this a first fine careless rapture. The closing lines of Blake's original draft, "O dark secret love / Doth life destroy," with only two fewer anapests, are much weaker.

These poems illustrate what is perhaps most characteristically Blakean in the metric of the *Songs*, their repeated use of mixed measures. About one-third of the *Songs* are in mixed iamb-anapest meters; some like "The Sick Rose" and "Laughing Song" combining the two kinds of feet in almost every line, a few like "Night" juxtaposing whole lines of each. Another third mix iambic and trochaic lines, usually with the trochees dominating, for one of Blake's favorite devices was to relieve a too insistent trochaic beat with an occasional iambic line. In "The Little Girl Lost" and "The Little Girl Found," the few iambic lines enhance Blake's studied effect of naïveté. It is as if the lisper of these poems could not manage to keep straight even so simple a pattern as the trochaic trimeter. In "A Poison Tree," however, there is deliberate drama. After the situation of suppressed wrath against a foe has been established in the first stanza, succeeding stanzas erect a kind of grisly mockery of the tune in the "Introduction" to *Innocence*. There the tune was of free creativity, here it is of perverse creativity, the nourishment of hate's poison tree: "Ând Ĭ wátĕrd . . . Ând Ĭ súnnĕd . . . Ând ĭt gréw . . . Ând mў fóe . . . ." It is all in trochaics, until the last line; but then the relief of tension, the relaxation from trochees to an iambic line, is the relief of death:

And into my garden stole.
When the night had veild the pole;
In the morning glad I see;
My foe outstretchd beneath the tree.

(*Experience*, p. 218)

A final example of how Blake employed mixed meters for expressive ends is "The Tyger," where an iambic line serves at several points like a water boy among the hammering trochees and spondees. The first stanza is preparation:

> Tyger Tyger. burning bright,
> In the forests of the night;
> What immortal hand or eye,
> Could frame thy fearful symmetry?
>
> (*Experience*, p. 214)

The final iambic line here provides a break, or breath, preventing the poem from building up too rapidly. The second stanza is entirely trochaic. The third stanza sandwiches two regular iambic lines between the trochaic-spondaic ones:

> Ănd whát shóuldĕr, &̆ whát árt,
> Cŏuld twíst thĕ sínĕws ŏf thy̆ héart?
> Ănd whén thy̆ héart bĕgán tŏ béat,
> Whát dréad hánd? &̆ whát dréad féet?

Here there is already something insinuating and ominous in the iambic lines. The fourth stanza, in which the creation of the Tyger culminates, is again all pounding trochees. The fifth, quieter and more fearsome, is again half-and-half:

> Did he smile his work to see?
> Did he who made the Lamb make thee?

Note how the accent shifts: first "Díd hĕ," then "Dĭd hé." *Did he?* And the final stanza, answering nothing, returns to the opening—with a difference:

> Tyger Tyger. burning bright,
> In the forests of the night;
> What immortal hand or eye,
> Dáre fráme thy fearful symmetry?

It is no longer a matter of "Could frame," the phrase of physical might, but "Dare frame." In closing his fearfully symmetrical circle, Blake opens the question of moral power. The longer vowel, and the sound-link of the *r*'s, make us dwell on this spondee which has replaced the first stanza's iamb. It is only a slight touch; but it completes the poem.

T. S. Eliot has paid Blake a high compliment by finding in him "merely a peculiar honesty, which, in a world too frightened to be honest, is peculiarly terrifying. It is an honesty against which the whole world conspires, because it is unpleasant. . . . And this honesty never exists without great technical accomplishment." [11] The technical accomplishment of Blake's candid lyrics involved a double temerity. In the first place, he dared to write serious poetry with the basic rhythmical and linguistic tools of a prattling child. In the second, he dared to think thoughts and hear melodies whose precise expression required breaking some universally accepted metrical conventions. The latter achievement, which it is easy for the lens of prosodic history to magnify, should not obscure the former, which was at least as essential to Blake's lyric gift. They dovetail, one defining the particulars of emotion and idea, the other the generalities of simplicity and purity.

Probably Blake did not realize the extent of his boldness, for his "peculiar honesty" kept company with a peculiar oblivion to certain things in the world about him. His friend Cunningham wrote that Blake at the outset of his career "thought that he had but to sing songs and draw designs, and become great and famous." [12] To be sure, he knew that he was not writing like Pope or Dr. Johnson; but did he know that he was writing like no one else? His acquaintance was artistic, not literary. He would hardly have paid attention to the finer points of contemporary prosodic faith, and perhaps not even to some of the cruder ones, despite owning a copy of Bysshe.[13]

[11] T. S. Eliot, *The Sacred Wood* (London, 1934), p. 151.

[12] Allan Cunningham, *Life of Blake*, in Arthur Symons, *William Blake* (New York, 1907), p. 401.

[13] It is likely that Blake worked by ear, not by rule, but we cannot be sure of this. Notwithstanding his inclinations to expound, sometimes at

The Blake of *Innocence* and *Experience* is like a choirboy in the back row singing sweet and sour songs to please himself, unaware of what the rest of the chorus is doing. He differs more by inadvertence than by conscious rebellion. In the Prophetic Books, the case is altered to deliberate rebellion. Before considering the technique of the Prophetic Books, however, it will be necessary to discuss the other half of Blake's lyric music, its vowel and consonant patterns; and also to review the later lyrics, which deviate in both ends and means from *Innocence* and *Experience*.

---

tedious and cranky length, his theories and practices in the visual arts, we have from him only the barest, most equivocal clues about his poetic methods. Perhaps one reason for this is that, considering himself a professional artist rather than a professional poet, he did not feel so much called upon to enter the lists of self-defense, or to spend time on intramural squabbles, in the field of poetry. Thus he may have developed a theory or theories of prosody comparable to his theory of outline in drawing and painting, but not written on it. It seems more plausible, however, that he felt words did not require explanations, even to himself, in the same way pictures did; and that the spirits that guided his hand, and of whom he dared not "pretend to be any other than the Secretary" (*Letters*, p. 825), simply kept their own counsel.

6

Sound-Effects: Rhyme, Alliteration, Assonance

Poetry admits not a Letter that is Insignificant.

(*VLJ*, p. 611)

The music of poetry does not consist entirely in its metric frame, or even in its rhythmic run. If meter is poetry's golden cage, vowels and consonants are the singing birds inside. Unfortunately, although the melody of verse may contribute even more to its music than the rhythm, almost nothing is known about it.

Critics may make arbitrary or educated guesses on what sounds are "euphonious" or "cacophonous," but little will come of this. On the question of whether sound can create or reinforce meaning, the argument persists between critics of sensibility and those of sense, the former picking virtually onomatopoeic significance out of every sound in a line, the latter insisting that such correlations have been read into the poetry after the fact. This controversy, a lively one in the eighteenth century, provoked some words from Samuel Johnson in a *Rambler* essay "On Sound and Sense in Milton."

Johnson's literalism provides the dogma that "sound can resemble nothing but sound, and time can measure nothing but motion and duration." Theories of correspondence he finds "like the blind man, who, after long inquiry into the nature of the scarlet colour, found that it represented nothing so much as the clangour of a trumpet." However, although Johnson shrewdly observes, "it is scarcely to be doubted that on many occasions we make the music which we imagine ourselves to hear; that we modulate the poem by our own disposition, and ascribe to the numbers the effects of the verse," he also admits that "it would be too daring to declare that all the celebrated adaptations of harmony are chimerical." [1]

In the twentieth century, many people might leap to defend the trumpetlike qualities of the color scarlet. Even among those who will not, a few basic points about the possible effects of sound in language may be granted.

It is evident that physiologically based distinctions between sounds may associate themselves with psychological phenomena; that consonant clusters, being relatively difficult to articulate, may more easily suggest difficulty or slowness or harshness than will liquids or nasals; that vowels like *ee* and long *i* (the *y*-glides) do not suggest depth or resonance so well as *o* or *oo* (the *u*-glides). Linguists, I believe, would also agree that certain sounds or sound combinations acquire certain associations through use in words with related meanings. Two instances that come to mind are the suggestion of *sli*pperiness in slick, slide, slink, slither, or the suggestion of comedy or violence in crash, bash, gash, hash, splash, smash, etc. Most of us have many private associations of certain sounds with certain ideas. Poets also have these, but make systematic use of them. A poet may be expected to develop his diction in accordance with private sound-significance correlations, which his readers will temporarily absorb due to his repetitions. If, for example, he habitually used *squ* for *squ*eal, *squ*awk, *squ*int, *squ*ash,

[1] *The Rambler* (London, 1794), II, No. 94, pp. 230, 227. The same points are made, less succinctly, but perhaps more palatably to modern ears, by I. A. Richards, *Practical Criticism* (New York, 1929, paperback), pp. 340–42.

*squ*irm, he might reasonably expect a comic or negative response to his (otherwise neutral) *squ*are.

These observations give us the best approach to Blake's sound-effects, for theories which explain poetic sounds in terms of physical representation do not apply to Blake, any more than theories which completely deny their significance. Pope's doctrine that "the sound must seem an echo to the sense," as interpreted physically to mean that

> ... the smooth stream in smoother numbers flows;
> But when loud surges lash the sounding shore,
> The hoarse, rough verse should like the torrent roar,

suits Pope, and inspired many other poets in the tradition of sensibility. It can also fit the Romantics. But it does not fit Blake, as we shall see, at least in his lyrics.

Any reader of Blake's lyrics will immediately sense two things about his sound-effects: their limited range, and (partly as a consequence) their striking emotional impact. Blake in his sound patterns as in his diction and phrasal structure loved nothing better than to repeat himself. These repetitions serve several functions.[2] They furnish a primitive esthetic pleasure comparable to that produced by a regular rhythmic beat, and they accentuate, when placed in crucial positions on accents and especially at the end of the line, the poem's rhythmic structure. These effects are obvious, and have obvious value in Blake's style of lyric. In addition, and this is less immediately apparent, they serve to intensify emotion, and often help create it.

Repetition of sound in poetry is like a burning glass which can focus the harmless white light of the sun on one spot until that spot blazes up. Any poet with a good ear will use some repetition in his verse; those who use a great deal are usually asking us to respond with our passions first, and only afterwards, if at all, with our heads. Blake is among these.

[2] See Henry Lanz, *The Physical Basis of Rime* (Stanford, 1931), ch. 1, *passim.*

Consider, for example, his use of rhyme. Some poets choose to subtilize this most conspicuous of sensuous pleasures by placing their rhymes far apart, using soft sounds for them, or dissipating their effect through enjambment. Blake, unlike these, shoots his rhymes out one after another, sometimes so fast that the rhyme comes every five syllables, as in

> The Sun does arise
> And make happy the skies (*Innocence*, p. 116)

or even every three:

> Sound the Flute!
> Now it's mute. (*Innocence*, p. 123)

Where his lines are long, there is often the suggestion of interior rhyme, so that we are never too far away from jingle.

Moreover, Blake consistently rhymes almost twice as much on long vowels as on shorts and diphthongs, with an extraordinary proportion of long *e*'s and *i*'s, seconded only by *a*'s.[3] Nor does he hesitate on many occasions to use these piercing *y*-glides throughout whole stanzas, or even groups of stanzas, at a time, in the fashion of:

> My mother bore me in the southern w*i*ld,
> And I am black, but O! my soul is wh*i*te;
> White as an angel is the English ch*i*ld;
> But I am black, as if bereav'd of l*i*ght.
> (*Innocence*, p. 125)

(and note too the internal "My . . . I . . . White . . . I," as well as the short *i* of "*i*n . . . *i*s . . . Engl*i*sh . . . *i*f") or:

> T*i*red with kisses sw*ee*t
> They agr*ee* to m*ee*t,

[3] The proportion of rhymes on long *e* and *i* to the total number of rhymes (391) in *Innocence* and *Experience* is 40%. In 100 rhymes taken from each of the following: Watts, Gray, Collins, Coleridge, Shelley, the proportions are: Watts, 19%; Gray, 23%; Collins, 31%; Coleridge, 24%; Shelley, 20%.

When the s*i*lent sl*ee*p
Waves o'er heaven's d*ee*p;
And the w*ea*ry t*i*red wanderers w*ee*p.
(*Experience*, p. 219)

The effect of high-pitched chant works in each case like the subsidiary arrows Cupid is supposed to have shot, that "drave the first dart deeper more and more." They make the feeling more intense, keener. It is also significant that Blake's favorite rhyme-words, words like day, chain, weep, sleep, fears, light, mild, laden with import as they are for him, often set the tone of whole poems at a time.

Blake sometimes repeats his rhyme-words, as if his *Songs* were not hypnotic enough already. This occurs most conspicuously in "The Lamb," but also in "The Blossom," "Infant Joy," ("I have no name . . . Joy is my name"), "On Another's Sorrow" ("O! no never can it be. / Never never can it be"), "The School Boy," and "The Little Vagabond." These repetitions, of course, are only foam on the larger wave of verbal and syntactic parallelism with which he imitates the child's way, or the Biblical way, of using language; they are more integral to his meaning than Coleridge's self-conscious

Is the night chilly and dark?
The night is chilly, but not dark.

was to the meaning of Coleridge.

Like his rhyme, Blake's alliteration often seems childlike. Many of his alliterative phrases, such as "wild winds weep," "cold as clay," "maker meek," "little Lamb," "bleak & bare," suggesting the staple phrases of folk song or nursery rhyme, enhance the effect of spontaneity. Nor does he hesitate to alliterate important words to make sure they stand out, as in "*T*y*g*er *T*y*g*er. *b*urning *b*right," "*Sh*all *sh*ine like the gold. / As I guard o'er the fold." "So *s*ung a little *Cl*od of *Cl*ay," "*L*ovely *L*yca *l*ay," and a multitude of other places. Usually the device has an accretive effect: one word strengthens the other, as in "Marks of *w*eakness, marks of *w*oe."

But sometimes, in *Experience*, the effect is ironic; the second word changes our opinion of the first. For example, *mind* and *pity* should be positive terms, but consider what happens in "*m*ind-forg'd *m*anacles" and "*P*ity would be no more, / If we did not make somebody *P*oor."

Just as the vowel sounds long *e* and *i* are "intensifiers" which Blake slips into rhymes when he wants to spike our drink, so several of the consonants seem to connote distinct emotions which alliteration purveys in strength. Blake's *l*'s usually suggest sweetness or joy:

Lovely Lyca *l*ay (*Innocence*, p. 112)

Then down a green p*l*ain *l*eaping *l*aughing they run
(*Innocence*, p. 117)

The *l*ittle ones *l*eaped & shouted & *l*augh'd
(*Innocence*, p. 121)

his *b*'s very often sorrow or anger:

That free Love with *b*ondage *b*ound
(*Experience*, p. 211)

And their fields are *b*leak & *b*are
(*Experience*, p. 212)

And Priests in *b*lack gowns, were walking their rounds,
And *b*inding with *b*riars my joys & desires.
(*Experience*, p. 215)

This negative association for *b*, as well as the context, produces a bitterly ironic inflection for "best" and "breast" in "Infant Sorrow":

Struggling in my father's hands:
Striving against my swadling *b*ands:
*B*ound and weary I thought *b*est
To sulk upon my mother's *b*reast.
(*Experience*, p. 217)

The transformation of rebellion to resentful acquiescence in "*Str*ugg*ling* ... *Str*iv*ing* ... *s*wad*ling* ... *s*u*l*k," ending abruptly in the monosyllable, is also important.

It is interesting to note that Blake did not feel "London" was completed until the verbs he tried tentatively for the last line, "hangs," then "smites," became "*bl*ights" to alliterate with "*bl*asts" and "new *b*orn." And *b*'s (black, bereav'd, bodies, sun*b*urnt) contend with *l*'s (live, light, lambs, love) in "The Little Black Boy," with the *l*'s winning in the end. Other thematically significant instances of alliteration include the soothing *s*'s of "A Cradle Song," the cheerfully explosive *p*'s of the "Introduction" to *Innocence,* and the cold *d*'s in "Earth's Answer," "*d*arkness *d*rea*d* and *d*rear ... fle*d* ... *d*rea*d* ... *d*espair."

As should have been suggested by now, Blake habitually echoed sounds within his words. This habit, along with the rhyme and alliteration, gives his most characteristic lyrics several chains of like sounds strung from line to line, with relatively few vowels or consonants left unduplicated. The more this is done, the stronger is the emotional intensity. An average passage is the opening of "The Chimney Sweeper" in *Innocence:*

> When my mother died I was very young,
> And my Father sold me while yet my tongue,
> Could scarcely cry weep weep weep weep.
> So your chimneys I sweep & in soot I sleep.
>
> (*Innocence,* p. 117)

There is the sequence "Wh*e*n ... m*o*ther ... v*e*ry y*ou*ng ... y*e*t ... t*o*ngue," the short vowels dominated by *o* giving, I think, the sense of gravity, deepened by the solitary long *o* of "sold," to the first couplet. The more numerous but less conspicuous vowels of m*y*, d*ie*d, *I*, m*y*, wh*i*le, m*y*, along with the several *m*'s and *d*'s and the off-rhyme of *mother-Father,* tape the lines together. The second couplet has, besides the dominant *ee*'s and the slight sad echo of *could-soot,* the rather matter-of-fact crisp *c*'s in "*c*ould s*c*ar*c*ely *c*ry," softened by the *s*'s of *s*carcely, *S*o, *s*weep, *s*oot, *s*leep.

The degree of echo in "The Chimney Sweeper" is average. "The Tyger" is packed about twice as tight, and its last stanza is a musical miracle of rare device to express, through sound, the synthesizing energy of Creation, and the fearfulness of the thing created.

> Tyger Tyger burning bright,
> In the forests of the night:
> What immortal hand or eye,
> Dare frame thy fearful symmetry?
>
> (*Experience*, p. 214)

Almost every word is knit up through sound with every other word, and this in itself suggests the idea of the demiurge's infinitely painstaking design. Of the vowels, the long *i* with its great symbolic impact dominates. It is balanced by the deeper vowels of b*ur*ning, f*o*rests-*o*f, imm*or*tal-*or*, which in turn become the broader, almost rhyming *Dare-fear*ful. Short *i*'s appear in burn*i*ng, *I*n, *i*mmortal, s*y*mmetry, one per line. Of the consonants, which Blake piles more thickly than usual in order to suggest "difficulty and labour hard," *t*'s and *r*'s, which one imagines Blake pronounced quite hard, run right through; *n*'s almost through. The ominous *f* of *f*orest is picked up again with a gain in power by "*f*rame . . . *f*earful"; and countering its softness is the firmness in "i*mm*ortal . . . fra*m*e . . . sy*mm*etry." Immortal is significantly assonant with fearful. And, for a symmetry which is fearful indeed, consider the mirror-image pattern of consonants in "immo*rt*al . . . *fr*ame . . . *f*ea*rf*ul symme*try*": *rt fr f rf tr.*

Blake's sound-effects, in the intensity of their economy, gather to a greatness like the ooze of oil crushed. But he does not overdo them. His confined power resembles not at all the mental fresh air of a Pope, who used alliteration and assonance just enough to give his lines muscularity, and otherwise spread their tones as broadly as possible; nor on the other hand does it resemble the hothouse atmosphere of a Swinburne, where alliteration and assonance are applied with a ladle, and where reading is like walking through honey. As a rule, the Augustans tried for health and breadth in their sound-effects. Tennyson and the late Victorians—Swinburne, Rossetti, Morris—tried for euphony. The Romantics in between, and Blake with them, were mainly interested in expressiveness.

Blake most resembles Coleridge, Keats, and Shelley, who had subtler ears than Wordsworth and Byron. He is, however, divided from them, and from most other poets, by one thing: after *Poetical Sketches*, he did not attempt through the sound of his poetry to represent the physical outside of his world, but only its spiritual inside. Blake deals exclusively, as most other poets do occasionally, in symbols; his child, lamb, tiger, and rose are colored glass through which we are to behold "portions of eternity" (*MHH*, p. 151). Each one focuses congruent truths. "Lamb" is God's love, incarnate Christ, the soul's trustfulness in the state of Innocence, and the dumb animal life of the body. "Tyger" is God's wrath, the energy embodied in Creation, personified Evil, the baneful influence of reason and order. In themselves the named objects of Blake's lyrics have only minimal value compared with the spiritual essences to which they point, and Blake expends only minimal effort describing them.

This is why we hear scarcely anything of the tiger but his name; no talk of stripes, grace or speed of movement, diet; no retention from the manuscript version of the terms "cruel," "horrid," "eyes of fury," all of which the reader will supply for himself, given that double opening invocation and a few judicious hints.[4] Blake concentrates on the beast's fearsome Spiritual Form, as seen through the incomplete vision of a man in the state of Experience, whose unanswered questions and ungrammatical, unfinished exclamations make clear that this portion of eternity is "too great for the eye of

[4] Martin K. Nurmi, "Blake's Revisions of 'The Tyger,'" *PMLA*, LXXI (1956), 669–85, noting that the poem's first version is too strongly and frighteningly phrased, the second too weak, and the final version a balance, seems to conclude that Blake was at first unsure of what he meant the tiger to signify. I think it likelier that Blake's problem was one of how much he needed to tell his audience.

man." If the poet could answer his own questions, the tiger might look quite different. Or perhaps not; we are not told. The glory and terror of its framing remains real enough, for the "Organ that beholds it"; and it is this glory and terror, and not a corporeal splendor, which the poem's rhythm and sound express.

The alliteration of forests, frame, fearful, fire, and furnace, in this poem, gives us no picture of a forest, a fire, or a furnace. It does give us a chain of associations, and it does tell us that Blake thinks Creation is a terrifying affair. The doubling of "*T*yger *T*yger. *b*urning *b*right" may suggest the tiger's two bright eyes, if we are ingenious, but it primarily conveys the idea of "symmetry" and the mood of ritual incantation. Even with the phrase "twist the sinews" (from "And what shoulder, & what art / Could twist the sinews of thy heart"), which wants to be onomatopoeic, Blake prevents us from seeing a concrete image by having "shoulder" and "art," instead of "hand," in the previous line. "Twist" remains mentally strenuous, but the shoulder looms between us and a picture of physical contortion.

We can find the same avoidance of the physical in quite a different poem, "Infant Joy." Coleridge's criticism of the antepenultimate line "Thou dost smile" of "Infant Joy," on the grounds that "a babe two days old does not, cannot smile. . . . Infancy is too holy a thing to be ornamented," [5] misses the point of a lyric which deals with the inner, not outer, infant. One might as well complain that no babe two days old can declare, "I have no name. I am but two days old." Clearly the infant neither speaks nor smiles with its corporeal lips but with its spiritual.

Blake in this poem wastes not a single word on physical description. Our realization of a symbolic essence depends upon the crooning, wandering rhythms of the infant; on the monosyllabic lines which can be spoken with equal stress on each word—"I—have—no—name—I—am—but . . . ;" on the careless

[5] Samuel Taylor Coleridge, *Letters,* ed. E. H. Coleridge (Boston and New York, 1895), II, 687.

rhyming of *name-am-name*. It depends on the statement "I am," which is given twice, and which could very easily be a deliberate echo of God's self-identification to Moses in Ex. 3.14, and on the repeated open vowel of h*a*ve, *a*m, sh*a*ll, h*a*ppy. It depends upon the mother, who serves the same creative function as beholder that the speaker in "The Tyger" serves, falling sympathetically into the infant's language and rhythms. There is no image anywhere here; there is only symbol.

Coleridge, closest in "The Rime of the Ancient Mariner" to Blake's symbolic approach, nevertheless often depends on imagistic detail: the "long grey beard and glittering eye" or "his skinny hand" fixing the Mariner visually; the onomatopoeic "It cracked and growled, and roared and howled;" the tactile hideousness of

> Yea, *sl*imy things did craw*l* with *l*egs
> Upon the *sl*imy *s*ea.

All this is excellent, but Blake has nothing like it. Still less has he anything like the sensual effects, from "*sil*v*er* *snarl*ing trumpets" to "bu*rst* Joy's *grap*e again*st* his *p*ala*t*e fine," of Keats, who not only saw distinctly "with" not "through" the eye, but also smelled with the nose, tasted with the tongue, heard with the ears, and felt—smooth and rough, warm and cool—with the entire surface of his skin, more frankly than any other poet. Even Shelley, whose assumed neoplatonism cannot disguise a love of sensation, uses sound to far more physical effect than Blake, whether heavily as in "a wave to *p*ant beneath thy *p*ower" or finely as in "Breathing the *s*oul of *s*wiftne*ss* into it," which latter, although it shows a love inhering in things "extreme, and scattering bright," is no less material for all that.

Blake's attempts to make sound represent sensation never went further than

> Let thy west wind sleep on
> The lake; speak silence with thy glimmering eyes,
> And wash the dusk with silver

in *Poetical Sketches*, although a few passages of natural description in *Milton* go almost as far. In the Prophetic Books, the will to broaden his scope and technique sometimes led Blake to indulge in representational, imitative sound. In *Innocence* and *Experience*, his sound-effects exist only for the sake of his symbolism.

Some mention should be made here of Blake's importance in prosodic history due to his freedom with the convention of rhyme. Wicksteed notes that Blake's rhyme, especially in *Innocence*, often seems to dictate the verse, but that he saves it from cloying either by omitting the rhyme altogether at times, or by introducing "bad" rhymes.[6]

Blake's attitude toward rhyme is fairly cavalier. He could skip it, even for the length of a stanza, as in the fourth stanza of "Earth's Answer" (otherwise rhymed abaab) whose terminal words are joy, grow, sower, night, plow. The strong rhythm and the previous rhymes carry the reader along without a jolt. Or he could deceive the reader into thinking that sense-linked words like *cold-warm* rhyme, as in the first lines of "The Little Vagabond." Often, as mentioned above, he simply repeated words instead of rhyming them.

His use of false rhyme is most interesting. *Innocence* alone contains thirty-three examples like *shade-bed*, *lick-neck*, *weary-merry*, etc., where the consonants agree but the vowels differ. In this license he anticipates Yeats and Wilfred Owen. He also has a few instances of the type where the vowels agree but the consonants differ, as *dawn-scorn*, *vault-fraught* ("Mad Song"), *lambs-hands* ("Holy Thursday") and *gowns-rounds* ("The Garden of Love").

It is an open question whether or not Blake misrhymed deliberately. In the early lyrics it would seem that he did, for he uses off-rhymes in patterns. The first three quatrains of "Fresh from the dewy hill" contain nothing but off-rhymes: *year-car*, *shade-head*,

[6] Joseph H. Wicksteed, *Blake's Innocence and Experience* (London, Toronto, and New York, 1928), pp. 36–37.

lawn-morn, etc. "Love and harmony combine" plays with quatrains rhymed aaaa, with one off-rhyme per quatrain to soften an otherwise oversweet effect. There are several similar things in *Innocence*, perhaps the most interesting of which is the second half of the coupleted "Lamb," where a favorite off-rhyme appears twice, in conjunction with identical rhyme, to form one of Blake's most economical patterns:

> Little Lamb I'll tell thee, (a)
> Little Lamb I'll tell thee; (a)
> He is called by thy name, (b)
> For he calls himself a Lamb: (b)
> He is meek & he is mild, (c)
>
> He became a little child: (c)
> I a child & thou a lamb, (b)
> We are called by his name. (b)
> Little Lamb God bless thee. (a)
> Little Lamb God bless thee. (a)
>
> (*Innocence*, p. 115)

It seems appropriate that the poet who was later to complain of "the modern bondage of rhyming" should have played these tricks. However, the frequency of his odd rhymes declines steadily after *Poetical Sketches*, throughout his lyrical work (see Appendix B). This might be attributed to either waxing or waning ingenuity. If the former, we should say that Blake was correcting an early tendency to carelessness, or at least thought he was. If the latter, we should say that the carelessness consisted in letting himself sink back into ordinary rhyme instead of treading water with head and hands above it. This seems more plausible, since the falling-off occurs as Blake finds more fulfillment in unrhymed prophetic works and thus loses interest in expanding lyric technique.

7

Later Lyrics: A Compromise with Prophecy

The lyrics written after *Songs of Experience* exhibit two trends. They cast about for ways to express Prophetic matter; and they show declining concern with lyric form as such.

As early as *Innocence* and *Experience*, a few signposts point toward the future. The typical lyric in those books was implicitly, not explicitly, didactic; built its symbolism on significances already accepted in daily life, or popular imagination, or the Bible, or pastoral tradition; and derived force from confinement, as a stream enclosed in narrow banks will rush more swiftly. It expressed the partial point of view either of Innocence or of Experience, each unmodified by its contrary.

But there were exceptions. "The Divine Image," "Holy Thursday" and "The Voice of the Ancient Bard" in *Innocence* are to varying degrees explicitly didactic, written not from the innocent's but from the outsider's point of view. "The Voice of the Ancient Bard," with its querulous tone and prophetic protagonist inviting the reader to enter Experience, particularly deviates from its context, and was perhaps written later. In *Experience*, with consciousness of ill a reigning motif, a didactic approach becomes more natural. Yet we must remember that didacticism, which is especially noticeable in "Earth's Answer," "Holy Thursday," "London," "The Human Abstract," and "A Divine Image," will be a standard feature of the prophecies. And Blake shifts nearer prophecy in several other ways. The "Introduction," "Earth's Answer," and "To Tirzah" clang for the first time with a symbolism which strikes discords instead of harmonies with traditional understanding; "To Tirzah" presents Blake's first overt symbolic personage; and "The Human Abstract," whose intellectual jigsaw puzzle integrates poorly with the rather mechanical "snare" and "tree" symbols, prefigures many passages in the Prophetic Books. On the other hand, these poems still fit the limitations of their state in that, although they bubble with indignation, they do not yet spill over into the vision necessary for redemption. Experience may inspire terror ("The Tyger"), pity ("The Sick Rose"), indignation ("London") or cynicism ("The Clod and the Pebble"). Of itself it can cure nothing.

Technically these exceptional songs still show only slight impatience with the lyric mold. "The Voice of the Ancient Bard" is structurally weak, with a lopsided rhyme-scheme and a disorderly mixture of three- and four-beat iambic, trochaic, and anapestic lines. "The Human Abstract" has several clumsy lines, especially in its last stanza. "London," on the other hand, has its well-known force; and the "Introduction" and "Earth's Answer," more complex in form than the other songs, show great rhythmic drive. Of the two stanzas beginning "O Earth O Earth return!" Saintsbury declared that he "would rather have written these lines than anything in English poetry outside of Shakespeare." [1]

The *Songs of Experience* as a group lack the serene sweetness of *Innocence*, although they often compensate in power. The Notebook lyrics written contemporaneously with *Experience* resemble their fellows in range of theme and technique. Several Notebook pieces from this period are independently remarkable. "Never seek to tell thy love" and "I asked a thief" convey hypocrisy by an

[1] George Saintsbury, *A History of English Prosody* (London, 1906–10), III, 15 n.

elegant slipperiness of image and sound unduplicated in *Experience*. "I saw a chapel all of gold," with its religious-sexual-animal symbolism, is sensually more shocking than anything in *Experience*. And the gemlike quatrain "He who binds to himself a joy" slips quietly past the realm of experience into that of vision, which gives answers instead of questions. As in the *Experience* lyrics, there are a few hints of future developments. Blake's myrtle tree, his fairies, and the appearance of Nobodaddy, all move toward private symbolism and nomenclature. The several epigrams and the two longer pieces "Let the Brothels of Paris be Opened" and "When Klopstock England defied," are deliberate doggerel like "The Everlasting Gospel."

The care Blake took to perfect his lyrics is evident in the MS revisions of this period, where in several instances he changes his meter or sound in order to wheedle the latent impact out of his sense. The replacement in "Never seek to tell thy love" of the last line "He took her with a sigh" by "O was no deny" exchanges a heavy, thick-sounding explicitness for a smooth, cool (note the two *o*'s), compactly ironic allusiveness which enhances the theme of slyness and secrecy. The new line, moreover, ironically parallels the earlier "Ah she doth depart." Again, the second stanza of "I saw a chapel all of gold" originally read:

> I saw a serpent rise between
> The white pillars of the door
> And he forcd & forcd & forcd
> Till he broke the pearly door. (*Notebook*, p. 163)

This is fairly obscene, but the new last line, "Down the golden hinges tore," makes it more so. The revision eliminates the extraneous "Till he" and gives a stronger verb. The sound is more resonant. The strong accents, distributed throughout the line instead of concentrated on the one word "broke," suggest a sustained effort of ripping down rather than a single blow, thus rendering the line more powerful, more suspenseful, and more a part of the poem's gradual motion toward its unholy climax. Still again, in "Earth's Answer," the verb of

> Break this heavy chain
> That does close my bones around
> (*Notebook*, p. 169)

changes to "freeze my bones," which is not only more vivid, but provides a more striking sound pattern: one high sound amid many low ones, instead of just another low. These are typical changes, and they thoroughly refute the Woodnotes Wild theory of Blakean composition.

Blake's subsequent lyrics, appearing in the Notebook, the Pickering MS, the letters, one or two prophetic works, and a few spare leaves, may be divided into several types: prophetic lyrics, mythic lyrics, autobiographical pieces, didactic poems, and epigrams. Except for the epigrams, almost the entire body of this work employs the four-stress line Blake was most relaxed with, either in couplets or in quatrains rhymed xaxa. Damon writes that Blake sustained his lyrical technique in these poems: "His prosody became increasingly sensitive to the subtler variations of word-music; while the thought was more and more fully expressed." [2]

But while admitting the clause about Blake's thought, one must note that Blake's prosody in these lyrics sometimes becomes like a pair of well-worn overalls: pliant to the wearer's figure, handy for all kinds of clean or dirty work, but not in itself decorative. As in his prophecies, Blake grows less and less concerned with appearances.

Very few of these later poems sustain the condensed symbolic mode of *Innocence* and *Experience*, and only four develop it into prophetic lyric which passes beyond the mire of experience onto the firm ground of vision. "The Crystal Cabinet" I take to be an

[2] S. Foster Damon, *William Blake, His Philosophy and Symbols* (Boston, 1924), p. 128.

exposition of Beulah, the state of triple vision achieved through sex,[3] which is lovely but insufficient and impermanent, since when the Cabinet is "burst," the poet lapses back to single vision. This is Blake's equivalent of "La Belle Dame Sans Merci." "Mock on, Mock on, Voltaire, Rousseau," "And did those feet in ancient time," and the Epilogue to "The Gates of Paradise" attain a higher vision. The language of the first two is the completed apocalyptic symbolism of *Milton* or *Jerusalem.* They blend passion and calm, they have rhythm and resonance as fine as "The Tyger" without reliance on childlikeness. They are to the Prophetic Books as the sound of the sea in a shell is to the sea itself. "To the Accuser who is the God of This World" is quieter but equally rare; Blake for once stops railing at his Satan and pities instead. Its music is quite subtle, especially in the second stanza, where the decelerating tempo and the two run-on lines seem to anticipate the figure of night's onset.

Blake has two groups of mythic, or narrative, lyrics. "William Bond," "Mary," and "Long John Brown and Pretty Mary Bell," all dealing with Blake's ideal of Love versus Prudence, try to imitate the style of topical ballad. They use proper English names, tell simple stories, have the insouciant rhythm of ballads; the latter two jog along in a doggerel anapest common for eighteenth-century street songs. "William Bond" is often supposed to be somehow autobiographical, and "Mary" to refer to Mary Wollstonecraft, although the doctrine that "sweet Love & Beauty are worthy our care" does not especially appear to suit a lady who dressed like a proletarian on principle. Whether or not these songs

[3] See *Ibid.*, ch. 15, *passim*, and particularly: "I believe that Blake was not emphasizing the sexual act entirely for its own sake. I think he found that it also induced the proper mental state in which to write poetry or imagine pictures. The ideal conditions for this are a perfectly relaxed body and a stimulated mind. The trouble with drugs and alcohol is that they generally deaden the mind with the body. So I believe that Blake, in the dreamy post-coitional state, found an unusual effervescence of ideas; and this was what he meant by passing into the World of the Poetic Imagination by the Fifth Window" (p. 102). From "The Crystal Cabinet," however, it would seem that vision occurred during, not after, the sexual meeting.

versify real incidents, their ballad-like style fails to mesh with their archetypal, mythological import. The confusion of intentions shows plainly in "Mary," where Blake cannot decide whether he wants a particular or a general heroine. He clings to literal-appearing detail because he wants to make the song balladlike and popular, and yet never enters wholly into the detail for fear of losing his symbol. He tries to squeeze an Oothoon out of the girl, but she crumbles in his grasp. Someone like Burns could use the popular style like a razor to slash establishment morality into tatters, as in "The Jolly Beggars." But Blake here is heavyhanded, more like Wordsworth, and so "Mary" and the other two narratives "come out with a Moral like a sting in the tail," [4] even though Blake's moral reverses the world's.

When he leaves proper names and explicit moralizing behind, as in "My Spectre around me," "The Golden Net," "The Mental Traveller," and—almost—in "The Grey Monk," he achieves finer results. These semi-dramatic narratives all rely on a self-consistent symbolic structure in the same way that Blake's prophecies do; that is, they make no compromise with popular understanding. Let the reader beware, now that Blake has entered the maze of his system and shut the door behind him. An outsider will receive only minimal assistance from the conventional meanings of some of Blake's key symbols.

"The Mental Traveller," most finished and best constructed of this group, employs meter with an almost passionate monotony which betrays all along what the last lines will declare plainly: that a cyclic futility poisons the veins of human history. We do not quite realize this until the conclusion. The ironic *seeming* significance of "such dreadful things" as the narrative relates is produced by the startling imagery, by the packed, declarative syntactical structure which makes almost every stanza appear a completed "episode," and by the individual fingering of his lines. Despite confinement to iambs, with a few trochaic inversions, almost no anapests, and only occasional emphatic pauses, Blake

[4] *On Homer's Poetry*, p. 778.

achieves sufficient variety by degrees of accenting and placing of slight pauses. A typical stanza is:

> Ănd íf thĕ Bábe ĭs bórn ă Bóy
> Hĕ's gívĕn tŏ ă Wómăn Óld,
> Whŏ náils hĭm dówn ŭpŏn ă róck,
> Cátchĕs hĭs shríeks ĭn cúps ŏf góld.
>
> (*Pickering MS*, p. 425)

There are also stronger lines like:

> Then he rénds úp his Manacles
>
> The stárs, sún, Móon, âll shrínk awáy,
>
> They cry "The Babe! the Babe is Born!"

The sound patterns, combining alliteration and a rich vowel range, give additional vividness. Note how "Catches his shrie*k*s with *c*ups of gold" modulates from harsh, to high, to deep and cold vowel. But this vividness is spurious, fantastic, like a surrealist landscape or a painting by De Chirico, where distinct detail only enhances the pervasive unreality, and one is uncomfortably conscious of the empty spaces. Blake was describing the tedium of abortive change in a world without apocalypse, a theme he expanded for the epics dealing with what Northrop Frye calls the "Orc cycle." [5]

The other poems in this group are strongest when, like "The Mental Traveller," they keep within the iamb-trochee gamut. They are weakest when they lapse loosely into anapests without structural or rhetorical justification. Nothing about them outrages the ear, for the poet has not lost his competence. Few things ravish it, either, for he has lost some of his interest in making every syllable of his lyrics count. Except for "The Mental Traveller," these poems are interesting mainly for their attempt to condense prophetic matter into lyric scope.

In quite a different vein, the two autobiographical poems to

[5] *Fearful Symmetry, a Study of William Blake* (Princeton, 1947), pp 207–35.

Butts make delightful reading. Not that they return to discipline; on the contrary, the spring of Blake's language bubbles along vagrantly after his ideas, only barely contained between the banks of rhyme. This freedom suits the enthusiasm and expansiveness in both poems, and helps give the feeling of live speech. The 1800 "first Vision of Light" (p. 804) is in an anapestic dimeter much like Skeltonics. Of Romantic poems, it most resembles Keats' "There was a naughty boy," which was grown-up Keats at his happiest when full of animal good spirits, as this was Blake in the same condition, when surrounded by Vision, with his "dross purg'd away," resting "Sun bright" in the bosom of the One Man. The vision of the Thistle-Old Man and of "Los in his might" which begins "With happiness stretch'd across the hills" (p. 816) appeared two years later, when Blake was less pleased with conditions at Felpham. A graver poem, in a longer (tetrameter) meter, mainly iambic, it retains the swiftness and vigor if not the sparkle of the earlier lyric.

"Auguries of Innocence" and "The Everlasting Gospel," two of Blake's most tantalizing shorter pieces, are difficult to judge as works of art. Both use pounding iambic tetrameter couplets. Both are overtly didactic, but proceed by trains of symbolic aphorisms or exempla rather than by abstract statement. Neither seems finished. The "Auguries," except for its exquisite opening and closing quatrains, is simply a succession of ill-connected couplets. Its leitmotifs of animal significance, doubt, politics, the human condition of Joy and Woe, and so on, appear and reappear without discernible order or evolution. Many points are overworked by excessive repetition:

> He who mocks the Infant's Faith
> Shall be mock'd in Age & Death.
> He who shall teach the Child to Doubt
> The rotting Grave shall ne'er get out.
> He who respects the Infant's faith
> Triumphs over Hell & Death....
> The Questioner, who sits so sly,

> Shall never know how to Reply. . . .
> A Riddle or the Cricket's Cry
> Is to Doubt a fit Reply. . . .
> He who Doubts from what he sees
> Will ne'er Believe, do what you Please.
> If the Sun & Moon should doubt,
> They'd immediately Go out. (*Pickering MS*, p. 433)

Each couplet, alone, is fine; several are as good as the best Proverbs of Hell; but one of those Proverbs applies stingingly to them: "Enough! or Too much" (*MHH*, p. 152). They pop out of Blake too glibly, as if he were some sort of gumdrop machine and they the gumdrops.

Damon feels that "Auguries of Innocence" was not a complete poem, but only "elaborate notes" for a poem.[6] More likely (since the poem is a fair copy like the other lyrics in the Pickering MS), the *radix malorum* is not incompletion but Blake's theories. Repetition of a truth six different ways in part illustrates its infinite expansibility; we explore the "world" inherent in the "grain of sand" which that truth is. Blake's prophecies use for the same purpose the image of a pulse of time opening out into six thousand years, or the space of a globule of blood opening at the center into infinitude by the grace of a daughter of Beulah. Similarly, lack of structure may illustrate the principle that all truths are equal, and equally imply one another. Evidently Blake felt that any imposition of logical order in the "Auguries" would have falsified his position by capitulating to Reason and Doubt. By taking the stance of the illogical child implied in the poem's title, Blake "does not argue his case in the world, but tries to set forth, to present merely, the towering tyranny of his material."[7] Josephine Miles observes that this is pre-eminently the method of Blake's Prophetic Books. Those books, too, exhibit excessive repetition and the deliberate avoidance of rational structure. Thus in the technical

[6] Damon, *Blake*, p. 133.
[7] Josephine Miles, *Eras and Modes in English Poetry* (Berkeley, 1957), p. 97.

foibles of the "Auguries" we begin to see Blake swimming upstream for expression's sake while the current of precedent flows down.

"The Everlasting Gospel" must have been one of the last items recorded in Blake's Notebook, since its fragments occur at several different spots for want of space, and ultimately overflow onto separate sheets. It is impossible to hypothesize about the poem's intended structure, except to say that its central portion would have consisted in such parallel questions as "Was Jesus gentle?" "Was Jesus Humble?" "Was Jesus Chaste?" "Was Jesus Born of a Virgin . . .?" with the negative replies Blake drew from his New Testament. Like "Auguries of Innocence," which it resembles in assertiveness and in form, "The Everlasting Gospel" "is simply a collection of unfinished and unpolished fragments. Some of the couplets are unsurpassable, both rhythmically and from the standpoint of the compression of thought. Others are weak. Still others are audaciously undignified." [8] The unfinished state of the poem may account for several metrically awkward lines among its tetrameters, like the couplet:

> He must mean the meer love of Civility
> And so he must mean concerning Humility

or the first line of

> He who loves his Enemies betrays his Friends
> This surely is not what Jesus intends.

or:

> And Pride & Vanity of the imagination
> (*EG*, pp. 750, 751, 752)

[8] Damon, *Blake*, p. 293. Compare, however, Jack Lindsay, "The Metric of William Blake" in *Poetical Sketches*, ed. Eric Partridge (London, 1927), pp. 14–15: "In the *Everlasting Gospel*, by a rapid shifting of accents, by swooping monosyllabic substitutions and nervously alternating trisyllabic ones, Blake manages to achieve a continuous flaming agitation, a feeling of apocalyptic delight. . . . Always the rhythm has this almost shuddering tautness; and when it snaps, the effect is like an orchestral fortissimo."

but even discounting these, the rhythmical terrain is consistently rugged, good for tripping up metrical purists just as Blake's revolutionary, commandment-breaking Christ "speaks in parables to the Blind" (p. 748). With any other subject, passages like the following would be mere doggerel:

> And when he humbled himself to God,
> Then descended the cruel rod....
> If thou humblest thyself, thou humblest me
> Thou also dwelst in Eternity
> Thou art a Man God is no more
> Thine own Humanity learn to Adore (p. 750)

> He did not die with Christian Ease
> Asking pardon of his Enemies
> If he had Caiphas would forgive
> Sneaking submission can always live (pp. 751–52)

> Was Jesus Chaste or did he
> Give any Lessons of Chastity
> The morning blushd fiery red
> Mary was found in Adulterous bed (p. 753)

No two lines can be scanned alike for long stretches, and the rhythm jumps along clownishly. Only Blake's epigrammatic gift ties this package together, and his blatant enjoyment of paradox and shock wraps it up.

If "Auguries of Innocence" and "The Everlasting Gospel" strike lyric's limits, Blake's epigrams finally cross the borders. We have no right to expect anything poetic out of these primarily splenetic jottings with which Blake thrashed for life and self-respect in his sea of troubles; their most significant virtues, for him, were violence, vehemence, and tooth-gnashing humor:

> The only Man that eer I knew
> Who did not make me almost spew

Was Fuseli he was both Turk & Jew
And so dear Christian Friends how do you do
(*Notebook*, p. 551)

Blake's weapon is the bludgeon, not the dagger. The revisions which occur among these verses simply try to make the blow heavier rather than to improve its form. Sometimes this involves technical improvement, as in the changing of "Thank God I never was sent to school / To learn to admire the works of a Fool" to the alliterated "To be Flogd into following the Style of a Fool" (p. 550). Blake's hit-or-miss method does produce a number of sound venomous hits. And hidden among his fathomless caves there are also a few gems of purest ray serene, like the triplet about "The Angel that presided oer my birth" (p. 541), and the quatrain "I give you the end of a golden string" (p. 551), which later came to head *Jerusalem*. But the poet at the time of writing may have valued the coarsest, least metrical, most clogged-sounding of his epigrams as much or more than the artistically finished ones, because their ugliness gave shape to the ugliness in the world at which he raged.

As a summary of Blake's later lyrics one may say that, seemingly written in the intervals between more protracted works, they form a series of sorties toward regions which the Prophetic Books were occupying in force. They move toward private symbolism and then into outspoken didacticism, just as the prophecies do. They tell stories of mythic import, even if they do not supply Ossianic names for the characters. Blake in them begins to make high argument out of his personal history in a way he never did in *Innocence* and *Experience*, but did supremely in *Milton* and bewilderingly in *Jerusalem*. And in form, these lyrics turn gradually from beauty of sound to power of sound, from metrical control to metrical devil-may-carelessness. As the epigrams in many spots break through poetry to doggerel, so *Jerusalem*, the last of the Prophetic Books, breaks the bones of meter for the sake of something Blake called "oratory." Some of these lyrics succeed, some do not. As a group, they never formed so complete a vehicle for Blake's thought as either the early lyrics or the Prophetic Books. They have neither the flawless intensity of the former nor the flawed might of the latter; neither the purity of the one nor the scope of the other. They shoot off in different directions, each a compromise between lyric and prophecy.

PART III

The Prophetic Books

8

The Case Against the Prophecies

And they inclos'd my infinite brain into a narrow circle.

(*VDA*, p. 191)

According to Saintsbury, "Blake could have distilled everything that was valuable from *Tiriel* to *Jerusalem*... into the forms of 'Broken Love' and 'Auguries of Innocence' and 'The Everlasting Gospel' "[1] and the world would be none the worse. De Selincourt, who complains that in depending on private "unintelligible" symbolism Blake writ no language, felt that "the few short lines in which Blake says that God is in the lamb or asks if he is in the tiger have more meaning, more of true mysticism ... in them, than the whole bulk of his prophetic books."[2]

However offensive such opinions may be to those who enjoy elucidating the ineluctable in Blake's work, they are understandable. Blake's prophetic books seldom have the immediate esthetic and emotional appeal of his *Songs*. They seem turgid and overwrought, chaotic or oversystematized (depending on the reader), raw vision insufficiently translated into the terms of art. They do not please; they puzzle; and the beginning reader may well ask himself whether they will begin to please any more when they

[1] *A History of English Prosody* (London, 1906–10), III, 20.
[2] Basil de Selincourt, *William Blake* (London and New York, 1911), p. 289.

cease to puzzle. We have no such difficulty with the *Songs*. The cause of this heavy change, of course, is that Blake meant to accomplish certain things with the Prophetic Books which he could not accomplish with the lyric, and that the difference in approach precipitated a difference in style.

To anticipate quarrels, it is useful to consider the main objections which critics have made against the prophecies; for although the tide of protest has been steadily receding among the scholars, the general reader will, at the outset, probably feel his own protests in full flood. These criticisms may usually be classified as doubts of Blake's meaning, disagreements with his general approach to art, or disparagements of stylistic particulars.

Scholarship has already driven back one wave of criticism: the early notion that Blake's prophetic works were nonsense, or the fruit of madness, or dangerous blasphemy, or all three. These views were held by many who coupled enthusiasm for Blake's art and lyrical verse with complete bafflement over the later poetry. Exhibit A of the sort of thing they said may be the statement of James Smetham, printed in Gilchrist's second volume:

> As to any serious consideration of Blake's vocation to teach aught of morals; of theology, or non-theology; of Christian Atheism, or Atheistic Christianity; we . . . on a general glance at the tone and tenor of these portentous scrolls of *Thel* and *Urizen*, these *Marriages of Heaven and Hell*, which would look blasphemous if we did not tenderly recollect by whom they were written, refuse any serious further investigation of their claims, and must dismiss them, not scornfully, though it may be sorrowfully. We regard them rather as we regard the gentle or exalted incoherences of a dear friend's delirium; for our theory of the mental structure of Blake renders them as harmless to us as his gentle *Songs of Innocence*.[3]

Gilchrist himself, although more charitable about Blake's sanity, could offer nothing but generalities about his poetry. Even Swinburne, the first critic to suggest that we should not pass Blake's

[3] Alexander Gilchrist, *Life of William Blake*, 2nd ed. (London, 1880), II, 335–36. Reprinted from *London Quarterly Review*, January, 1869.

prophecies unalarmed, retreated behind a fog of Carlylean prose when confronted by his latest works. But Swinburne contributed a consistent, if partial, summary of Blake's main ideas; and these first timbers having been hewn, nothing could prevent others from clearing the whole woods. The discovery that Blake had something to say has been gradual, like the discovery that began in the eighteenth century and is still proceeding today, that the Middle Ages were not entirely barbaric. Ellis and Yeats, Berger, Sloss and Wallis, all attempted to clarify Blake's system; Damon in 1924 singlehandedly opened vast tracts; and after him have come Frye, Schorer, Erdman, Percival, and many others. At each stage it becomes clearer that Blake touched no province of thought, whether psychology, politics, esthetics, ethics, or religion, which his persistent intelligence and stubbornly insular honesty did not adorn. With each new exposition Blake grows more sane, more contemporary; it seems only a question of the world catching up with him.

Still, if the value of Blake's thought is granted, the value of his poetry remains questionable. Suppose a thing is Truth; is it necessarily Art? Blake would say yes, but not many people would agree with him. One may reasonably charge that the Prophetic Books "are marvellously strange and powerful; but, except for passages of rare energy and magnificence, almost smothered in the obscurity and involution of their context, they are notably deficient in lucidity, in wholeness, in vitality, and in beauty—in all the essentials of great literature and great art."[4] If it were so, it were a grievous fault. Had Blake any explanations for his deficiencies?

On the matter of obscurity, the poet was always forthright. "You say that I want somebody to Elucidate my Ideas," he wrote the Reverend Dr. Trusler in 1799.

But you ought to know that What is Grand is necessarily obscure to Weak men. That which can be made Explicit to the Idiot is not worth my care. The wisest of the Ancients consider'd what is not

[4] Helen C. White, *The Mysticism of William Blake,* Univ. of Wisc. Stud. in Lang. and Lit., No. 23 (Madison, 1927), p. 225.

too Explicit as the fittest for Instruction, because it rouzes the faculties to act.... What is it sets Homer, Virgil & Milton in so high a rank of Art? Why is the Bible more Entertaining & Instructive than any other book? Is it not because they are addressed to the Imagination, which is Spiritual Sensation, & but mediately to the Understanding or Reason? [5]

Some years later, alluding directly to his own work, he writes of his intention to

speak to future generations by a Sublime Allegory, which is now perfectly completed into a Grand Poem.... I consider it as the Grandest Poem that this World Contains. Allegory address'd to the Intellectual powers, while it is altogether hidden from the Corporeal Understanding, is My Definition of the Most Sublime Poetry.[6]

Noting here the "altogether hidden from" as opposed to the earlier "but mediately addressed to," we may ascribe the difference either to Blake's being more at ease with Butts than Trusler, or to his advancing mistrust of this world's corporeality.

Certain critics have posited other reasons for Blake's retreat from clarity. Those who emphasize the influence on him of Boehme and Swedenborg, Paracelsus, Taylor, and the obscurer visions of the Bible, sometimes suggest that he not only learned from them the virtue of symbolism in communicating high matters, but fell into the error of mistaking accident for essence—obscurity for wisdom. George Mills Harper believes he picked up from Taylor the esotericist's notion that Plato and other Greek philosophers, instead of using "clear and explicit diction, adopted fables and enigmas, metaphors and similitudes; and under these, as veils, concealed [their wisdom] from the profane and vulgar eye," because of "a profound conviction that the sublimest truths are profaned when clearly unfolded to the vulgar." [7]

[5] *Letters*, pp. 793–94.
[6] *Letters*, p. 825.
[7] Thomas Taylor, *The Metaphysics of Aristotle* (London, 1801), p. iv; *The Dissertations of Maximus Tyrius* (London, 1804), I, iv–v. Quoted by George Mills Harper, *The Neoplatonism of William Blake* (Chapel Hill, 1961), p. 49.

Another suggestion, proposed by critics who emphasize the social and political aspects of Blake's thought (and sometimes rather wish he had not diluted it with other matter), is that after 1791 and during the period of political reaction in England, when "the radicals were dispersed . . . Blake went underground with them and his poetry in a very real way went underground with him." [8] Bronowski declares outright that the poet disguised a concern with revolution under symbolic names: "he chose now to call these forms Orc, Rintrah, and Palambron, because he dared not call them Lafayette, Pitt, and George III." [9] Erdman, whose understanding of Blake's life is unsurpassed today, also insists upon his "nervous fear of censorship," [10] and considers the withdrawal damaging to his art.

Yet Blake had legitimate cause enough for obscurity in his Prophetic Books. These books deal, as many competent studies have indicated, with Blake's problems in private life; with the various states of the human soul and the progression thereof; with a theory of art and the imagination; with contemporary political events; with world history in both the temporal and theological sense, using the poet's own Creation myths, eschatology, and metaphysical geography; and as often as not, they deal with all these matters at once. Blake had the drive of the true allegorist, who automatically identifies any single happening in any single man's life with a shift of balance on every stratum of the cosmos.[11]

[8] Mark Schorer, *William Blake, the Politics of Vision* (New York, 1946), p. 17.

[9] Jacob Bronowski, *William Blake, 1757–1827: A Man Without a Mask* (London, 1944), p. 52.

[10] David V. Erdman, *Blake, Prophet Against Empire* (Princeton, 1954), p. 139.

[11] We should not be deceived by Blake's differentiation of Vision from Allegory at the apparent expense of the latter: "Fable or Allegory are a totally distinct & inferior kind of Poetry" (*VLJ*, p. 604). It is a purely verbal distinction; Blake uses "Allegory" as a synonym for "the superficial," without defining it. If by the allegorizing temperament we mean that which produces a *Piers Plowman*, a *Pearl*, or a *Divine Comedy*, a temperament which sees all things under the form of eternity, a vision which presumes that a single symbol may represent precise ideas to several levels of the imagination, and a sense of the infinite in the individual which allows the

He wrote in all seriousness that "A Robin Red breast in a Cage / Puts all Heaven in a Rage" ("Auguries," p. 431). He felt every level of life, from below the robin to above the heavens, moving in concentric, interdependent spheres. This is the subject of his epics. Thus he did not exchange the title "Lafayette" for the title "Orc." Orc is not simply one man figuring in one revolution. He is also the spirit of revolution itself; an aspect of Blake's own personality and of the collective personality of Man; a child of Time, which is the labor of poetic imagination to recreate cosmos out of chaos; and a force driving toward the Christian Apocalypse. If all these things are one, why have several names for them? Blake's awareness of unity here forced him to invent Orc. Similar amalgamations produced his other symbols. When he wrote that "Men are admitted into Heaven... because they have Cultivated their Understandings" (*VLJ*, p. 615), he meant by "Understanding" only this, the ability to discover a real unity in an apparent diversity.

A probable reason for the transfer from public to private symbolism was Blake's mistrust of other people's free associations. Tiger and Lamb, like Orc and Urizen, symbolize many things. But would this be understood? "To the Eyes of a Miser a Guinea is more beautiful than the Sun.... The tree which moves some to

---

poet, without romantic egoism, to make himself the theme of his song, then Blake had an allegorizing temperament. "Auguries of Innocence" is an anatomy of the allegorical method; and Blake's few comments on literature indicate that allegorical interpretation came naturally to him. In his lengthiest piece of literary criticism, the analysis of characters in the *Canterbury Tales,* he writes as follows: "The characters of Chaucer's Pilgrims are the characters which compose all ages and nations: as one age falls, another rises, different to mortal sight, but to immortals only the same; for we see the same characters repeated again and again, in animals, vegetables, minerals, and in men; nothing new occurs in identical existence; Accident ever varies, Substance can never suffer change nor decay....the characters themselves for ever remain unaltered, and consequently they are the physiognomies or lineaments of universal human life, beyond which Nature never steps....As Newton numbered the stars, and as Linneus numbered the plants, so Chaucer numbered the classes of men." (*Descriptive Catalogue,* p. 567.) In effect, Blake out-medievalizes the fourteenth-century writer; the habit of allegory was more pervasive, more systematic, in him than in Chaucer.

tears of joy is in the Eyes of others only a Green thing that stands in the way" (*Letters*, p. 793). And again, " 'What,' it will be Question'd, 'When the Sun rises, do you not see a round disk of fire somewhat like a Guinea?' Oh no, no, I see an Innumerable company of the Heavenly host crying 'Holy, Holy, Holy is the Lord God Almighty.' I question not my Corporeal or Vegetative Eye any more than I would Question a Window concerning a Sight. I look thro' it & not with it" (*VLJ*, p. 617). But to others, the windows might prove opaque. To others, the children and animals of the *Songs* might be *merely* children and animals, and the delightful poetry merely poetry.

All the anecdotes about Blake, as well as his letters, bespeak a man intensely eager to communicate with others, yet clearly preferring not to be understood at all than to be misunderstood. When he decided to "speak to future generations," he took his stand here. This is not esotericism. One remembers that Blake, to Dr. Johnson's insistence that the unlearned must have the Bible explained to them by notes, observed that "Christ & his Apostles were Illiterate Men; Caiphas, Pilate & Herod were Learned." [12] Annotating Berkeley, he remarked that "Jesus supposes every Thing to be Evident to the Child & to the Poor & Unlearned. Such is the Gospel." [13] He said children could best interpret his own paintings, and Crabb Robinson found him speaking casually of his "faculty of vision," saying that "all men partake of it, but it is lost by not being cultivated." [14] These are not the statements of obscurantist snobbery. Blake did not become obscure because he wanted to hide his truths from the vulgar. It was the learned, the casuist, the doubter, whom he loved to confound with apparent paradoxes. In the truly vulgar, the simple believer, he placed his faith. "When I tell any Truth it is not for the sake of Convincing those who do not know it, but for the sake of defending those who do" (*PA*, p. 597).

[12] *Annotations to Thornton*, p. 786.

[13] *Annotations to Berkeley*, p. 774.

[14] Henry Crabb Robinson, *Diary*, in Arthur Symons, *William Blake* (New York, 1907), p. 264.

Admirers of the lyrics might contend that the *Songs* were sufficiently obscure themselves, that they too were always resonating on a scale of meanings, echoing off into anagogy at either end. Certainly, the best of Blake's lyrics do give us an Eternity in the palm of our hand. The problem is that Blake had a whole host of Eternals, of which he wished to speak in a manner more complex than his lyric form afforded. He wanted to show how they related to each other, how they fought together, how they were born from each other, murdered each other, became each other. And a lyric, as Blake wrote lyrics, could present but one truth, or one chain of consonant truths, at a time. It could not present conflict, being single. It could not present change, being static. When he tried to press more of his system into lyric form, the results were only partially successful. For such effects, he was ultimately forced to write epics.[15]

A charge related to that of obscurity is the accusation that Blake erred in creating his own system instead of working within "the tradition." Sometimes this argument shallowly disguises the critic's personal preference for *a* tradition, as when T. S. Eliot discovers that Blake's ideas, exhibiting "a certain meanness of culture . . . illustrate the crankiness, the eccentricity, which frequently affects writers outside of the Latin tradition," [16] and concludes therefore that Blake is only "a poet of genius" instead of a classic like Dante. This very intelligent essay pretends merely to be pointing out the defects of Blake's virtues. Eliot suggests that a poet can feed us a pill if only the sugar coating is his own, but not the medicine. Yet in complaining that Blake "must needs create a philosophy as well as a poetry," [17] he seems here as elsewhere to begrudge a poetry which is too conspicuously philosophical partly because it presents ideas he disbelieves in. When he finds ideas he more or less agrees with, or can interpret in his own way, he can safely insist that he is disregarding the doctrinal

[15] Cf. Robert Gleckner, *The Piper and the Bard* (Detroit, 1959), pp. 275–76.

[16] T. S. Eliot, *The Sacred Wood* (London, 1934), p. 157.

[17] *Ibid.*, p. 156.

aspect—that doctrine is only a frame for poetry, and that "poetry is a superior amusement." [18] The argument for tradition appears more objectively in Yeats, who is not afraid of letting poetry swallow up religion and philosophy, and would not have cared whether Blake used Dante's Christianity, or Norse, or Irish tales, but who felt that the texture of the poetry suffered by its lack of a given myth, that Blake fell into incongruities and arbitrariness which he might have avoided.[19]

The wisdom of ages as a source, and communal consent in an audience, are two definite advantages for a poet. Most of Blake's defenders therefore assert that Blake does belong to a tradition. Some, notably Kathleen Raine, claim very broad antecedents for him. "Blake was working in a tradition—some would say in *the* Tradition—of the perennial philosophy of absolute spiritual knowledge and its unchanging symbols." He used "symbolic language with the same almost mathematical exactness that we find in Cabbalism, Neoplatonism, and Vedantic literature." He got his inspiration from all the right people: "not in the late and secularized copies of ancient myths, but in the Eddas, in Homer, Hesiod, the Hymns of Orpheus; not in the disputations of 17th century English theologians, but in the works of Plotinus and Proclus, the Pymander of Hermes, the Baghavad Gita, Ovid and Virgil, Plato, Plutarch, Porphyry and Apuleius." Even the alchemists Blake read are now becoming respectable, says Miss Raine.[20]

[18] *Ibid.*, p. viii. When divorced from Eliot's admirably partisan passion, the "superior amusement" theory appears foolish. An essay by B. Ifor Evans on "Thomas Gray and William Blake" in *Tradition and Romanticism* (London, 1940) suggests that "Any unique human experience is *somehow* an extension of life, not always desireable if judged socially, but in *devious* ways an enrichment." (Italics mine.) But soon the ink-stained finger is shaking: "With Gray no problem of belief arises, for the verse is to be enjoyed as a picture or statue, or a vase elaborately chased and burnished . . . Blake, on the other hand, immediately challenges one's conception of the universe, usurping for poetry the place of religion and philosophy" (pp. 104–5). Precisely; and Blake felt he had ample precedent for his usurpation in the Hebrew prophets.

[19] W. B. Yeats, "William Blake and the Imagination" in *Ideas of Good and Evil* (New York, 1903), pp. 173–74.

[20] Kathleen Raine, "Blake and Tradition," *Encounter*, Nov. 1956, pp. 51–53.

This exaggerates a case to make one, since analogue does not prove source, and since much of Blake's culture came through eighteenth-century filters.[21] It is questionable, moreover, whether a common denominator reduction of sects and philosophies constitutes a "perennial philosophy of absolute spiritual knowledge" which anyone would personally endorse. Blake's very eclecticism excludes him from the advantages of a writer who shares a single received body of myth with his audience; nor has he the position of Milton, who overtly played Christian and pagan traditions against each other, claiming both as his own. Nevertheless, the work of scholars like Frye, Percival, and Harper, as well as Miss Raine, in establishing parallels to Blake's myths in other cultures, has this value: it makes his ideas and symbolism seem less arbitrary than formerly. It is not important whether Blake discovered certain symbols in books or in his head, if the parallels exist. Nor is it required that Blake should give his egg symbol the same moral interpretation that the Neoplatonists gave theirs, or that his Albion should serve the same exact purpose as the Cabbalists' Adam Kadmon, if a basic meaning is shared. We do not yet have a universal vocabulary of symbols. But the research already completed shows Blake to have such varied affinities, that, if a theory of psychological and literary archetypes ever is proven valid, he may be expected to assume a central position in it. Then, if the common reader grows as well acquainted with the furniture of his non-rational mind as Blake was with his, the issue of Blake's "tradition" may evaporate.

Meanwhile, it will be useful to remember that Blake was English, that he was soaked in Biblical lore, and that his faith in individual insight was in effect a "traditional" Protestant one. He assumed that his audience would know the Bible and Milton backwards and forwards, as he did; and such knowledge would in

[21] The case Harper makes for Taylor's influence is quite strong; and we remember also that Blake was reading classic poetry with Hayley, and began learning Greek and Latin at Felpham. See *Letters*, pp. 806, 821.

fact give a standard context to many, although not all, of his apparent idiosyncracies. Northrop Frye has analyzed Biblicism and radical individualism as English traits which coalesce in romanticism's insistence on the value of the creative process as an end in itself. "This combination of Protestant, radical, and Romantic qualities is frequent enough in English culture" to account for work like Blake's. It is opposed only by "cultural evangelists who came from places like Missouri and Idaho, and who had a clear sense of the shape of the true English tradition, from its beginnings in Provence and mediaeval Italy to its later developments in France." [22]

To explain is not to forgive. But even if we dispose of "obscurity" and "lack of culture" along with "madness" as pertinent objections to Blake's prophecies, there yet remain other charges of a more esthetic sort. These have not been so thoroughly answered.

Blake has been called too great a literalist of the imagination,[23] and charged with trusting his visions and voices so implicitly that he failed to transform them to art. If this refers only to his claim of composing his poetry "without Labour or Study" (*Letters*, p. 823), it is meaningless. The one manuscript we have of a prophetic work almost topples under its revisions of content, if not of form. There is no reason to doubt that the other prophecies were similarly worked over. As to his form, Blake like Milton trusted his Muses, or Daughters of Beulah, to express themselves adequately without pencil-and-paper struggles. On the other hand,

[22] Northrop Frye, "Blake after Two Centuries," in *English Romantic Poets, Modern Essays in Criticism*, ed. M. H. Abrams (New York, 1960), p. 66.

On the present value to most readers of a non-English Blake, see W. W. Robson, "Kidnapping Blake," *Spectator*, Dec. 6, 1957, p. 806: "Miss Raine's efforts to show that Blake was not 'an isolated crank' with a home-made philosophy can only succeed in making him seem more of a crank than ever, one with an esoteric, derivative, literary philosophy instead." The point is more than a quibble. If Blake be not traditional to me, what care I how traditional he be?

[23] Yeats, "William Blake and His Illustrations," in *Ideas of Good and Evil*, p. 182.

if it is objected that Blake transcribed his system unselectively, that he mistakenly tried to squeeze every detail into print, there may be a fair grievance. Schorer argues that the very subtlety and complexity of his thought was intrinsically "too vast" for poetic form.[24] Or the complaint may be that of Yeats, who felt that by sacrificing "every grace of style that might obscure" the lineaments of his thought, Blake sacrificed something essential.[25]

Sometimes it is charged that Blake was by nature a lyricist, and did not know how to give structure to an epic poem.[26] To round off this allegation, one might add that in prose Blake was an aphorist, and either could not or would not construct a "great argument."

Many complain that Blake's characters or personifications fail to come alive. "If Blake had had Bunyan's magic power of vitalizing abstractions, so that a vice or a virtue becomes, in the twinkling of an eye, a character, and puts on flesh and blood .... then we might have had something very different." [27] "Urizen, Urthona, Luvah, and Tharmas—how do we distinguish them? Are they not all the same loose-limbed giant in habiliments only so slightly different as not to be distinguishable at all except in wholly abstract terms?" [28]

Even the symbolic technique comes into question. Stanley Gardner, in his little book *Infinity on the Anvil*, finds steady "disintegration" of the poet's symbolic control after *The Book of Urizen* and *Songs of Experience*.[29] To Gardner, the symbolism of the late books is meaningless. Others find it merely monotonous or redundant. "Many of his images are not images at all, but ideas expressed through force of habit in figures of speech." [30] We can

[24] Schorer, *Blake*, p. 338.
[25] Yeats, "William Blake and His Illustrations," p. 182.
[26] W. H. Stevenson, "Blake's Jerusalem," *Essays in Criticism*, IX (1959), 254, 264.
[27] Lawrence Binyon, ed., *Poems of Blake* (London, 1931), p. xxxiii.
[28] Schorer, *Blake*, p. 424.
[29] Stanley Gardner, *Infinity on the Anvil, a Critical Study of Blake's Poetry* (Oxford, 1954), pp. 132 ff.
[30] Stevenson, "Blake's Jerusalem," p. 260.

discount the implied assumptions that all images must be palpable, and that "ideas expressed . . . in figures of speech" are somehow wrong for poetry; but "force of habit" is a dart that will stick painfully in any author's skin.

A final criticism of the Prophetic Books is that they are impossible, or ugly, to read as verse. "Even the loosest arrangements of the iambic and anapestic feet that were his favorites often vanish completely in passages that defy all metrical system. . . . Their arrangement into lines is the merest irrelevance. Blake assuredly escaped from the prosodic cage. But the rights of poets, like those of men, involve their duties. He was freed to chaos." [31]

Few of these stylistic criticisms support themselves by textual analysis. But those who raise shields in defense of Blake's honor do not usually refer to the text either. The following discussion of the prophetic versification cannot deal, except incidentally, with all the other problems of poetic worth or worthlessness in the prophecies. It is one candle in the cavernous, ill-lit question of Blake's esthetics. But other applications are possible, since the principles which govern his verse, or fail to govern it, may also underlie his treatment—or nontreatment—of structure, character, and symbolism.

[31] Schorer, *Blake*, p. 411.

9

The Line of Freedom

Poetry Fetter'd Fetters the Human Race.
(*Jerusalem*, p. 621)

To understand Blake's prophecies, we must understand their technique; we must consider why Blake required a new type of versification, as far removed as possible from lyric, what sources he drew from, and how the verse itself is meant to be read. On the first point, we will see that his new technique conveys the devotion to complexity, the passion for freedom, and the mistrust of formal beauty, which distinguish the prophetic side of his temperament from the lyric.

Complexity is to the Prophetic Books what simplicity was to the lyric. Although Blake always retained his sense of the mind's essential unity, what impressed him more and more about that unity was the multiplicity it embodied. How much more excellent a piece of work was Man, if he could contain ages, nations, universes of weal and woe, if he could contain huge struggling Zoas and their emanations and children, if in his body could be enacted endless historical cycles, and if with all this he could yet rise from his sleep single and whole at the moment of resurrection! How much simpler and more self-evident did the ethic of forgiveness of sins seem if one looked at the ramifications of evil which followed from neglect of it! How much more wonderful was the real unity of God and Man if one realized the distance Error placed between them.

As he proceeded in his Prophetic Books, Blake pushed God, his idea of ultimate unity, ever further back from the fallen world, apparently the better to enjoy the reunion of God and Man when it came, as it comes on the final plate of *Jerusalem*. Vegetated men on earth are subject to the four Zoas, who parallel Jung's division of the mental faculties into reason, emotion, sense perception, and intuition. The four Zoas comprise Albion or Man. Albion is only one of a great family of Immortals or Eternals. These Immortals or Eternals, when united, are identical with Jesus or the Divine Vision. There is cloud behind cloud, for the sake of clarity.

The cosmic geographies of Dante and Milton are cosy compared to Blake's cosmos. With its superimpositions of Biblical locales on Britain, its vortexes, its intersecting universes, and its multidimensionality, Blake suggests a sheer vastness of distance and duration unsurpassed outside of astronomy texts. This is another form of "O Altitudo" at the oneness of the universe when seen by spiritual eyes. Rebelling against Newtonian absolute space and time, he developed a system which parallels the theory of relativity in modern physics. Like the physicists, he presumes relative values of time and space depending upon co-ordinate systems, only in order to discover the conditions under which time and space cease to be relative. "Time was Finished!" is the cry which announces the close of *Jerusalem* (94.18; see also *FZ*, IX.568), although in Eternity, of course, the Immortals can go about "Creating Space, Creating Time" (*J*, 98.31) for fun.

Treating human experience, Blake could not always afford to neglect the involutions, the deformations of life, for the sake of its simplicity. He told the truth in his lyrics. In his prophecies he chose to tell the whole truth, altering nothing, leaving nothing out. The lyric form, the lyric line, would not do for this. He needed a form more spacious, more elastic, more able to sustain itself despite severe distortions.

The new wine shatters the old bottles for another reason. Blake in his lyrics does not stress his gospel of freedom. In *Innocence*, freedom was an assumed thing, an absence or pliancy of restraints.

The child who wanted to play a little longer would be permitted to do so. Often the absence of restraint was less important than the immanence of protection; the lost child would be found, the sleeping child would be cradled, the sad child would be comforted "till our grief is fled & gone." In *Experience* and the early MS lyrics, restrictions become palpable. There are the myrtle-tree of marriage, the swaddling bands binding infant joy to its mortal prison, the mind-forg'd manacles of the social contract, the iron chain of holiness. Yet the hero of these songs is at best the victim, not yet "a man who has come through."

The Prophetic Books, even before *Experience*, speak in terms of revolution, in terms of the "Energy" which is "Eternal Delight." *Tiriel*, a study of energy perverted, only gropes toward this. *Thel*, until its close, is a shady interlude before the onset of red Orc. In *The French Revolution* naked energy blasts forth, and continues raging to the end of the prophecies. Blake, believing in a heaven whose chief activities were "War & Hunting" (*M*, 35.2), thought any action, even the writhing of error, was better than passivity. Only the fool folds his hands and eats his own flesh, and "The Fool shall not enter into Heaven let him be ever so Holy" (*VLJ*, p. 615). To reinforce his message of freedom and energy, Blake developed a verse-form which openly flouted conventions and proclaimed its author's "mental fight."

The form is not designed for esthetic delectation. Blake no doubt felt that his songs, even when they pleased, were not understood; were not understood precisely because they did please. As a visionary, he cared only for that "beauty" which Dostoevsky called "the battleground where God and the devil contend with one another for the heart of man." Lesser types of literary or artistic beauty had to be sacrificed for higher ends. The test of poetry was not pleasure, as Wordsworth and Coleridge thought, but truth.

If poetry was a servant of Blake's vision, then prosody was the servant of a servant. Blake's search for a line that would transcend ordinary meters corresponded with his search for that "most

Sublime" mode of poetry which would be "addressed to the Intellectual Powers, while altogether hidden from the Corporeal understanding." Here is what he says he found, in the preface to *Jerusalem:*

When this Verse was first dictated to me, I consider'd a Monotonous Cadence, like that used by Milton & Shakspeare & all writers of English Blank Verse, derived from the modern bondage of Rhyming, to be a necessary and indispensible part of Verse. But I soon found that in the mouth of a true Orator such monotony was not only awkward, but as much a bondage as rhyme itself. I therefore have produced a variety in every line, both of cadences & number of syllables. Every word and every letter is studied and put into its fit place; the terrific numbers are reserved for the terrific parts, the mild & gentle for the mild & gentle parts, and the prosaic for inferior parts; all are necessary to each other. Poetry Fetter'd Fetters the Human Race. (*J*, p. 621)

This manifesto essentially contains two assertions: first, that the prophetic verse is irregular; second, that it is minutely adjusted to the content. One of these assertions is valid; the other is partially misleading.

For the first, we will find even at the beginning that Blake unmoors himself from the short line and simple childlike beat of the lyrics. In time that green and stable shore vanishes over the horizon. The prophetic verse becomes progressively more irregular, and this irregularity is the conscious expression of rebellion against traditional forms.

Second, however, we find that the adjustment of technique to content exists, but is rather massive than minute. The declaration that "every word and every letter is studied and put into its fit place" is a bit of bravado, or rather, an attempt to explain the poet's expressive approach in terms more suitable for lyric than for prophecy. Blake applies his prophetic paints with a broad, not a delicate brush. In the minor prophecies, and less frequently in the three major ones, he does occasionally convey fine shades of emotion or idea through his metrics. What we usually encounter, however, is not infinite variety, but a limited number of distinguishable styles, which must be taken in large amounts to have their effect. If a wall of bricks suddenly fell on us, we would not concern ourselves about the texture and pattern of each brick. We would simply be flattened. So do the prophecies try to flatten us. This is not, by any definition current then or now, an "esthetic" experience. But then, Blake can give us what other literature cannot: an experience of raw immensity.

The balance of styles varies from book to book. In *Tiriel*, the prevailing mood is grotesque and hysterical. In *Thel* it is elegiac. In *Visions of the Daughters of Albion* and *America*, built on a larger scale, a sense of power dominates. The tripartite division of styles into "terrific," "mild & gentle," and "prosaic" applies quite well to *The Four Zoas*, which is more intensely emotional than the other two major prophecies which followed it, and also more like a pageant or sequence of poetic tours de force in plainly distinguishable styles. Blake's mood becomes more intellectual in *Milton* and *Jerusalem*, and his style more consolidated. In these books, moreover, the bulk of "prosaic numbers for the inferior parts" increases, for Blake's concern with his system eventually crowded out all other interests. This phenomenon will be dealt with at greater length in the discussion of the major prophecies.

Septenary, the line Blake chose to use for most of his prophecies, already had a long history in English verse. In its long form it was the meter of didactic poetry beginning with the twelfth-century *Poema Morale;* it combined with six-foot lines to form the popular Poulter's Measure of early Elizabethan drama; and smoothed out, it appeared in Warner's *Albion's England* and Chapman's *Iliad*, after which it disappeared, replaced in serious poetry by the less cumbrous form of blank verse.

Broken up into four- and three-foot lines, septenary had been the meter of ballad. The samples of early, rough ballad that Blake saw in Percy's *Reliques* presented a model and precedent for his free stanzaic style which could also have served for his long-line technique. The seventeenth- and eighteenth-century literary ballad, prettified and regularized as it was, may also have influenced him. In a letter to Butts he quotes a stanza from Thomas Tickell's lachrymose *Colin and Lucy*, and writes it out long:

> I hear a voice you cannot hear, that says I must not stay,
> I see a hand you cannot see, that beckons me away.
>
> (*Letters*, p. 813)

The immediate inspiration for Blake's septenary was probably the prose-poetry of Macpherson's *Ossian*, which had stunned all Europe with its two-handed engine of sublimity and sentiment. Blake in 1789, still attracted by the novelty of its hybrid form, and now angered by the English hostility to Macpherson, needed to take only a short step from the Ossianic imitations in *Poetical Sketches* to the exclamatory, hair-raising *Tiriel*.

Macpherson's "rhythmic prose" was really a rather languid affair. Its sentences were strings of iambs, commonly of septenary length with a central pause, varied by alexandrines, and only rarely extending as far as eight feet, or stopping as short as five or fewer feet. At times, by shortening or extending its lines, and by the usual metrical variations, it could achieve some drive:

> A tale of the times of old! The deeds of days of other years. / The murmur of thy streams, O Lora! brings back the memory of the past. / The sound of thy words, Garmaller, is lovely in mine ear. / Dost thou not behold, Malvina, a rock with its head of heath! / Three aged pines bend from its face; green is the narrow plain at its feet; / there the flower of the mountain grows, and shakes its white head in the breeze.[1] [Divisions mine.]

Otherwise, it merely loped along:

> Many a voice and many a harp, in tuneful sounds arose. / Of Fingal noble deeds they sung; of Fingal's noble race; / And sometimes, on the lovely sound was heard the name of Ossian. / I often fought, and often won in battles of the spear. / But blind, and tearful, and forlorn, I walk with little men! [2] [Divisions mine.]

[1] "Carthon," in *The Poems of Ossian*, translated by James Macpherson, Esq. (New York, 1806), pp. 222–23.
[2] "Fingal," in *The Poems of Ossian*, pp. 328–29.

Blake was never so bland as Macpherson. Even in his earliest prophecies, the phrase and sentence are somewhat longer, the rhythm somewhat less regular. Later on, scarcely any resemblance remains, except the habit of varying his line-length from the staple septenary to other lengths. This habit, however, is one of the chief devices by which Blake keeps his distance from the "monotonous cadence" of normal verse.

Blake had other guides to a mighty line within the tradition of the English sublime: its finest flower of prose, and its boldest of verse, the Bible and Milton.[3] These sources stand in the same relation to Blake's Prophecies as nursery rhymes to *Innocence* and *Experience*. Blake was so steeped in them that his poetry and prose are filled with allusions and even puns on their texts. He assumed an equal knowledge in his audience. Just as the style of nursery rhyme would be familiar to his audience, so, he thought, the styles of the Bible and Milton would be. Just as the child's piping voice might disarm the reader and make difficult material seem easy, so the voice of the prophets—the Hebrew ones and the English one—funneled through Blake, might make the strange idea seem as if it were already known, and the revolutionary doctrine as if it resembled the doctrine of accepted authority. And of course this was not simply clever strategy. Since Blake thought he was inspired in the same way, and for as great a purpose, as the authors of Job and *Paradise Lost*, he echoed their manners, just as he echoed

[3] Josephine Miles, *Eras and Modes in English Poetry* (Berkeley, 1957), p. 18, gives some of the characteristics of sublimity in English verse: "The phrasal mode of Sylvester, Milton, and the eighteenth century, with its lofty phrases and cadences, its figures larger than life, and its high passions, was a clear part of what the century itself called the high or sublime style, not so much heroic as cosmic, not so much active as receptive and 'passionate,' in Pindar's richly ceremonious sense." This mode is (p. 45) "atmospheric in its terminology, cosmic in its reach, Platonic and Biblical and Protestant, overbalanced in structure and least regular in linear metrics in ode and blank-verse forms." In the prose of Blake's day, many of these qualities could apply to writers as diverse as Burke and Macpherson. Their extraordinarily consistent presence in Blake's prophecies, and their almost total absence in his lyrics, is one measure of the disparity between Blake's lyrical and prophetic impulses.

the child's manners when he wanted to convey the child's vision.

Most of the Biblical influences are in diction and symbolism rather than rhythm and structure. The Old and New Testaments offered Blake an endless banquet of narrative material, phrases, and images; they provided models for the rhetoric of lamentation, song of praise, pastoral, aphorism, invective. A few of the Biblical structural devices are also conspicuous in Blake; for example the concrete noun-abstract noun linkages like "Rock of Eternity," "Furnaces of affliction," "Tree of Mystery"; genealogical catalogues and formula statements like "And the number of his Sons is eight millions & eight" (*M*, 28.30); sentences beginning with "For" or "Behold" or "Lo." Parallelism, which is considered the most important structural principle of Biblical poetry, is very common in Blake, both in couplets: "The heavens are shaken & the Earth removed from its place" (*FZ*, IX.16), "From his mouth curses & from his eyes sparks of blighting" (*FZ*, V.3), "Does not the worm erect a pillar in the mouldering church yard / And a palace of eternity in the jaws of the hungry grave?" (*Thel*, 5.41–6.1); and in triplets: "The Stars flee remote; the heaven is iron, the earth is sulphur" (*J*, 66.81), "My tents are fall'n! my pillars are in ruins! my children dash'd / Upon Egypt's iron floors & the marble pavements of Assyria" (*J*, 79.1–2).

Sometimes Blake's Authorized Version supplied the rhythms, as well as the language, he needed. Compare:

> For out of Zion shall go forth the law, and the word of the Lord from Jerusalem. (Isaiah 2.3)

> And I heard the Name of their Emanations they are named Jerusalem. (*J*, 99.5)

Both are septenary lines with emotional emphasis on the center and close, and with the extra syllables of "Jerusălĕm" at the end giving a sense of further thrust as if the end were but a beginning. Or compare how Blake finds pointedness of rhythm as well as diction in:

And many among them shall stumble and fall, and be broken, and be snared, and be taken. (Isaiah, 8.15)

which he first transcribed in rather stumbling six-foot lines:

> That he who will not defend Truth may be compelled to
> Defend a Lie, that he may be snared & caught & taken.
> (*M*, 8.47–48)

Later, although he kept his own six feet to Isaiah's seven, he filled out the rhythm:

> That he who will not defend Truth, may be compelld to defend
> A Lie, that he may be snared and caught and snared and taken.
> (*J*, 9.29–30)

Or consider the rhythms of the Song of Songs:

For, lo, the winter is past, the rain is over and gone. . . . / The fig tree putteth forth her green figs, and the vines with the tender grapes /give a good smell. Arise, my love, my fair one, and come away. . . . / My beloved is mine, and I am his: he feedeth among the lilies. (S. of Sol. 2.11, 13, 16)

This divides easily into six- and seven-foot lines. Blake took from it, among other things, the lines from Book IX of *The Four Zoas*, "For Lo the winter melted away upon the distant hills" (*FZ*, IX.600) and "he cast them wailing into / The world of shadows thro the air till winter is over & gone" (*FZ*, IX.797–98), as well as the pastoral interlude in that same book beginning:

> Where dost thou flee O fair one where dost thou seek thy happy place
> To yonder brightness there I haste for sure I came from thence
> Or I must have slept eternally nor have felt the dew of morning. . . .
> Then O thou fair one sit thee down for thou art as the grass
> Thou risest in the dew of morning & at night art folded up
> (*FZ*, IX.401–3, 408–9)

Blake's most conspicuous rhythmic source in the Bible is the Book of Job, from which he learned how to construct a throbbing lamentation, and from which he took and used time and time again the device of the repeated rhetorical question:

Doth the hawk fly by thy wisdom, and stretch her wings towards the south? Doth the eagle mount up at thy command, and make her nest on high? (Job, 39.26–27)

Does not the great mouth laugh at a gift? & the narrow eyelids mock
At the labour that is above payment, and wilt thou take the ape
For thy councellor? or the dog for a schoolmaster to thy children?
(*VDA*, 5.7–9)

The style of the Prophecies comes closest to converging with the Bible in passages like these, in pastoral sections, in passages of lists and catalogues and genealogies, and wherever the poet is striving for simplicity. His divergences lie in his tendency to exaggerate, to build ornately where Biblical poets had built chastely. He is very fond of adjectives; he likes to repeat as well as rephrase ideas; he often prefers using ten words to one word. A single example must suffice here. Describing a tumultuous natural upheaval, I Kings 19.11–12 reads "And, behold, the Lord passed by, and a great and strong wind rent the mountains, and brake in pieces the rocks before the Lord; but the Lord was not in the wind: and after the wind an earthquake; but the Lord was not in the earthquake: and after the earthquake a fire; but the Lord was not in the fire: and after the fire a still small voice." A similar passage, Ezekiel 1.4–5, reads "And I looked, and behold, a whirlwind came out of the north, a great cloud, and a fire infolding itself, and a brightness was about it, and out of the midst thereof as the colour of amber, out of the midst of the fire. Also out of the midst thereof came the likeness of living creatures." The language in both passages is remarkable for its sobriety. The corresponding lines in Blake are (*FZ*, III.135–53):

A crash ran thro the immense The bounds of Destiny were broken
The bounds of Destiny Crashd direful & the swelling Sea
Burst from its bonds in whirlpools fierce roaring with Human voice . . .
From the Crash roared a flame of blue sulphureous fire from the flame
A dolorous groan that struck with dumbness all confusion
Swallowing up the horrible din in agony on agony

Thro the Confusion like a crack across from immense to immense
Loud strong a universal groan of death louder
Than all the wracking elements. . . .
But from the Dolorous Groan one like a shadow of smoke appeard.

This amplification, this tendency to lengthen and twist the sentences, to pile up accents, to lay emotional coloring on thickly, is Miltonic. If Blake in his reinterpretations of Christianity was producing his "Bible of Hell, which the world shall have whether they will or no" (*MHH*, p. 158), in his poetic career he was giving the world a reincarnation of Milton, the true Milton who was "of the Devil's party" (*MHH*, p. 150).[4] Wherever in his prophecies Blake seems overblown, he is probably trying to outdo Milton. Among the particular devices attributable to this source are the sudden explosion into Latinisms, the accretion of epithets, the adverbial use of adjectives and participles as in "swift writhd his neck / Involuntary" (*FZ*, IV.291–92) or "waters / That roll'd perplex'd, lab'ring" (*BU*, 4.2–3), the flanking of a substantive by adjectives as in "With dismal torment sick" (*Eur*, 12.18). Blake sometimes succeeded in investing the Miltonic anaphora with a Miltonic pathos; compare:

that be from thee far,
That far be from thee, Father, (*P.L.* III. 154–55)

And all that has existed in the space of six thousand years:
Permanent, & not lost not lost nor vanishd, (*J*, 13.59–60)

The parallel between Milton's note on the verse of *Paradise Lost* and Blake's on that of *Jerusalem* shows that Blake considered himself not only an imitator but a successor to Milton in prosodic matters. His stretching of pentameter to a longer line was a first step.[5] It seems to be true in general that the longer the line of a poem, the greater its capacity for dignity, moral seriousness, physical stress. It is impossible to say whether the reason for this is

[4] The standard comparative work on the two poets is Denis Saurat, *Blake and Milton* (London, 1935). Most of the material offered there is elementary, however, and no comparison of styles is attempted.

[5] One commentator amusingly demonstrates the verbal and metrical kinship between the two poets by transcribing some lines from *Paradise Lost*

physiological association (of long lines with long breaths, for example, or strenuous muscular activity) or historical accident. But very short lines are slight or volatile—think of Skeltonics or Ralegh's "The Lie"—there is nothing visceral in them. Four beats is the line of song, from "O Western Wind" to Burns and beyond; in morality it is Hudibrastics or Swift on the death of Dr. Swift; in reflective verse it is "L'Allegro" and "Il Penseroso" or "In Memoriam." Pentameter is for drama and epic. You can stretch lyrics to a longer line, but you cannot squeeze *Macbeth* or *Paradise Lost* into a shorter one. Blake, feeling he had to deliver more weighty matter than any other poet, chose the broadest line he could fit on his page. Then he proceeded to incorporate, in his longer rhythms, the techniques of metrical variation which Milton had employed, plus a few of his own.

This creates certain problems for the reader. Thanks to four hundred years of blank verse composition in English, readers know how to tolerate a good deal of irregularity in the pentameter line. This line is now familiar enough so that Donne, Milton, or Browning can do some of the queerest things with it—things which in their own day were considered disgraceful violations of prosodic decorum—yet we have no trouble reading them as verse. We do not complain like Ben Jonson that Donne deserved hanging for murdering meter, or declare like Sam Johnson that Milton's barbaric metrics should be tolerated for the sake of his wholesome doctrine. Instead we praise Donne and Milton for expanding the expressive possibilities of verse. Blake's septenary is a different matter, for Blake deals with meter as with myth: he

---

(X, 867–75) in the form of Blake's septenaries. So written, they do look as if they came from one of the prophecies:

Out of my sight, thou serpent! That name best befits thee, with him leagued,
Thyself as false and hateful; nothing wants but that thy shape
Like his, and colour serpentine, may show thy inward fraud
To warn all creatures from thee henceforth, lest that too heavenly form,
Pretended to hellish falsehood, snare them. But for thee
I had persisted happy, had not thy pride and wandering vanity ....

See Jack Lindsay, "The Metric of William Blake" in *Poetical Sketches*, ed. Eric Partridge (London, 1927), p. 19.

virtually invents his own, and then treats it as if it were already traditional, as if he did not have to make it easy for his readers.

Except in its simplified ballad form, few readers today have much practice with the seven-foot line. So when Blake tampers with it, even when he works by the rhythmic principles that apply in blank verse, we may find him daring. When he begins to violate those principles as well, we may find him unreadable. We need therefore to understand the system he worked by, to learn to read his lines as he learned to write them, and to abstain from applying to Blake's verse standards of harmony which may seem absolute and necessary to our ears only because our ears are too lazy to change their habits. Blake demands of us, as Los demands of his Spectre:

> Take thou this Hammer & in patience heave the thundering Bellows;
> Take thou these Tongs, strike thou alternate with me, labour obedient.
> (*J*, 8.39–40)

The first possible stumbling block is that of pause. Septenary seems to divide naturally, as in the ballad, into four- and three-foot sections, and we take this division to be "melodious." Divisions which come a half foot later or earlier also seem to run smoothly; and a pause after the third foot, though not quite so natural-sounding, passes too:

> The daughters of Mne Seraphim / led round their sunny flocks,
> (*Thel*, I.1—pause after fourth foot)

> To fade away like morning beauty / from her mortal day:
> (*Thel*, I.3—pause dividing fifth foot)

> But now his eyes were darkned. / & his wife fading in death
> (*Tiriel*, I.4—pause dividing fourth foot)

> Curse on your ruthless heads. / for I will bury her even here
> (*Tiriel*, I.33—pause after third foot)

As in the first three examples, a secondary pause at or about the second foot is also common. But the instinct for a pause about the fourth foot is so strong that one may distort the sense-reading to obtain it. In the line just given one tends to pause, irrationally, after "I"; and in the following lines, if we have become used to the ballad cadence and expect it to continue, we tend to pause after "intricate," "weak," "every," and "universal," instead of only after "years," "women," "bliss," and "stroke":

> One hundred years. pond'ring the intricate mazes of Providence
> (*M*, 2.17)
>
> He will give it thee for we are weak women & dare not lift
> (*FZ*, IV.255)
>
> Arise and drink your bliss, for every thing that lives is holy!
> (*VDA*, 8.10)
>
> Trembling & strucken by the Universal stroke the trees unroot.
> (*FZ*, IX.52)

When the sense-reading is correctly followed, Blake's pause patterns may seem queer. So, to Milton's contemporaries, did the Miltonic pause which cut off one syllable from the rest of its line:

> Day, / or the sweet approach of Ev'n or Morn
> (*P.L.* III.42)
>
> And bush with frizl'd hair implicit: / last
> Rose . . . . (*P.L.* VII.323)

"The early defenders of *P.L.* [*sic*] when still fewer than fit, were scandalized by the verse 1 + 9."[6] But we are used to it now. The advantage of a varied pause pattern, to Blake as to Milton, was that it gave the impression of strength and energy, of muscle that could contract or relax at will. By avoiding symmetry, it also helped the writer to build paragraphs.

Another problem is the accenting. Blake like Milton felt free to weigh his rhythms with extra stresses, to lighten them with dropped stresses, and to invert his accents anywhere, including a line's last foot. This too causes difficulties beyond those encoun-

[6] Robert Bridges, *Milton's Prosody* (Oxford, 1921), p. 44.

tered in pentameter. For example, a peculiarity of the ballad septenary is that it tends to fall into a "dipodic" rhythm in which the second and fourth feet take lighter stresses than the first, third, and fifth:

> The kíng sits ĭn Dumférling tòune
> Drínking the blude-reid wine.
> (*The Ballad of Sir Patrick Spence*)

> The dáughters ŏf Mne Séraphìm led róund their sunny flocks,
> (*Thel*, I.1)

Blake often prefers to leave a first, third, or fifth foot unstressed, and the reader must perforce inhibit his desire to stress it. In each of the following cases, the displaced accents give an emphasis of which the flowing ballad line is incapable:

> Tŏ thĕ | fóur wínds | ăs ă | tórn bóok, & none shall gather the leaves
> (*Am*, 8.6)

> Horrid to think ŏf whĕn enquired deeply into; and all
> (*J*, 28.8)

> But she can howl incessant wríth|ĭng hĕr | sóft snówy limbs
> (*VDA*, 2.12)

> Orc listend to the song compell'd húng'rĭng | ŏn thĕ | cóld wínd
> That swággd | héavў | wĭth thĕ accursed dough. the hoar frost ragd.
> (*FZ*, VII.99–100)

In his varied pause pattern and accenting, Blake was simply applying blank verse techniques. His use of enjambment and of extra light syllables, however, constitute freedoms of his own. Enjambment is a device where Blake's radicalism unfolds in several distinct stages. Early blank verse writers had used enjambment systematically for the purpose of building paragraphs. Milton refers to it when he speaks of having "the sense variously drawn out from one line to another." [7] His heir apparent improved on the lesson. The earliest prophecies are bound by Blake's lyric habit of

[7] John Milton, *Paradise Lost*, ed. Merritt Y. Hughes (New York, 1935), p. 6.

end-stopping lines, and enjambment scarcely appears. The next ones mainly use enjambment of the type which has syntactic run-on but still allows the final foot to be accented:

> Now thou maist marry Bromions harlot, and protect the child
> Of Bromions rage, (*VDA*, 2.1–2)

> Ah vision from afar! Ah rebel form that rent the ancient
> Heavens, (*Am*, 9.14–15)

> Their oak-surrounded pillars, form'd of massy stones, uncut
> With tool: (*Eur*, 10.7–8)

The latest books go beyond Milton by ending lines with unaccentable conjunctions, particles, and prepositions:

> The rocks groan horrible & run about the mountăins &̆
> Their rivers cry with a dismal cry the cattle gather together.
> (*FZ*, IX.53–54)

> And then rush forward with me into the glorious spiritual
> Vegetation: the Supper of the Lamb & his Bride; ănd thĕ
> Awaking of Albion.... (*M*, 25.60–62)

> he infolded her in his garments
> Of wool: he hid her from the Spectre in shame and confusĭon ŏf
> Face; in terrors & pains of Hell & Eternăl Déath, thĕ
> Trembling Globe shot forth Self-living.... (*J*, 17.52–55)

This device is relatively uncommon in *The Four Zoas*, and usually serves some obvious expressive function, as in the above lines where the metrical disjunction supports the theme of apocalyptic uprooting. By *Jerusalem* it has become habitual. There, its only function seems to be to uproot—by flagrant disregard—our expectations concerning the distinctions between line and line in poetry.

Blake has another trick which he plays with line-ends, and sometimes in the vicinity of his caesurae. This derives from his observation of blank verse feminine endings, where in such lines as

Of Rebel Angels, by whose aid aspirĭng (*P.L.*, I.38)

the syllable -ing is felt as extrametrical, not requiring consideration in the abstract scansion, although of course it cannot help but affect the rhythm. Blake extended the principle by allowing himself more than one extra syllable at his line-ends, and at his pauses as well.[8]

In thoughts perturb'd they rose from the bright ruins silent follŏwĭng (*Eur*, 10.1)

And first he found the Limit of Opacĭtў / & nam'd it Satăn, (*FZ*, IV.271)

He often achieves an effect of enjambment simply by hooking to one line unstressed extrametrical syllables which might as easily have been hooked to the next:

Enraged & stifled without & within: in terror & woe he threw hĭs
Right Arm to the north. (*M*, 3.24–25)

This cavalier approach toward syllable count also had its effect on his foot-substitution. While in the lyrics he had often let a three-syllable foot take the place of a disyllable, he now extended his hospitality to feet of four syllables:

His primĭtĭve tўrán|nĭcăl ăttémpts | on Los: with most endearing love (*M*, 7.7)

Awake! awake O sleepĕr ŏf thĕ lánd of shadows, wake! expand! (*J*, 4.6)

Attractĕd bў thĕ rê|vŏlútions of those Wheels the Cloud of smoke (*J*, 5.61)

For not one sparrow can suffĕr. ˘& thĕ whóle Universe not suffer also. (*J*, 25.8)

[8] We do not know whether Blake had any acquaintance with Jacobean drama; but his metrical freedom in this respect parallels the frequency of feminine endings in Fletcher, or the general looseness of the pentameter in, for example, Middleton.

The first two lines read smoothly, with a kind of paeonic swing. The third seems awkward, partly because there is a slight pause after "Attracted," partly because the hard consonants prevent elision, and partly because the "rev-" of "revolutions" is not accented fully enough to pull the weight of what precedes it. The fourth, despite its disarming reminiscence of "Auguries of Innocence," has no distinctive rhythm. This brings up a point which has been mentioned before, and will be further discussed in connection with the three major prophecies; namely, that Blake has what he calls a "prosaic" or "inferior" style, where his rhythms become either awkward or nondescript. As shall be seen, Blake's "inferior" verse usually occurs when he is concentrating too exclusively on philosophical matter.

If these were all the irregularities Blake's verse offered, even a fairly mechanical scansion would pose no great problem. Every line could simply be divided into seven parts as bars divide music. One final difficulty remains, which complicates the rest. This difficulty is that Blake did not always confine himself to seven-beat lines. Alexandrines play an increasingly important distaff part in his verse, and octameter also becomes frequent. Sometimes there are lines of four or five beats, and sometimes there are lines nine beats long or longer. The alexandrine when it uses central caesura works in smoothly, since the pause tends to serve in effect as an extra beat, and, conversely, the light stress Blake often leaves in the fourth foot of his septenaries makes them approach alexandrine quality:

Wondring she saw her woof begin to animate & not (7)
As Garments woven subservient to her hands but having a will (6–7)
Of its own perverse & wayward Enion lovd and wept. (6)
(*FZ*, I.83–85)

The octameters and other line-lengths give more trouble. They, along with the alexandrines, are of course subject to as many rhythmical peculiarities as Blake imposes on his septenaries. And these odd-size lines appear unpredictably, so that we can never be certain how many beats a line is going to have until we finish reading it.

With so many hindrances to metrical reading, it might seem simpler to take these books as prose rather than verse. Such a solution has been proposed by several commentators.

Saintsbury, most cautious, suggested that the bulk of Blake's prophetic work from the *Visions of the Daughters of Albion* on is "neither pure verse nor . . . rhythmical prose, but a hybrid between them," with the "regular or almost regular fourteeners and sixteeners" gradually waning. Of *Milton,* he says, "Metre almost disappearing, but a strong rhythmical split, at or a little beyond the middle, prevailing, as if in a sort of lengthened *Piers Plowman* scheme. . . . Of course there is what may be called a substratum of fourteener generally." *Jerusalem* he finds sometimes pure prose, sometimes verse, and mostly "not unlike the *Milton,* but with the central break less obvious, more enjambment, and every now and then a distinct hexametrical suggestion." [9]

Symons also feels that the prophecies steadily approach prose, declaring that "In *Milton* there was still a certain approximation to verse . . . but in *Jerusalem* . . . I am by no means sure that Blake ever intended the lines, as he wrote them, to be taken as metrical lines, or read very differently from the prose of the English Bible. . . . Read the whole book as if it were prose, following the sense for its own sake, and you will find that the prose . . . has generally a fine biblical roll and swing in it, a rhythm of fine oratory." [10] A third ballot cast for prose reading is Damon's. In his opinion, all the prophecies "are to be poured out in a great flood of oratory, stressing the natural accents, and passing rapidly over the unaccented syllables. . . . Each line represents a breath; and this breath is the real metrical unit, around which all the variations are formed." [11] A fourth opinion is Laurence Binyon's, who feels that

[9] *A History of English Prosody* (London, 1906–10), III, 26, 28.
[10] *William Blake* (New York, 1907), p. 156.
[11] *William Blake, his Philosophy and Symbols* (Boston, 1924), p. 57.

from *The French Revolution* onwards, Blake meant his work "to be read as one would read prose, giving each word its normal accent. . . . Finally, in *Jerusalem* he abandons all pretense to metrical strictness, aiming at oratory rather than verse: indeed in many passages of the poem the division into lines has no significance or value." [12]

"Oratory," from Blake's phrase "a true Orator," seems to be the order of the day. On the other hand, since Blake did print these works in the form of poetry, and presumably with some cause called even *Jerusalem* a "Poem" and "verse" in the same paragraph which speaks of the "true Orator," it might seem reasonable that the burden of proof should rest with those who declare otherwise. None of these commentators scan passages of *Milton* or *Jerusalem* as either prose or verse to prove their point. Moreover, the idea implied by Symons, Damon, and Binyon that "following the sense for its own sake," or "stressing the natural accents," or "giving each word its normal accent" is somehow the method of prose but not of verse, suggests a possible confusion of terminology. Even so, the voice of instinct deserves a hearing; for a case may be made on either side.

The problem will be clarified if we understand, through the help of studies in the psychology of rhythm, what we mean by "verse" and "prose." The first definition which will occur to most people is the rule-of-thumb distinction between language which "has" and language which "has not" a regular sequence of stresses. This cannot be sufficient. Rhythm does not simply inhere in objects; it is a subjective sense based on our perception of events felt to occur at equal or approximately equal time or space intervals, which in turn depends on the psychological fact that even when the intervals are not objectively equal we tend to adjust our perceptions in order to perceive them as such.[13] It has also been

[12] Laurence Binyon, ed., *Poems of Blake* (London, 1931), pp. 365–67.

[13] See the discussion of isochronism in André Classe, *The Rhythm of English Prose* (Oxford, 1939), pp. 85–88. Mr. Classe shows by experiment that people will try to organize aural stimuli into a semblance of rhythm. Raymond MacDonald Alden, writing on "The Mental Side of Metrical

shown that some people are more "aggressively rhythmic," i.e., better skilled at mentally ordering disordered aural stimuli, than others.[14] Thus the rule-of-thumb definition should be altered to say that verse is language which *may be perceived* as having a regular sequence of stresses, with the provision that it will be easier for some people to feel regularity than for others.

But obviously there is a continuum rather than a dichotomy between verse and prose, at least in theory. At one extreme, that of "pure" verse, the stresses would presumably fall at perfectly regular intervals, like a metronome, and be perceivable to everybody. At the other, that of "pure" prose, the stresses would fall in perfectly random sequence, without forming any sort of pattern for anyone. Since human language does not yield either perfect order or perfect disorder, we may expect our reading matter to fall between the extremes. With "poetry," we find accents repeated regularly enough to establish a subjective beat—a kind of metrical metronome which we call "meter"—and when the accents perceptibly diverge from regularity, we are still able to perceive the divergences as syncopations counterpointed against the meter. So long as regularity predominates over syncopation, we will expect it to continue so, and will read the material as verse. With "prose," although fragments of rhythm may occur, accent patterns may repeat, phrases of varying lengths may form pleasing conjunctions with each other, there is not enough to establish an expectation of regularity in us for any great length of time. In borderline cases, such as Biblical prose or free verse, the factor of expectation may be crucial: we will work harder to establish a

---

Form," *MLR*, IX (1914), notes for himself (pp. 298–300) that pauses in poetry may be perceived as part of a metrical pattern, and may even, though not pronounced, be felt as stresses; that syllables "may be thought of as stressed and yet be uttered without stress"; and that so far as isochronism of verse-feet is concerned, "for me the stable time-interval is always present *in consciousness*, though I do not know how fully experiment would show me to observe it in practice." The point is that what is present *in consciousness* is what counts.

[14] William Morrison Patterson, *The Rhythm of English Prose, an Experimental Investigation of Individual Differences in the Sense of Rhythm* (New York, 1916), *passim*. This is the standard work in its field.

subjective beat if we think something is supposed to be poetry, than if we think it is supposed to be prose.

To summarize: when writing or speech seems to conform more than it diverges from a subjectively felt beat we call it poetry. When it diverges more than it conforms, we call it prose.[15]

By this definition, Blake's minor prophecies should be verse for the average reader. The verse may often be clumsy, as we shall see, but the elements of order so outweigh the elements of disorder that it is impossible to doubt Blake's intentions. Of the major prophecies, *The Four Zoas* and *Milton* grow more rugged, but the verse line is still there. *Jerusalem* is borderline. What Saintsbury calls the "substratum" of septenary is in fact so pervasive everywhere that it is impossible not to fall, again and again, into verse reading. Blake as it were interrupts himself with phenomena like three or four light syllables between stresses, or three or four stresses in a row, or patterns of enjambment that seem to make distinctions between line and line meaningless. Even more disconcerting are Blake's habits of alternating between incompatible rhythms without apparent cause, or of moving along fairly steadily in one rhythm except for an impossible line or two in another.[16] For many readers, the best solution might be to read the prophe-

[15] *Ibid.*, pp. 74–76.

[16] Examples. No special reason seems discernible for the odd-length lines (my italics) in:

For the monsters of the Elements Lions or Tygers or Wolves
Sound loud the howling music Inspir'd by Los & Enitharmon sounding loud terrific men
They seem to one another, laughing terrible among the banners.
(*FZ*, VIII.120–22)

Guide thou my hand which trembles exceedingly upon the rock of ages,
While I write of the building of Golgonooza, & of the terrors of Entuthon:
Of Hand & Hyle & Coban. of Kwantok. Peachey. Brereton. Slayd & Hutton.
(*J*, 5.23–25)

Or notice the switch into paeonic rhythms in:

In all the dark Atlantic vale down from the hills of Surrey
A black water accumulates, return Albion! return!
Thy brethren call thee, and thy fathers, and thy sons,
Thy nurses and thy mothers, thy sisters and thy daughters.
(*J*, 4.9–12)

cies sometimes as quite regular verse, sometimes as quite dull prose, and typically as rhythmical language which leaps back and forth between verse and prose. This is close to what Saintsbury advises. It would have the advantage of acknowledging Blake's startling range. Precedents and models might be cited not only in the Bible and Macpherson, but in pulpit oratory and political rhetoric, two forms with which Blake was well acquainted. A serious disadvantage of such reading is that it allows the reader's rhythmic sense to slacken. The less we look for rhythm, the less we find it. Although it is quite possible to find a continuum in Blake, and it is necessary to keep an ear open for Biblical echoes, I believe that the most exciting and most invigorating reading of him comes if we keep his center of gravity on the side of verse.

Blake's figure for the prophet Los imprisoned in the vegetated world is that of a "bird in a blue shell" (*FZ*, I.350) straining to be born; but the shell is the sky. Blake's meter is an elastic shell. Sometimes he lives at ease in it; sometimes he pecks at it furiously, distorting its shape, making it bulge; sometimes he cracks it. To read the prophecies as verse one must more and more firmly keep in mind a sense of the basic accentual pulse and the larger unit of line-length, because Blake syncopates more and more, playing one rhythm off against another just as a drummer can beat ¾ time

---

Or into and out of anapests:

> Then Los uttered with Hammer & Anvil: Cahunt! revoice!
> *I mind not your laugh; and your frown I not fear! and*
> *You must my dictate obey* from your gold-beam'd Looms: trill
> Gentle to Albions Watchman. on Albions mountains reeccho.
> (*J*, 56.29–32)

Or the incompatible rhythms in:

> If you account it Wisdom when you are angry to be silent and
> Not to shew it, I do not account that Wisdom, but Folly.
> Every Man's Wisdom is peculiar to his own Individuality.
> O Satan, my youngest born, art thou not Prince of the Starry Hosts
> And of the Wheels of Heaven, to turn the Mills day & night?
> (*M*, 4.6–10)

> O Swedenborg! strongest of men, the Samson shorn by the Churches!
> Shewing the Transgressors in Hell, the proud Warriors in Heaven:
> Heaven as a Punisher & Hell as One under Punishment: (*M*, 22.50–52)

with one hand and 5/8 with another. This requires effort; one needs a trained ear to follow what the drummer, or Blake, is doing. The rewards are also similar.[17]

Suppose the opening of *Jerusalem* is read as prose, i.e., without any expectation of a regular pulse and therefore with no effort made to hear such a pulse. "Of the Sléep of Úlro! and of the pássage through Etérnal Déath! and of the awáking to EtérnalLífe." This has a good rhythm in itself, organized in units of two beats—three beats—three beats, with longer intervals between the units than between the stresses within each unit. In a verse reading we can keep this rhythm and have more besides:

> Of the Sléep of Úlro! ànd of the pássage thrôugh
> Etérnal Déath! and òf the awáking to Etérnal Lífe.

First of all, we habitually read verse more slowly than prose. This fits Blake's portentous tone, and also gives us more chance to notice small rhythmic details like the contrast in structure between the first two phrases: "Ŏf the Sléep" and "ŏf Úlrŏ." The sense of pulse produces slight emphasis on some of the syllables which would remain unaccented in prose, but not enough to make them conflict with the primary accents. Thus there is a greater fineness in the degrees of stress perceived. Finally, the secondary pauses after "through" and "awaking" (the latter is simply the natural septenary caesura discussed above) add subtlety to the

[17] John Dewey, *Art as Experience* (New York, 1958, paperback), p. 164, observes: "Rhythm involves constant variation . . . variation is not only as important as order, but it is an indispensable coefficient of esthetic order. The greater the variation, the more interesting the effect, provided order is maintained."

This idea is elaborated in Paull Franklin Baum, *The Other Harmony of Prose, an Essay in English Prose Rhythm* (Durham, 1952), p. 24: "Rhythm is a series of units or elements or groups which are similar not necessarily in themselves or necessarily in their duration, but the more alike they are in both characteristics the more obvious is the rhythm, and the more unlike they are in one characteristic or the other, provided the impression of similarity is maintained or is induced, the more interesting the rhythm is." The difference between a rhythm which is satisfyingly obvious and a rhythm which is satisfyingly "interesting" is the difference between Blake's lyrics and his prophecies.

pause pattern and help emphasize "Eternal Death" and "Eternal Life." The fact that one of these lines is a pentameter and one a septenary does not disturb the sense of roughly equivalent time values, because the extra syllables of the first line help compensate for its temporal brevity.

To be sure, the bulk of *Jerusalem* does not move so pleasantly as its opening lines. But in most of the "inferior" passages prose cadences would prove no more satisfactory than the verse. Certainly the idea of reading Blake like "the prose of the English Bible" would hardly apply to his more run-on, involved, overweight periods, with their extremes of pounding at one end and slurring, skipping, and dragging at the other. Deliberate prose reading of such passages would improve nothing, would spoil the cadences which do exist, and would deprive us of whatever satisfaction may be gained from reading poetry as poetry.[18]

[18] Interestingly enough, Saintsbury changed his mind when he came to consider Blake's Prophetic Books as prose, in an Appendix of his *History of English Prose Rhythms* (London, 1922) devoted to neither-fish-nor-fowl authors like Whitman and Blake. Whitman, he found, was differentiated from highly rhythmic prose only by virtue of typography; but Blake must willy-nilly be returned, for the most part, to the domain of verse (pp. 469–72).

10

The Minor Prophecies

Thus My Picture is a History of Art &
Science, the Foundation of Society,
Which is Humanity itself.
(*VLJ*, p. 613)

The early Prophetic Books record a restless hunt for ways of talking about evil: what it was, how it came into the world, how it might be eradicated. Blake stalked round his subject in a sort of guerrilla warfare, attacking now one flank, now another, apparently never satisfied that his weapons were lethal enough. Two allegories—one dramatizing the overripe end of Innocence, the other attempting to portray the bitter results of Experience through its villain symbol of father-priest-king—are followed by three inflammatory pieces of immediate topical interest.[1] Then comes a time of consolidation in which Blake invents myths to embody his ideas. These books also record the search for a technique, for it did not happen all at once with prophecy as with lyric that the muses were willing to

Come into my hand,
By your mild power: descending down the Nerves of my right arm
From out the Portals of my brain. (*M*, 2.5–7)

[1] David V. Erdman, *Blake, Prophet Against Empire* (Princeton, 1954), ch. 10, shows that *Visions of the Daughters of Albion* is a tract on slavery as well as on sexual morality.

The impatience which characterizes the poet's earliest work in *Poetical Sketches* reappears. He interrupts his gradual strengthening of the iambic septenary twice by experiments in other forms, and as soon as the septenary becomes a satisfactory vehicle in the *Visions of the Daughters of Albion* and *America*, he tosses it aside and begins experimenting all over again. The assurance of the late prophecies came only after trial and error.

For his first poetic essay in the mechanics of Experience, Blake reverted to the spirit of *Island in the Moon*. Like the early satire, *Tiriel* is a parade of grotesque puppets who perform jerky pointless actions and make melodramatic speeches in *No Exit* fashion talking at, not to, one another.[2] The tone grates, as if we had a sound-track of Edvard Munch's *Der Schrei:*

Serpents not sons. wreathing around the bones of Tiriel
Ye worms of death feasting upon your aged parents flesh
Listen & hear your mothers groans. No more accursed Sons
She bears. she groans not at the birth of Heuxos or Yuva
These are the groans of death ye serpents These are the groans of death
Nourishd with milk ye serpents. nourishd with mothers tears & cares
Look at my eyes blind as the orbless scull among the stones
Look at my bald head. Hark listen ye serpents listen
What Myratana. What my wife. O Soul O Spirit O fire.

(*Tiriel*, 1.22–30)

[2] Josephine Miles, *Eras and Modes in English Poetry* (Berkeley, 1957), p. 83, quoting the opening lines of *Tiriel* as exemplifying Blake's prophetic style, finds in them "alliterative and repetitive balance" and "the sense of massive deliberate motion, with repeated order and echo." "Balance" and "order," however, do not accurately describe Blake's attempt in *Tiriel* to convey mechanism, nor do these terms take into account his efforts in later books to portray a powerful *dis*order. On the other hand, Robert Gleckner, *The Piper and the Bard* (Detroit, 1959), finding these same lines to be "inept poetry" (p. 145) "symptomatic of the many technical failings of *Tiriel*" (p. 293), also ignores Blake's expressive intentions. It is not quite fair to say that "the general stiffness, lack of feeling, and immature, melodramatic effects" simply "confess to the author's embarrassment outside the lyric form," especially in the light of his prior performance in "King Edward the Third," which more nearly approached the norm of drama. We may still assert that the poetry of *Tiriel* is bad, but we will come closer to the mark if we say that it was bad on purpose.

The passage has considerable metrical variety, with inversions both in the first foot (Sérpĕnts, Lístĕn, Thése ăre, etc.) and internally (wréathĭng ăróund, etc.), with spondees (Nó móre), enjambment (accursed Sons / She bears) and one trisyllabic foot (nourĭshd wĭth móthers). Yet instead of developing a paragraph structure with this as Milton would do, Blake moves no further than the repetition and parallelism of ll. 22–23, 26–27, 28–29. Possibly Tiriel is capable only of such abortive rhetoric. Other devices also fit the character. The multiple first-foot inversions emphasize Tiriel's aggressiveness, as if he must start each sentence with a shout; the frequent full stops and the many pauses early in the line punctuate his exclamatory gasping style, preventing any fulness of motion.

The sound pattern is full of *s*'s and *r*'s, wherewith Tiriel inadvertently imitates the serpent's hiss and curl. Consonants cluster and impede the motion. Cacophonous off-rhymes like *wreathing-feasting* set a shrill tone. The clawing repetitions, especially of "serpents," reveal Tiriel's hysterical obsessiveness, his self-imprisonment, his mistaking of words for things. The last line reads like the absurdest kind of melodrama because that is what Blake means it to be. Although Tiriel is partly Lear,[3] Blake will not allow his father-priest-king Lear's dignity of heroism, or even of poise. Tiriel can only rage and posture, for Blake's absolute tyrant, like Shelley's, as he glares out of his darkened eyes, is nothing but a dummy.

Most of the other characters are similarly grotesque. Tiriel's sons, in spite of rebellion, sound like himself. Perhaps Blake already felt that mere rebellion without a change of heart to some new idea changes nothing. Ijim and Zazel, respectively representing Superstition and the reversion to savagery which religious and political tyranny forces on its subjects, somewhat parallel Edgar and the Fool in *Lear*. But here too Blake forfeits the opportunity of creating distinctive speech-patterns, although Zazel the Fool has one melodious Fool-like line:

[3] Gleckner, *The Piper and the Bard*, p. 147.

Shout beautiful daughter of Tiriel. Thou singest a sweet song.
(*Tiriel*, 7.10)

The imbecilic Har and Heva, and the earth-mother Mnetha, do have consistently differentiated patterns. Mnetha's speeches are calmly regular. Har and Heva, the parents who deny Experience in order to enjoy an eternal perverse Innocence, rear up an exaggerated symmetry of rhythm and language to disguise their fears of "the king of rotten wood," the bogey man whom they wish tamed:

God bless thy poor bald pate. God bless. thy hollow winking eyes
God bless thy shriveld beard. God. bless. thy many-wrinkled forehead
Thou hast no teeth old man & thus I kiss thy sleek bald head
Heva come kiss his bald head for he will not hurt us Heva.
(*Tiriel*, 2.35–38)

Toward the poem's close, Tiriel's speeches gain rhythmical firmness. His last speech, denouncing both Har and himself, consists of an essay in the manner of Proverbs on the theme "Dost thou not see that men cannot be formed all alike," followed by a passage which symbolically recapitulates the causes of Tiriel's soul-sickness. Blake deleted the first part, perhaps because he recognized it to be too much in his own style and not enough in Tiriel's. He later gave similar speeches to characters like Oothoon and Orc. The remainder sustains Tiriel's manner somewhat better, although nothing in the poem has prepared us for his moment of self-revelation:

The father forms a whip to rouze the sluggish senses to act
And scourges off all youthful fancies from the new-born man
Then walks the weak infant in sorrow compelld to number footsteps
Upon the sand. And when the drone has reachd his crawling length,
Black berries appear that poison all around him.[4] Such was Tiriel . . .
Compelld to pray repugnant & to humble the immortal spirit
Till I am subtil as a serpent in a paradise. (*Tiriel*, 8.30–37)

[4] Keynes prints "round" but the manuscript very clearly reads "around."

This last speech is metrically somewhat more irregular than the rest of the poem, having several alexandrines and at least one eight-foot line. Possibly it was written later; or possibly this "freedom" represents Tiriel's mental liberation.

Tiriel suffers as a poem in several ways from the limitations of its idea, which is, in brief, that the wages of untranscended Experience is death. Most conspicuously, it is ill-constructed as narrative. Good narratives, even of the episodic type, usually follow a simple curve, with an expected conclusion giving meaning to the episodes as they seem to advance or recede from that conclusion. Odysseus is getting home to Penelope, and meanwhile is demonstrating and improving his manhood by all sorts of adventures. Don Quixote is becoming worthy of Dulcinea, and meanwhile transforming chaos and injustice into order and justice. Tom Jones is going to win Sophia, and meanwhile is learning about Life. In failing to bestow any such unity on the zigzag plot of *Tiriel*, with its double homecomings and unexplained final change of heart, Blake perhaps meant to demonstrate the inanity of mechanical motion without ethical purposefulness. It is questionable whether such a theme can by itself produce interesting narrative poetry.

Similarly, the flatness of the characters, while compatible with Blake's idea of soullessness, seems incompatible with his attempt to write a semidramatic poem. Drama requires a degree of sympathy with all one's characters. Shakespeare, whom Blake admired, never drew a villain without becoming villainous for the nonce. Even devils like Richard III or Iago have wit and eloquence to recommend them. But Blake was a curious phenomenon among poets in that, while he was intellectually obsessed by the problem of evil, he believed with St. Augustine that true evil did not "really" exist—it was a "Negation" not a "Contrary"—and therefore he could not involve himself enough in its various manifestations to write good poetry about it. In England he is paralleled only by Shelley, whose poetry also suffered when he attempted to portray the objects of his detestation. Blake's *Songs of Experience* succeed where *Tiriel* fails, partly by their brevity, partly because they take the point of view of the oppressed rather than the oppressor.

The poem's pervasive shrillness forms a related problem. It is as if Shakespeare had written *Troilus and Cressida* with all the characters being duplicates of Thersites, or Swift had written *Gulliver's Travels* with nothing but Yahoos. All satirists must wrestle with the danger of becoming so possessed by hatred that they can do nothing but scream and stamp their feet like children; Swift sometimes comes perilously close to being overwhelmed; Blake does not seem even to realize that this is a danger.

In his later prophecies Blake circumvents these limitations to some extent. His plots improve when hinged to historical events or to a developed cycle of fall and redemption. The need for rounded characterization disappears when he stops pretending to portray persons and concentrates on symbols. "We are not individuals, but States, combinations of individuals," his characters keep reminding us later. The problem of shrillness also subsides as Blake begins to take this world more seriously and at the same time learns to present the frozen soul as declined from something better. Not until *Jerusalem* does he again confront us with a poem devoted almost entirely to horror.

The poet had an easier time with his second allegory, *The Book of Thel.* Having explored the terrors to which the soul subjects itself when it submits to "mind-forg'd manacles," he now moved backward in his analysis. *Thel*, using the Neoplatonic idea of the unborn soul facing the world of Generation which to it is death, explores the reluctance of Innocence to enter Experience.

Blake did not condone this reluctance. Thel's self-awareness, her fearfulness, her dissatisfaction, show that she is past the prime of true Innocence, and ripe for a fall or a rise. In the illustrations, she is an adolescent girl. Her wishes to be happy, to live forever, to be taken care of, are therefore out of place, selfish in a bad sense, as the child's thoughtless egotism is selfish in a good sense. In her wish to be "useful," she merely parodies the teachings of lily, cloud, and clod of clay, for usefulness to her is a form of power. "Thy perfume," she tells the lily, "Revives the milked cow, and tames the fire-breathing steed." Or it is a source of fame, and she fears for her reputation that "all shall say, Without a use this shining woman liv'd." Desiring to pass painlessly to the higher innocence, she ignores the humility of lily, cloud, and clod, their willingness to "fade away," and their surrender to nuptial bonds. Saying "I am not like thee" to each, instead of discovering identity with all, she finds only vanity for herself everywhere. Naturally, she flees the vision of Experience.

Thel is selfish, and a coward. If she continues so, never surrendering herself to "her own grave plot," she will end like Heva in *Tiriel.* Yet Blake sympathizes with the youth and grace she still retains, and shares her dread of Experience. Thanks to this sympathy, he can present in attractive guise, without too much irritable reaching after moral facts and reasons, an existence which he morally condemns. He shows Thel as she sees herself, lovely and mournful, wandering through a pastoral paradise with a sweetly elegiac song on her lips.

Thel is thus the nearest of Blake's prophetic works to lyric, in both matter and manner. It flows almost uniformly smoothly and sweetly:

> The daughters of Mne Seraphim led round their sunny flocks,
> All but the youngest: she in paleness sought the secret air.
> To fade away like morning beauty from her mortal day:
> Down by the river of Adona her soft voice is heard:
> And thus her gentle lamentation falls like morning dew.
>
> (*Thel,* 1.1–5)

Pleasant vowel sounds flow from line to line, in d*au*ghters, *A*ll, s*ou*ght, m*or*ning, m*or*tal, s*o*ft, f*a*lls; in s*u*nny, b*u*t, y*ou*ngest, th*us*; in p*a*leness, f*a*de aw*ay*, d*ay*, lament*a*tion. Instead of the harsh consonant clusters of *Tiriel*, we have the languid and soft consonants of *l*ed, *fl*ocks, pa*l*eness, morta*l*, gent*l*e, *l*amentation; *f*locks, *f*ade, so*f*t, *f*alls. Except in "secret," the *s*'s bear no ill connotation. Thel's lamentation continues a few of these sounds for several lines before turning to something else:

> O life of this our spring! why fades the lotus of the water?
> Why fade these children of the spring? born but to smile & fall.
> Ah! Thel is like a watry bow, and like a parting cloud,
> Like a reflection in a glass. like shadows in the water.
> Like dreams of infants. like a smile upon an infants face.
> Like the doves voice. like transient day, like music in the air;
> Ah! gentle may I lay me down and gentle rest my head.
> And gentle sleep the sleep of death. and gentle hear the voice
> Of him that walketh in the garden in the evening time.
>
> (*Thel*, 1.6–14)

The musical *l*'s, *f*'s, and *s*'s now have more explicitly melancholy associations. The disparate *a*'s of f*a*de and f*a*ll also reappear; but the dominant vowel finally is the four-times repeated *e* of g*e*ntle, allied pointedly with r*e*st, h*ea*d, d*ea*th, and with the other *e* of sl*ee*p, *e*vening. "Gentle," with such companions, has a sly twist like that of "For the *gentle* wind doth move" in "Never seek to tell thy love." Passivity, the elegiac mood, always reminds Blake of hypocrisy.

The rhythms of *Thel* are slightly more regular than those of *Tiriel*, with fewer inversions and spondees, and the spondaic constructions usually mild, as in "Ó lífe," "whý fádes," or "dóves vóice." The internal inversions, as in "bórn bŭt," do not break the rhythm. There are very few trisyllabic feet, and feminine endings are only half as frequent as in *Tiriel*. The sense of flow comes from the fact that the phrases are longer and far less jolted by exclamations and queries than *Tiriel*'s. Pauses appear at the line's center, commonly dividing it into the smooth four and three feet of ballad measure, but sometimes into slightly different divisions. The small variations keep *Thel* from monotony, and also assist development of its rudimentary paragraph structure, a thing scarcely found in *Tiriel*. Where the units of rhetoric in the earlier poem rarely exceeded two lines' length, they are often longer here. The four central lines of the passage just quoted, for example, form a unit which coheres rhetorically by parallelism, while it varies in accent pattern and caesura placement:

> Áh! Thél is lìke a wátry bów, / and lìke a párting clóud,
> Like a refléction in a gláss. / like shádows in the wáter.
> Like dréams of ínfants. / lìke a smíle upon an ínfants fáce.
> Like the dóves vóice. / like tránsient dáy, / like músic in the áir.

The pause comes twice after the fourth foot, then recedes to divide the third, then divides the last line into units of two feet—two feet—three feet. The weak accenting seems to bring out Thel's lyric frailty, while the triple comparative of the final line seems to show her overwhelmed by ideas and becoming a little insistent about her point.

Blake does not metrically differentiate the speeches of the advising lily, cloud, and clod of clay from Thel's, except that the cloud, sole masculine voice of the poem, speaks with somewhat fuller accenting and more pauses. The reader must discern for himself that the charm exuded equally by the Virgin of Har and the wedded creatures of Paradise conceals infinite disparity, where the creatures resemble the calm surface of a lake fed by hidden springs, but the maiden is like the calm surface of a stagnant pool which ultimately "breeds reptiles of the mind" (*MHH*, p. 156). Just as he used beauty ironically to criticize the tradition of courtly love poetry in "How sweet I roamed" or "Never seek to tell thy love," so here he uses it to criticize the tradition of elegy.

Blake realized that regret is always regret for oneself. "It is the blight man was born for, / It is Margaret you mourn for." But he was not so sympathetic as Hopkins. So he gave his self-pitying heroine a foretaste of her potential Experience. The close of *Thel*, even more than that of *Tiriel*, is somewhat irregular. There is an uncomfortable accent pattern in the line "Till to her own grave plot she came, & there she sát dówn" (4.9), with its echo of Psalm 137; and the "voice . . . breathed from the hollow pit" not only uses a much greater proportion of trochees and anapests than the rest of the poem, but breaks up into line-lengths varying from five to eight feet, anticipating a later habit of Blake's:

Why cannot the Ear be clos'd to its own destruction? (6)
Or the glistning Eye to the poison of a smile! (5)
Why are Eyelids stord with arrows ready drawn, (6)
Where a thousand fighting men in ambush lie? . . . (5)
Why a Nostril wide inhaling terror, trembling & affright (8)
Why a tender curb upon the youthful burning boy! (7)
Why a little curtain of flesh on the bed of our desire? (7)

This plate may have been a late addition to the poem,[5] but its abrupt harshness nevertheless forms a fitting conclusion to Thel's lament, as she discovers that her fate is far worse than she imagined. Instead of merely fading away and dying gracefully, she will have to undergo a storm of passions and restraints in which she will lose even the vision of the higher innocence which she now has. "Serve her right," one imagines Blake thinking. But he pitied her too, and the passage's metrical irregularities underline his pity by emphasizing the fearsomeness of Generation.

After *Tiriel* and *Thel*, the minor prophecies contain a good deal of experimentation, some of it successful, some requiring considerable tolerance on the reader's part.

These books include the public prophecies of *The French Revolution*, *The Marriage of Heaven and Hell*, *Visions of the Daughters of Albion*, and *America*, which were written and printed in the years 1790–93 when Blake still believed that social revolution might produce the wished-for human apocalypse; and the mythic new start embodied in *The Book of Urizen*, *The Song of Los*, *The Book of Los*, *Europe*, and *The Book of Ahania*, written in 1794–95, when Blake was disillusioned with the French Revolution and frightened by the reaction in England. In the first group the main technical trend is toward rhetorical strengthening, with a beginning of muscular irregularities in the verse. The

[5] See D. J. Sloss and J. P. R. Wallis, eds., *The Prophetic Writings of William Blake* (Oxford, 1926), II, 267; and George Mills Harper, *The Neoplatonism of William Blake* (Chapel Hill, 1961), pp. 247–48.

second group forms a series of trials and false starts in forms which Blake later abandoned.

After completing *Tiriel* and *Thel*, Blake apparently decided that his long and flexible iambic septenary was not quite long or flexible enough. For *The French Revolution* he therefore used anapests, which according to Frye are "thundering anapests,"[6] and thunder was certainly Blake's intention. His ambition led him into trouble immediately:

> The dead brood over Europe, the cloud and vision descends over chearful France;
> O cloud well appointed! Sick, sick, the Prince on his couch, wreath'd in dim
> And appalling mist, his strong hand outstretch'd, from his shoulder down the bone
> Runs aching cold into the scepter, too heavy for mortal grasp, No more
> To be swayed by visible hand, nor in cruelty bruise the mild flourishing mountains. (*FR*, 1–5)

The opening phrase is metrically confusing. If the line is to be read as anapests, this should be "Thĕ dĕad bróod," which creates the false impression that "dead" is an adjective modifying the noun "brood." If, to give the correct noun-verb intonation, we accent both "dead" and "brood," with a faint pause between the words, we lose the anapest. Somehow this does not become a problem in the second line, "O cloud well appointĕd! Síck, síck, the Prince on his couch wreath'd in dim," where in fact the double accent on "Síck, síck" provides a strong dramatic focus for the hexameter. But then the third line is retarded by the successive accents and thick consonants of "hĭs stróng hánd ôutstrétch'd"; the fourth reads like a hexameter with one extra foot stuck on after the pause; and Blake thus does not strike the rhythmic norm of his poem until its fifth line.

This passage suggests the difficulties of *The French Revolution*.

[6] Northrop Frye, *Fearful Symmetry, a Study of William Blake* (Princeton, 1947), p. 184.

The poem has many smooth sections, but it also has many instances of rhythmical confusion, badly jointed octameters and nine-foot lines, and lines with gaping spots between stresses, like:

And fed on the body. She refus'd to be whore to the Mínĭstĕr, ănd wĭth ă knífe smóte hĭm. (*FR*, 37)

Yet Blake's boldness wins him a few prizes. His new tendency to replace the central ballad-measure pause by less regular line divisions, along with the frequent enjambment, helps him construct verse-paragraphs of considerable length without relying like *Thel* on simple syntactic parallelism. As far as paragraphing is concerned, the poem's opening is after Milton's heart. The rhythm drives forcefully from the slow "Sick, sick" (which can refer either backwards or forwards), to the prince, the prince's hand, the scepter held by that hand, the mountains bruised by that scepter, until in five lines a honeycomb of associative symbolism has been established.

Thanks to his new freedom, Blake now sustains a narrative style which can shift moods easily to produce variegated effects, a feat not contemplated in *Tiriel* and *Thel.* Early in the poem there is a long macabre passage describing the prisoners in the Bastille, full of lines like "Eternally rushing round, like a man on his hands and knees, day and night without rest" (46). Suddenly we have a movement of freshness; the prisoners "listen,"

Then laugh in the dismal den, then are silent, and a light walks round the dark towers:
For the Commons convene in the Hall of the Nation, like spirits of fire in the beautiful
Porches of the Sun, (*FR*, 53–55)

Note how the extra syllable of "silĕ*nt,* ănd ă líght" gives a sense of quickening; the rhythm of "and a light walks round the dark towers" has a dancelike stateliness; and the next line seems to rise like a cup being filled until it overflows with "in the béau*tĭfŭl* / Pórches of the Sún." Shortly after this, a single, oddly accented octameter gives a solemnly momentous feeling:

The voíce céas'd: the Nátion sát: And the tríple forg'd fétters of
tímes were unlóos'd. (*FR*, 62)

The poem has many such changes of pace. Its declamations, too, show advances. Where Tiriel could do nothing but rage and whine, the royalist villains of *The French Revolution* hold forth with some solidity, perhaps because Blake has been impressed in spite of himself by the oratory of Burke.[7] He allots some of the poem's strongest lines to the Duke of Burgundy. This title is fictitious, but the "winepress" later became Blake's symbol for war, and so Burgundy is a warmonger:

"Shall this marble built heaven become a clay cottage, this earth an oak
stool, and these mowers
From the Atlantic mountains mow down all this great starry harvest of
six thousand years? . . .
Till our purple and crimson is faded to russet, and the kingdoms of the
earth bound in sheaves,
And the ancient forests of chivalry hewn, and the joys of the combat
burnt for fuel . . . ?" (*FR*, 89–93)

These villainous speeches are an auspicious sign, since all Blake's later books will represent conflicts between good and evil, and he will have to make evil a believably formidable antagonist. Although this is a far cry from the subtlety of Milton's Council in Hell, the poet does succeed in making wickedness temporarily attractive, as he did not in *Tiriel*.

Blake evidently found anapestic rhythms too bulky to handle, in spite of his limited success with them. In 1793 he returned to iambic septenary with the *Visions of the Daughters of Albion* and *America*, bringing with him the technical licenses of *The French*

[7] Mark Schorer, *William Blake, the Politics of Vision* (New York, 1946), p. 412, points out the similarity between Blake's prophetic rhetoric and the Burkean purple passage.

Revolution, but leaving the awkwardness behind. For the first time, a few distinct styles are clearly discernible. Narrative and declamation remain vigorous. The turbulent spirit of both poems, which in *Visions* depends on high rhetoric and in *America* on violent action, elicits new and powerful cadences:

I cry. Love! Love! Love! happy happy Love! free as the mountain wind!
Can that be Love, that drinks another as a sponge drinks water
(*VDA,* 7.16–17)

The moment of desire! the moment of desire! The virgin
That pines for man; shall awaken her womb to enormous joys
(*VDA,* 7.3–4)

And as a plague wind filld with insects cuts off man & beast;
And as a sea o'erwhelms a land in the day of an earthquake;
Fury! rage! madness! in a wind swept through America.
(*Am,* 14.8–10)

There is some lyric, as in the Plate 6 rhapsody of *America* beginning "The morning comes, the night decays, the watchmen leave their stations," which reverts to ballad rhythm and end-stopped lines. Another development consists of a few slight hints of natural (as opposed to purely symbolic) description, where sound helps evoke image. In *America,* the repeated call to arms of Albion's Angel, "Sound! sound! my loud war-trumpets, & alarm my Thirteen Angels!" (9.1, 13, 21, 27) imitates the trumpet's call of military maneuvers. In the *Visions,* when Theotormon "severely smiles" to see his eagles rend Oothoon's heart,

her soul reflects the smile;
As the cléar spríng / múdded with féet of béasts / gròws púre & smíles.

She replies:

I cry arise O Theotormon for the village dog
Barks at the *breaking* day, the nightingale has done lamenting.
The lark does rustle in the ripe corn. (*VDA,* 2.18–19, 23–25)

The spring's gradual return to clarity is delicately suggested by the rhythm and vowel patterns, and the pastoral noises of barking and rustling are echoed by the sound of the verse.

Besides their vigorous narrative and oratory, their lyric sections, and their touches of naturalism, a final novelty in these poems is the appearance in them of the rhetorical question series, recalling the Book of Job, and usually moving in long parallel sweeps, or else in a cantering combination of long and broken cadences:

> Tell me what is the night or day to one o'erflowd with woe?
> Tell me what is a thought? & of what substance is it made?
> Tell me what is a joy? & in what gardens do joys grow?
>
> (*VDA*, 3.22–24)

> Does the whale worship at thy footsteps as the hungry dog?
> Or does he scent the mountain prey because his nostrils wide
> Draw in the ocean? does his eye discern the flying cloud
> As the ravens eye? or does he measure the expanse like a vulture?
>
> (*VDA*, 5.33–36)

Passages like these recur like green sheltered oases in the sandstorms of the Prophetic Books. However raw the weather outside, they are always composed. However abstract the landscape, here Blake always recalls the old themes, the old diction of poetry. This should not, however, distract a reader from noticing that Blake uses the query device for quite various purposes. Here, for example, the first series is meant to be virtually meaningless, unanswerable, part of Theotormon's self-indulgent theorizing on his own woe, while the second series shows Oothoon making a concrete point in defense of individuality.

The *Visions* and *America* represent Blake's last attempt to portray human-seeming characters before exploding into the titans of his myths. Oothoon, who comes closest to having a full personality reflected in her speeches, begins as a young and delicate maid with soft sound and hesitating speech-rhythms. Captured by Bromion, her cries to Theotormon are at first those of simple wild yearning; then they become argumentative; and finally she breaks forth in a rhapsody of hatred for the Father of Jealousy, and praise for Love. Bromion the slave-master for a few lines has a distinct voice, a tight-mouthed one:

> *St*amp*t* with my *s*igne*t* are the *s*warthy children of the *s*un:
> They are obedient, / they resist not, / they obey the scourge:
> (*VDA*, 1.21–22)

Elsewhere he is only a mouthpiece for legalism and natural philosophy, as Theotormon is a mouthpiece for the self-pity of desire which "is weak enough to be restrained" (*MHH*, p. 149). *America*, which uses no real characters with personal life-histories, nevertheless offers an interesting and surprising contrast between the antagonists Orc and Albion's Angel. Albion's Angel, self-appointed guardian of God's Law and the status quo, has all the rant; he splutters and howls with scarcely more self-control than Tiriel, while Orc, called the Terror, Serpent, and red Demon, speaks lyrically of how "morning comes," sternly of "That stony law" which "I stamp to dust," and firmly but calmly of Man:

> Fires inwrap the earthly globe, yet man is not consumd:
> Amidst the lustful fires he walks: his feet become like brass,
> His knees and thighs like silver. & his breast and head like gold.
> (*Am*, 8.15–17)

In making Orc's speeches rhythmically and tonally mild, Blake seems to be hinting at a stillness of spirit in the eye of the storm, an aspect of Orc's character which has not commonly been noticed. The illustrations to *America* depict the Red Demon once as a tame, smiling, lightly bridled serpent ridden by naked children, and once as a ram, against whose sides a boy and girl are sleeping, and over whose head birds sing in a delicate willow. In later works, when Blake lost faith in the spiritual value of material revolution, he kept Orc more purely horrific.

Blake's failure, despite these slight touches of personality, to create characters as real and whole as those which vivify the tradition of allegory from the *Romance of the Rose* to Bunyan, his failure to achieve even a Spenserian standard of reality, was the main reason why he could not continue working in the manner of these early prophecies. He could write lyric, and he could write poetry of ideas, but he could not write the saga of persons because he was not interested in persons. Although modern liberals may praise his devotion to "the individual," individuality to Blake meant the principle of truth to type, not uniqueness. He never defended idiosyncrasy; he cared no more than Johnson for the number of streaks on the tulip. The discovery that he and his poetic façade of personages did not suit each other was a prod to drive him deeper into myth.

Before considering the early mythic poems, two curious experiments of a different type must be noted. Some time between 1790 and 1793 Blake issued a manifesto on morality, *The Marriage of Heaven and Hell,* in which he planned to show the world that William Blake read black where the rest of mankind read white, and also to crack the once-loved wooden idol of Swedenborg over his knee. The *Marriage* is flanked by two remarkable poems, its "Argument" at the beginning, and "A Song of Liberty" at its close.

The "Argument" technically resembles, and may have had for inspiration, the freely rhythmed choruses of *Samson Agonistes.* The difference is that Milton, attempting to parallel the effects of Greek drama in English, almost certainly was writing according to a set of self-imposed prosodic rules,[8] while Blake almost certainly was trying to escape from rules.

> Rintrah roars & shakes his fires in the burdend air; (7)
> Hungry clouds swag on the deep. (4)
>
> Once meek, and in a perilous path, (4)
> The just man kept his course along (4)
> The vale of death. (2)

[8] Robert Bridges, *Milton's Prosody* (Oxford, 1921), pp. 50–66.

Roses are planted where thorns grow. (3)
And on the barren heath (3)
Sing the honey bees. (4)

(*MHH*, p. 148)

The principle is simple enough. Iambs, with the usual free metrical variations, are arranged in irregular line-lengths (as marked) which correspond to the natural length of phrases. Rhyme is omitted, and the poem's melody depends altogether on the balance of the phrases and the vowel and consonant patterns within the lines. In acknowledgment of Blake's intentions and his influence, we might call this our first bit of English free verse. It is not the sophisticated verse of the post-Eliot and Pound era which professes to base itself on speech rhythms rather than formal metric; but Pound and Eliot grew out of an earlier school of American free versers. Compare Blake's poem with Amy Lowell's "Wind and Silver":

Greatly shining,
The Autumn moon floats in the thin sky.
And the fish-ponds shake their backs and flash their dragon scales
As she passes over them.

The principle is the same, although the impressionistic language about rhythmic curves and breaths and tensions which Miss Lowell used in her defenses of free verse indicate that she either did not know, or did not choose to admit, how close her work and her friends' was to old-fashioned metrical poetry. In one essay Miss Lowell observed that "Blake was already attempting *vers libre*" in the eighteenth century,[9] but it is impossible to tell what area of Blake's work she is referring to, or how well she understood it.

The "Song of Liberty," a coda to *The Marriage*, is arranged in the form of Biblical prose verses, thus:

1. The Eternal Female groand! it was heard over all the Earth:
2. Albions coast is sick silent; the American meadows faint!

[9] Lowell, "Some Musical Analogies in Modern Poetry," *The Musical Quarterly*, VI (1920), 132.

3. Shadows of Prophecy shiver along by the lakes and the rivers and mutter across the ocean, France rend down thy dungeon. . . .

(*MHH*, p. 159)

There are twenty verses of varying length. Saintsbury took them to be "lyrical prose"; [10] Damon took them as "really alexandrines . . . but with a foot that varies from anapest to dactyl," [11] which in fact many of them are. Verse 3, for example, when divided after "rivers," forms two alexandrines. Others, however, seem to arrange themselves into septenaries or still longer lines.

By 1793 Blake had made of the iambic septenary, which thus far had formed the base line of most of his prophecies, a working vehicle. He could elicit narrative and lyric, dialectic and bombast from it. He could make it roar like a flood or slide like a stream.

In 1794 he began tinkering again. Perhaps he regretted the intellectual superficiality of poems which implied that an overt revolution in politics or morals could alone remove all men's woes, or perhaps he felt nervous about reprisals against his radicalism. Signs of restlessness with the character-centered semidramatic form had occurred in *America.* In his new series of poems Blake decided to trace human discomforts "inwards" to their springs in Man's mind back before the flood, before Creation, before Chaos itself, in Eternity. Beginning from the first lines in the *Book of Urizen,*

Lo, a shadow of horror is risen
In Eternity! (*BU*, 3.1–2)

Blake summarizes the original Fall, which he identifies with Creation, and brings us up to date in a series of brief prophecies which reinterpret universal history in terms of his own pantheon, his own myths, his own system. Blake thought that "Truth can never be told so as to be understood, and not be believ'd" (*MHH*, p. 152); and now there will be no more possibility of misunderstand-

[10] *A History of English Prosody* (London, 1906–10), III, 29.
[11] *William Blake, His Philosophy and Symbols* (Boston, 1924), p. 57.

ing, for we will see through Blake's glass brightly, or not at all. The sheer intellectuality of his new approach is evident at the opening of *The Book of Urizen,* where, in an intense effort to express the meaning of Urizen's split from Eternity, the first twenty-seven lines are thick not only with general negatives like "horror," "horrors," "horrible," "abominable," "tormenting," but with terms directly signifying nullity and nonentity. "Unknown" appears no less than five times, "unseen" three times, "unprolific" once. The terms "dark," "clos'd," "brooding," "silent," "shadow," each appear twice. All this abstract repetition has, at first, an unintended comic effect. It is as if a man, grimacing terribly, were assaulting us with a club made of air. Yet one wonders how else Blake could have gone about his task of demonstrating that even the smallest degree of a Fall makes all the difference between existence and extinction; that the Fall is a Fall into void, absence, non-being. His diction frontally attacks a difficult idea. The treble "horror" and the quintupled "unknown" do not in principle differ from the repeated "sweet," "mild," or "weep" in the *Songs,* since for Blake, the strongest way to say a thing always was to say it more than once. The difference is that where his vocabulary was affective, it is now intellectual, and remains so to the end of the prophecies.

For his plunge to the springs of time and space Blake chose new metrical gear as well as a new diction. Most common base line now is a trimeter, usually anapestic, sometimes lapsing into iambs. This is the form of *Urizen, Ahania,* most of the *Book of Los,* and the "Asia" section of the *Song of Los. Europe* employs several modes. The Preludium is in stanza-form iambs of varying length, the monodies of Los and Enitharmon are in two- to eight-stress iambs, and most of the narrative is septenary. The "Africa" section of the *Song of Los* is in free verse, part iambic, part anapestic, with short and long lines in no apparent order. The song of Eno at the opening of the *Book of Los* is also free verse, but restricts itself to the iamb-trochee gamut and to brief lines of two to four feet.

The trimeter gallop which dominates these poems is a queer

creature. Its greatest virtue is its power. A sense of resistless momentum appropriately informs poems dealing with a cosmic fall which is the collapse of energy, titanic battles which are the expenditure of energy, and revolution which is the restoration of energy.[12] Unfortunately, this energy often trips over itself.

In describing the initial cataclysm, Blake pulls out his stops. This is the Fall of Urizen (your Reason; horizon) from unity:

> Sund'ring, dark'ning, thund'ring:
> Rent away with a terrible crash
> Eternity roll'd wide apart
> Wide asunder rolling
> Mountainous all around
> Departing: departing; departing.
> Leaving ruinous fragments of life
> Hanging frowning cliffs & all between,
> An ocean of voidness unfathomable. (*BU*, 5.2–11)

The accretive sentence structure, the jaw-jamming consonants, and the deep vowels of "Sund'ring, dark'ning, thund'ring . . . asunder rolling," combined with this meter, give a sense of massive weight exerting itself against some great resistance.

The meter is also good for other purposes, for example the speech in which Urizen illustrates Blake's idea that "the enjoyments of Genius . . . to Angels look like torment and insanity" (*MHH*, p. 150), by declaring:

> Ĭ hăve sóught | fŏr ă jóy | wĭthŏut páin.
> Fŏr ă sól|ĭd wĭthóut | fluctuation
> Whý | wĭll yŏu díe O Eternals?
> Whý líve in unquenchable burnings? (*BU*, 4.10–13)

The fallen Reason contradicts itself, since "Eternals" cannot die, as he himself admits in the next line when he says they "live." Yet

[12] Jack Lindsay, "The Metric of William Blake," in *Poetical Sketches*, ed. Eric Partridge (London, 1927), p. 20, finds "dark revolutions of sound, palpitating eddies, a sense of the descending spirals of life which these books are intended to define."

there is real pathos in the lines, accompanied by a subtly varied rhythm. Note especially the repeated downbeat on "Why," first in the monosyllabic foot which is then emphasized by the rhyming "die," then in the spondee "Why live." A few lines later, Urizen's character expresses itself in a different style, when he tries to promulgate "Laws of peace, of love, of unity," thus:

> Let each chuse one habitation,
> His ancient infinite mansion,
> One command, one joy, one desire,
> One curse, one weight, one measure
> One King. one God. one Law. (*BU*, 4.36–40)

Notice how much more clipped the sound is, and how, as Blake tightens to straight iambs, and finally to those short monosyllables of the last line, one can hear the schoolmaster's rod tapping in the background, or, which would be the same symbol to Blake, the methodical tyrant's scepter pounding the floor.

Elsewhere Blake uses the brevity of his line to define the mechanical, metronome-like monotony of repeated action and reaction, in a situation where the conscious individual has lost control of his fate. He is describing the formation of the Chain of Jealousy, with Los (anagram of Sol; also loss—the fallen Intuition which becomes Prophecy in our world) the Oedipal father:

> Los awoke her: O sorrow & pain!
> A tight'ning girdle grew.
> Around his bosom. In sobbings
> He burst the girdle in twain.
> But still another girdle
> Oppress'd his bosom. In sobbings
> Again he burst it. Again
> Another girdle succeeds. (*BU*, 20.8–15)

The sound pattern, here based on the three explosive consonants *g* (Girdle, grew, again), *b* (*b*osom, so*bb*ings, *b*urst), and *t* (*t*igh*t*-'ning, burs*t*, *t*wain, s*t*ill), reinforces the repetition.

Despite these and other successful passages, Blake's trimeter may provoke more vexation than enjoyment in most readers. Irregularities protrude from these brief lines like toys in a bed too hastily made by an impatient child; a quilt might hide them, but the skimpy coverlet provided here does not suffice.

It is unpleasant, in the midst of a trimeter canter, to have to leap hurdles like the following lines, either squeezing their extra syllables into three beats, or letting them thump out as four.

> The Eter|năl Prŏphĕt héavd | the dark bellows.
> (*BU*, 10.15)

> And the voice cried: Ah Urizen! Love!
> Flówer of mórning! I wéep on the vérge
> Of Non-entĭtў̆; how wide the Abyss
> Between Ahania and thee! (*BA*, 4.52–55)

> He siez'd: beating incessant. condensing
> Thĕ sŭbtĭl párticles in an Orb. (*BL*, 5.29–30)

Again, Blake's heavy alliteration, compressed into this small scope, sometimes looks foolish; there is no excuse for turning "Earth's Answer" into such bad poetry as:

> Cruel jealousy selfish fear!
> Self-destroying: how can delight
> Renew in these chains of darkness
> Where *b*ones of *b*easts are strown
> On the *b*leak and snowy mountains
> Where *b*ones from the *b*irth are *b*uried
> *B*efore they see the light. (*BA*, 5.41–47)

The thick consonants Blake deploys to give a sense of "obstruction," as in:

> He arose but the *st*ems *st*ood *s*o *th*ick
> He with difficulty and great pain
> Brought his Books (*BA*, 3.71–73)

which is meant to improve Milton's "So he with difficulty and labour hard" (*P.L.* III.1021), often do their job of obstructing too well. The poetry's staccato bullet-mold construction makes passages of it read like Gilbert and Sullivan's most impossibly tongue-twisting patter. In general, too, it will be pointless to look for much subtlety or complexity in this verse. Its virtues are all on the surface; it is not a verse that pays dividends.

Of the free verse pieces, the worst is "Africa," less a poem than a brief Blake's Tour of the Early Religions, which travels as quickly as decency will permit from Adam and abstract Eastern philosophy to Newton, Locke, and Deism,

> Till a Philosophy of Five Senses was complete. (*SL*, 4.16)

There is no poetry in this line, nor in these:

> To Trismegistus. Palamabron gave an abstract Law:
> To Pythagorus Socrates & Plato. (*SL*, 3.18–19)

"Africa" is one of the few chapters in Blake's prophetic work which is most satisfactory as rhythmic prose. Unfortunately, since it does not show any larger unity of form, it falls short of his best prose, as it does of his poetry.

Europe, a collage of techniques, begins in a few copies with the famous Fairy's Song which pithily states Blake's theory of the senses. This song provides a good example of Blake's middle, expository style in septenary. Note the paragraphing, which divides the line into varying short and long phrases, the rhetorical lengthening of the clauses assigned to each successive sense, the strong stop preceding and isolating Blake's most important "fifth window" of Touch or Sex, and finally the mock sweetness in the meter and sound of the last line:

> Five windows light the cavern'd Man: / thro' one he breathes the air;
> Thro' one, hears music of the spheres; / thro' one, the eternal vine
> Flourishes, / that he may recieve the grapes; / thro' one can look.
> And see small portions of the eternal world that ever groweth; /
> Thro' one, himself pass out what time he please, / but he will not; /
> For stolen joys are sweet, & bread eaten in secret pleasant.
> (*Eur*, iii.1–6)

Septenaries reappear also in the Preludium, in stanzas of three long lines and a short one, and then later in solid blocks of the poem's narrative sections.

The poem proper opens with a reminiscence of Milton's *Nativity Ode*, in which the first two lines are Milton's meter, the second two Blake's:

> The deep of winter came;
> What time the secret child.
> Descended thro' the orient gates of the eternal day:
> War ceas'd, & all the troops like shadows fled to their abodes.
> (*Eur*, 3.1–4)

The rest of *Europe* slips in and out between septenary and free verse, the latter sometimes lyric, sometimes purely functional. Finally, toward the poem's close, we have more stanzas, irregularly combining septenary and short lines, which Blake possibly meant as a lengthened, unfettered version of the *Nativity* stanza. The subject significantly parallels Milton's roll call of the Pagan gods:

> Where is my lureing bird of Eden! Leutha silent love!
> Leutha. the many colourd bow delights upon thy wings:
> Soft soul of flowers Leutha!
> Sweet smiling pestilence! I see thy blushing light:
> Thy daughters many changing,
> Revolve like sweet perfumes ascending O Leutha silken queen!
> (*Eur*, 14.9–14)

In Blake's view, the first Christian era, whose commencement Milton had celebrated in his *Ode*, had been a failure. *Europe* describes the failure, but promises change. When Enitharmon calls her children, she is involuntarily announcing the Second Coming. It would be typical of Blake's little jokes to have her do this by parodying Milton's meter.

Europe, even though it is hardly more than a series of set pieces loosely linked together, does not seem to suffer by its lack of unity. As a group, however, these productions of 1794–95 are

Blake's least pleasant work, as they are his most monotonous. Their wild expenditure of energy, almost unrelieved by "mild & gentle parts," seems the energy of a Sysiphus. They contain some needlessly negligent tracts of poetry. Their thought, despite the first-glance obscurity, becomes all too simple once we have the key. Indeed, this is their main use: they provide footnotes and explanations to Blake's later, more expansive work.

But the variety of forms these poems pick up and put down gives us the right to call them transitional, and leave them there. Blake at this stage was still working out his system, and composing these poems almost as shorthand notes for it. Mentally, he seems a little like someone sitting on the edge of a chair in a strange house, looking about and trying to get all the impressions down quickly. He does not yet feel so accustomed, so at home, that he can afford to relax, move about slowly, do humdrum tasks, and let the rooms echo. His system has not yet become his tradition, as it will be in *The Four Zoas*, *Milton*, and *Jerusalem*.

11

The Major Prophecies

I must Create a System or be enslav'd by another Man's.
I will not Reason & Compare: my business is to Create.
(*J*, 10.20–21)

From the minor Prophetic Books to *The Four Zoas*, *Milton*, and *Jerusalem*, Blake accomplished a leap not only in scale but in poetic assurance. Where in the minor books he was in process of creating a system, the major books assume a system already created in which the poet can walk up and down at his ease, elaborating now one point and now another, applying color to the bare lineaments of doctrine, and co-ordinating new discoveries with what is known. Where the minor books separately concentrated first on psychological, then on social, and finally on mythical analysis, the major books push forward on all fronts at once, each telling the whole story of Man's fall and redemption. They advance from different angles. In *The Four Zoas* it is the story of Man's fallen, divided faculties, and how they overcame their divisions. In *Milton* it is the story of a single individual and how he overcame his Selfhood. In *Jerusalem*, it is the story not merely of Man quartered into his faculties, nor of Man the single striving soul, but of Man multiple as the children of earth, with special emphasis on the work performed by Prophecy through Time, and on what may be called Man's "subjective correlative," his Freedom, named Jerusalem. The three books also show an increasing emphasis on Christianity, but this is a discovery or unveiling of something necessary to his system from the beginning, rather than an alteration.

Where the minor books perpetually experimented with different formal techniques, *The Four Zoas*, *Milton*, and *Jerusalem* are of a piece. All adhere to the septenary, and differ from each other only as Blake, growing older, gradually shifted from a mode which was ornately emotional to a mode austerely and insistently intellectual. This involved a steady rise in degree of irregularity in the verse. It also involved, in *Jerusalem*, a sudden virtual cessation of imitative versification. Blake's manifesto for expressive technique, prefaced to *Jerusalem*, applies to all three: ". . . the terrific numbers are reserved for the terrific parts, the mild & gentle for the mild & gentle parts, and the prosaic for inferior parts." But the books, as we shall see, contain different proportions of mild, terrific, and prosaic.

Of all the prophecies, *The Four Zoas* offers the richest poetic treasure hoard. Possibly it is too rich for unity. The changes that came over *Vala* (Blake's first title for the poem) as it matured into *The Four Zoas* invariably show expansion rather than contradiction or contraction in Blake's thought. Among the most important additions are those which refer to Jesus and the Council of God, and those which allegorize contemporary events; these indicate that Blake's myth was alive enough for him to want to attach it to absolute Christian truths, and to the truths in history as he was discovering them. But G. E. Bentley feels that the revisions, occurring over a period of at least ten years, "left a wilderness of loose ends, incomplete ideas, sprained rhythms, and false starts which would have utterly condemned the work of a smaller mind." [1]

The unfinished state of *The Four Zoas* may excuse much of its disconnectedness. Its dream-framework may explain more.[2] The

[1] Gerald E. Bentley, Jr., "The Failure of Blake's *Four Zoas*," *Texas Studies in English*, XXXVII (1958), 103–4.

[2] Northrop Frye, *Fearful Symmetry, a Study of William Blake* (Princeton, 1947), p. 270.

real culprit is Blake's "Energy," which in this case was centrifugal. The poem remains a gaudy mental pageant, certainly a failure if judged by standards alien to Blake's. "Unity is the cloke of folly," he said (*On Homer's Poetry*, p. 778), and he composed accordingly. Since his habit was to let the totality of a work of art take care of itself while he labored at the parts, he did not feel obliged to glue together even the most disparate forms. In *The Four Zoas* he produced a work of extraordinary range, in which every mood is treated as intensely as if there were nothing else in the poem but that mood, as if salvation depended on that mood alone. The ground level of this epic takes up where *America* and the *Visions of the Daughters of Albion* left off. Beyond this, *The Four Zoas* resolves into several discrete styles which lie "at random, carelessly diffused," not given architecture until Night Nine.

Blake invokes "terrific numbers," of course, for the passages of loud noise and violent activity, for "The howlings gnashings groanings shriekings shudderings sobbings burstings" (VI.81) which cram the poem. These passages are always heavily, and usually irregularly, accented:

> The hammer of Urthona smote the rivets in terror. of brass
> Tenfold. the Demons rage flamd tenfold forth rending,
> Roaring redounding. Loud Loud Louder & Louder & fird
> The darkness warring with the waves of Tharmas & Snows of Urizen.
> (V.104–7)

In such passages spondaic formations (flámd ténfôld fórth réndìng . . . Lóud Lóud Lóuder) are important for emphasis, and enjambment and asymmetrical pauses build cumulative rhythms. The sound is strongly repetitive; here the consonant pattern moves from *m*'s (ha*mm*er, s*m*ote, fla*m*d) to *f*'s, to *l*'s and *d*'s culminating in the reiterated "*Loud*," and with strenuous *r*'s running all through. The vowels are broad and deep, with echoes and half-echoes like hammer-terror, brass-darkness. Most important, the rhythm, sound, and diction all imitate, in a sensuous as well as a symbolic way, the clamor and effort Blake means to express. It is quite a different technique from that used, for example, in "The Tyger," where the sense of effort was far more mental than physical.

One of the most sustained blood-and-thunder sections occurs at the close of Night III, when Ahania, spurned by Urizen, falls, and Urizen perforce follows, to the accompaniment of a crash, flame, and universal groan, and Tharmas rises as Chaos regnant:

But from the Dolorous Groan one like a shadow of smoke appeard
And human bones rattling together in the smoke & stamping
The nether Abyss & gnashing in fierce despair. panting in sobs
Thick short incessant bursting sobbing. deep despairing stamping struggling (8)
Struggling to utter the voice of Man struggling to take the features of Man. Struggling (9)
To take the limbs of Man at length emerging from the smoke . . .
Crying. Fury in my limbs. destruction in my bones & marrow
My skull riven into filaments. my eyes into sea jellies
Floating upon the tide wander bubbling & bubbling . . .
So Tharmas bellowd oer the ocean thundring sobbing bursting.
(III.153–76)

Here, in addition to the devices already mentioned of heavy and irregular accent patterns, and repetitive and imitative sound, Blake lets his struggling Chaos burst from septenary to an eight-foot and then a nine-foot line, as marked. Long lines like these are relatively common in *The Four Zoas*, as compared to *Milton* and *Jerusalem*.

Some of the lamentations, speeches of defiance, curses, and so on, though still fairly "terrific," are milder than this. When Urizen curses his daughters, the rage is controlled:

. . . for their colours of loveliness
I will give blackness for jewels hoary frost for ornament deformity;
For crowns wreathd Serpents for sweet odors stinking corruptibility
For voices of delight hoarse croakings inarticulate thro frost . . .
Go forth sons of my curse Go forth daughters of my abhorrence.
(VI.36–46)

Although the speech ends with a line from *Tiriel,* Blake has learned something from Isaiah about balanced diction and rhythm. Still, Blake's terrific passages are mainly brass and percussion. There is nothing subtle about them; nor is there anything subtle about the way Blake pulls them out for all occasions. The sort of trick which Milton dared play only once or twice in *Paradise Lost* in lines like

> O'er bog or steep, through strait, rough, dense, or rare,
> With head, hands, wings, or feet pursues his way, (II.948–49)

Blake plays many hundred times. He would not have seen the point of hoarding his purple effects, a niggardly, negative virtue, if "Exuberance is Beauty." As for Biblical influence, it is strong in the imagery of destruction and combat, but Blake's rhythms are usually more frantic than the Bible's in these passages.

A second style in *The Four Zoas,* commonly Biblical both in language and construction, is the lyric. Here the meter is regular and the matter is "mild & gentle"—although sometimes only in a very equivocal sense. Since Blake did not care about regularity or the appearance of regularity for its own sake, he often used it ironically, in the delusive tones of females, for songs of war and human sacrifice:

> In pits & dens & shades of death in shapes of torment & woe
> The Plates the Screws and Racks & Saws & cords & fires & floods
> The cruel joy of Luvahs daughters lacerating with knives . . .
> They Dance around the Dying & they Drink the howl & groan
> They catch the shrieks in cups of gold they hand them to one another.
> (IX.751–68)

> Now now the Battle rages round thy tender limbs O Vala
> Now smile among thy bitter tears now put on all thy beauty
> Is not the wound of the sword Sweet & the broken bone delightful
> Wilt thou now smile among the slain when the wounded groan in the field (VIIb.187–90)

Here once again is the "Prince of Love" motif from "How sweet I roamed from field to field," now carried to its conclusion, the explicit declaration that the god of love and passion (Luvah) is also the god of pain and mutilation. Yeats must have learned something from Blake about how "a terrible beauty is born." But what gives Blake's war lyrics force is that he couples a full perception of cruelty's beauty with a firm moral detestation of it, which Yeats (and Swinburne before him) was never able to do.

Another type of lyric in *The Four Zoas* is the lamentation:

> Why does the Raven cry aloud and no eye pities her?
> Why fall the Sparrow & the Robin in the foodless winter?
> (I.445–46)

> O did I keep the horses of the day in silver pastures
> O I refusd the lord of day the horses of his prince
> O did I close my treasuries with roofs of solid stone
> And darken all my Palace walls with envyings & hate....
>   I went not forth I hid myself in black clouds of my wrath
> I calld the stars around my feet in the night of councils dark
> The stars threw down their spears & fled naked away
> We fell. (V.210–13, 222–25)

Of the many lyrics of lamentation, the smoothest show characters nearest the state of regeneration, like Enion who never falls far, and Urizen in Night V temporarily perceiving his error. In these cases, metrical regularity bears morally positive implications. Both these lyrics, incidentally, may be interpolations originally written independently of *The Four Zoas;* for they, and a few other passages, are written in stanzaic form and have the quality of set pieces.

Finally, Blake also employs a flowing *Thel*-like meter for his lyrics of joy. The pastoral interlude of Night IX systematically recalls ballad; the diction, the hymeneal theme, the rhythms, are all from the Song of Songs:

> Where dost thou flee O fair one where dost thou seek thy happy place
> To yonder brightness there I haste for sure I came from thence
> Or I must have slept eternally nor have felt the dew of morning

Eternally thou must have slept, nor have felt the morning dew
But for yon nourishing sun tis that by which thou art arisen
The birds adore the sun the beasts rise up & play in his beams,
And every flower & every leaf rejoices in his light
Then, O thou fair one, sit thee down, for thou art as the grass,
Thou risest in the dew of morning & at night art folded up.

(IX.401–9)

The imitative music in *The Four Zoas*, whether bombastic or lyric, concurs with the sudden upsurge of natural description in this poem. After a few tentative sorties in the early books, Blake seems now to be observing the vegetative world for its sensory as well as its symbolic qualities. Not only does he give several catalogues of natural objects, like the list of trees, birds and animals in I.204–8, or the list of insects and small earth animals in IX.755–60. These might be padding. He also indulges in genuine imagery, of the sort which is every other poets staple, but which he had hardly trifled with since *Poetical Sketches*. To describe the sea's motion, he extends his line:

& helpless as a wave
Beaten along its sightless way growing enormous in its motion to
Its utmost goal, (I.193–95)

To describe Los at war, he brings the sun symbol back to the world of corporeal image:

Flaming his head like the bright sun seen thro a mist that magnifies
The disk into a terrible vision to the Eyes of trembling mortals.

(VIIb. 79–80)

In IX, when Urizen renounces authority, his Emanation appears from nowhere, dancing, "as when a bubble rises up / On to the surface of a lake" (195–96). Aural imagery is also important in *The Four Zoas*, although its source may be literary rather than natural. A passage in Night V describes the winter birth of Orc-Christ to the sound of music; its subject duplicates the opening of the *Nativity Ode*, and its technique may stem from Milton's musical passage later in that poem. In VIII (204) another bit of aural imagery has Los at work in Golgonooza; "The hard dentant hammers are lulld by the flutes lula lula" may have been suggested by the musical pastimes around Milton's Pandemonium.

In addition to the terrific parts and the lyrics, a third noticeable style in *The Four Zoas* is the ethically argumentative. This may be dramatic, as in the lament of Enion, Blake's "blind & age bent" Demeter (taken perhaps from Job 28.12 ff.): [3]

What is the price of Experience do men buy it for a song
Or wisdom for a dance in the street? No it is bought with the price
Of all that a man hath his house his wife his children [4]
Wisdom is sold in the desolate market where none come to buy
And in the witherd field where the farmer plows for bread in vain

It is an easy thing to triumph in the summers sun
And in the vintage & to sing on the waggon loaded with corn
It is an easy thing to talk of patience to the afflicted
To speak the laws of prudence to the houseless wanderer....
It is an easy thing to rejoice in the tents of prosperity
Thus could I sing & thus rejoice, but it is not so with me.

(II.397–405, 417–18)

Or it may be satiric. Blake's comment on Bacon's *Essays* was "good advice for Satan's kingdom," [5] and he probably meant Urizen's advice to his daughters to reproduce Bacon's curt style:

Compell the poor to live upon a Crust of bread by soft mild arts
Smile when they frown frown when they smile & when a man looks pale
With labour & abstinence say he looks healthy & happy

[3] Cf. "But where shall wisdom be found? and where is the place of understanding? Man knoweth not the price thereof; neither is it found in the land of the living. The depth saith, It is not in me: and the sea saith, It is not with me.... Whence then cometh wisdom? and where is the place of understanding? ... Destruction and death say, We have heard the fame thereof in our ears."

[4] The words "his house" unaccountably do not appear in Keynes, but are plain in the manuscript and in the facsimile edition: *Vala, or The Four Zoas*, ed. G. E. Bentley, Jr. (Oxford, 1963).

[5] *Annotations to Bacon*, p. 396.

And when his children sicken let them die there are enough
Born, even too many & our Earth will be overrun
Without these arts. (VII.117–22)

Technically these ethical passages fall between the terrific sections and the lyrics, with neither the rhythmic drive and the cacophony of the former, nor the rhythmic grace and mellifluousness of the latter. Their irregularities, like the ironic spondee of "sóft | míld árts," and the enjambment of "there are enough / Born," are rhetorically functional rather than imitative. The sound rather avoids than cultivates alliteration; there is just enough—"Com*p*ell the *p*oor to live upon a Crust," "healthy & happy," "ch*i*ldr*en* s*i*ck*en*"—to give the lines starch. At its worst, this middle style degenerates into "prosaic numbers for the inferior parts."

Blake, like Milton, wrote poorly when he wrote only to expound doctrinal points. Few critics claim great poetic value for God the Father's justification of Man's fall in Book III of *Paradise Lost*, although everyone agrees that the explanation given there of man's free will is central to the poem's conception. When Blake descends from poetry to explanation in lines like:

> But in Eternal times the Seat of Urizen is in the South,
> Urthona in the North Luvah in East Tharmas in West
> (VI.279–80)

> so permitted because
> It was the best possible in the State calld Satan to Save
> From Death Eternal (VIII.284–86)

And these are the Sons of Los and Enitharmon Rintrah Palamabron
Theotormon Bromion Antamon Ananton Ozoth Ohana
Sotha Mydon Ellayol Natho Gon Harhath Satan
(VIII.357–59)

> to Give his vegetated body
> To be cut off & separated that the Spiritual body may be Reveald
> (VIII.265–67)

Blake's catastrophe is severer than Milton's, because he lacks the ridge of a stable line to break his fall.

Except for Night VIII, *The Four Zoas* has rather few "inferior parts." In that Night the explanations, abstractions, catalogues, and genealogies come tediously thick and fast. Unfortunately, this was among the last sections of *The Four Zoas* to be written, and it ominously forecasts developments in *Milton* and *Jerusalem.* As it stands in the present poem, it is only the dark hour before the dawn.

Night IX, Blake's triumph, bursts from the poem like the final movement of Beethoven's Choral Symphony. It is the Last Judgment. "And all the while the trumpet sounds" (42; cf. also 65, 239, 263, 331, 615), amid tumult of flood and earthquake, human wailing and groaning, wakening the dead to judgment. The book resounds with musical imagery. "Vocal may" is mentioned early (194). There is a "noise of rural works" as horses, bulls, tigers, and lions "sing" (299, 302) and the Sons of Urizen "shout" (308). The Human seed is harrowed "To ravishing melody of flutes & harps & softest voice" (336). When Ahania rises in springtime,

A shout of jubilee in lovely notes responds from daughter to daughter
From son to Son as if the Stars beaming innumerable
Thro night should sing soft warbling filling Earth & heaven
And bright Ahania took her seat by Urizen in songs & joy.

(IX.350–53)

The Human Harvest is reaped to the sound "Of flute & harp & drum & trumpet horn & clarion" (586). The slaves of the earth, remembering Psalms 33.3, 40.3, Isaiah 42.10 and Revelations 5.9, "Sing a New Song" (683). The Human Wine is pressed to music, "to violins & tabors to the pipe flute lyre & cymbal" (721), and when the wine is finished, "the heavens rolld on with vocal harmony" (800). Even the structure of this Night is musical. After a tremendous apocalyptic prelude which corresponds to Winter in the Night's seasonal scheme and thus appropriately includes or announces bits of the various motifs to come, there are definite movements for the plowing and harrowing of springtime, vintage, and breadmaking, each interrupted by arias from the various characters.

All the styles of *The Four Zoas* appear at their best in this final Night, saved from the danger of overcrowding by the Night's good structure. As befits the theme of unification, and Blake's conviction that a whole Man was greater than the sum of his parts, something new also appears: a style which combines lyricism with a moderate degree of metrical irregularity to express the higher, firmer beauty of the new life:

The Sun has left his blackness & has found a fresher morning
Ănd thĕ míld móon rejoices in the clear & cloudless night
Ănd Mán wálks fórth from midst of the fires the evil is all consumd. . . .
The Expanding Eyes of Man behold the depths of wondrous worlds
Óne Éarth óne séa beneath nor Érrĭng Glóbes wándĕr but Stars
Ŏf fíre ríse ûp níghtlў frŏm the Ocean & óne Sún
Éach mórnĭng lĭke ă Néw bórn Mán íssŭes with songs & Joy.
(IX.825–33)

It is this firm, oratorical style, only barely discovered in *The Four Zoas*, which contributes most to the character of *Milton*.

Technically, *Milton* begins where *The Four Zoas* leaves off:

Daughters of Beulah! Muses who inspire the Poets Song
Record the journĕy ŏf immortal Milton thro' your Realms
Of terrŏr &̆ | míld móo|nў lúst|rĕ, ĭn sóft | séxŭăl | delusions
Of varied beautў, tŏ delight the wandĕrĕr ănd repose
His burning thirst & freezing hunger! Come into my hand
By your mild power: descending down the Nerves of my right arm
From out the Portals of my brain, where by your ministry
The Eternal Great Humanity Divine, planted his Paradise,
And in it caus'd the Spectres of the Dead to take sweet forms
In likeness of himself. Téll álsŏ | ŏf thĕ Fálse | Tóngue! végetated
Beneath your land of shadows: of its sacrifices and
Its offerings: (*M*, 2.1–12)

The opening invocation, patterned on that of *Paradise Lost*, uses long run-on sentences with the full stops occurring internally, so that the paragraph gathers momentum in its progress. Some of the strength comes from the many trochaic words—Dáughtĕrs, Béulăh, Músĕs, Póĕts, jóurnĕy, Míltŏn, móonÿ lústrĕ, etc.—played against the iambic pattern. The varied placement of dropped accents balanced against occasional spondees, here marked for the first few lines, continues through the passage. It is noteworthy that Blake restricts himself here much more than commonly to disyllabic feet. The trisyllables of "lustrĕ ĭn sóft | séxŭăl," "wandĕrĕr ănd," "powĕr dĕscénding," are easily elidible; and the extra syllables of "The Eternal Great Humanĭtў Dĭvíne" and "Téll álsŏ | ŏf thĕ Fálse" are in phrases intended for emphasis. In sound, the passage combines fairly broad range with the punctuation of a few echoes: B*eu*lah, M*u*ses; Rec*or*d, i*mmor*tal *M*ilton; *m*ild *m*oony; b*ur*ning th*ir*st; *d*escending *d*own, etc. There is a solidity here, seldom found amid the frenetic gyrations of *The Four Zoas*, but intrinsic to the spirit of *Milton.*

Milton is at once a more maturely simple and a more exasperatingly complex work than *The Four Zoas*. The main story illustrates two of Blake's important ideas: that "Whenever any Individual Rejects Error & Embraces Truth, a Last Judgment passes upon that Individual" (*VLJ*, p. 613); and that the poet as prophet embodies not only the conscience of the race, but also its fate. When Milton descends, taking a path similar to Christ's in *Paradise Regained*, renouncing Error, his Selfhood in Satan's form, and embracing the Truth of his prophetic destiny by uniting with Blake, Los, and his Emanation Ololon, a last judgment passes upon him and he regains his own Paradise. This simultaneously begins the redemption of Mankind. At the close of *Milton*, all creatures on earth are prepared "To go forth to the Great Harvest & Vintage of the Nations" (43.1). *Milton* belongs with the genre of quest poetry, as moral struggle. It is a kind of inverted *Purgatorio*, since the curve is downward from an unearned heaven to the earth of redemption. Affinities with the *Odyssey* include the fact that

Milton begins "unhappy tho' in heaven" as Odysseus is restless with Calypso; watched over by immortals, he rejoins Blake and Ololon (Telemachus, Penelope) and triumphs over the False Religions (suitors) which have infested the homeland. There is no evidence that Blake intended these parallels, but they are there.

Surrounding this simple story, which may be conceived as happening "Within a Moment: a Pulsation of the Artery," since such is the period in which "the Poets Work is Done" (29.1, 3), lies the vast territory of Blake's system. The system now has expanded to include new mythic characters, British and Near Eastern geographical symbolism, numerological symbols, places like Bowlahoola and Allamanda, and a good quantity of metaphysical and theological theory.

According to Schorer, "the central theme of *Milton* is not nearly adequate to fill the bloated structure of the whole."[6] One might make the same complaint of Dante, for Blake uses a method similar to Dante's in the *Paradiso*, introducing, at each stage of his narrative, mythic material or portions of doctrine appropriate to that stage. Thus we have the episode of the Prophet's Song to introduce us through a myth to Milton's dilemma. We have an explanation of Vortexes when Milton begins his journey and must pass from the vortex of heaven to that of earth (15). Beulah is explained (30–31) in order to clarify Ololon's situation before she goes to join Milton. The Seven Angels of the Presence expound Blake's doctrine of States versus Individuals (32) to instruct Milton in the task he is undertaking, and to explain to the reader the implications of that task. The catalogue of Monstrous Churches (37) expresses the history behind and within Milton's Puritanism, giving Error a verbal "body" that it may be recognized and cast off.[7]

[6] *William Blake, the Politics of Vision* (New York, 1946), p. 346.

[7] There are, of course, crucial differences. Dante's frame is composed of proportional parts. Each ring is equivalent to each other ring. In Blake's story, some important sections (e.g., Milton's struggle with Satan) are passed over very quickly, while some trivial ones (e.g., the exposition of the Churches) take up an inordinate amount of space. Furthermore, Dante

Metrically as well as structurally, *Milton* is more unified than *The Four Zoas*. It has no stanzaic interpolations. It has fewer too-short and too-long lines. Although on the whole it has shifted slightly to the left, toward a more consistent degree of irregularity, it lacks—except for passages incorporated from earlier poems—the extremes both of violent metrical distortion and of ballad-like smoothness.

There is still some imitative music. Part of this relates to Time, which is a main theme of the poem, and involves Blake in some interesting tricks with tempo. In the lines

> And every Moment has a Couch of gold for soft repose.
> (A Móment équals a pulsátion of the ártery) (28.46–47)

the line of "repose" moves slowly, the following line quickly, and the two together express Blake's paradoxical conception of Time. Most of the passages dealing with Beulah, the place of sleep, have a languid or moderate pace. But in the vegetated world where Blake stands, everything happens fast. Ololon appears:

> nor time nor space was
> To the perception of the Virgin Ololon but as the
> Flash of lightning but more quick the Virgin in my Garden
> Before my Cottage stood. (36.17–20)

The natural observation begun in *The Four Zoas* continues in *Milton*, and Blake now has a theory for it, to the effect that such phenomena as the stars, the "gorgeous clothed flies," and the trees that thunder in high winds, are all children of Los, "Visions of Eternity" (25.66–26.12). Similarly, birdsongs and the odors of flowers are "a Vision of the lamentation of Beulah over Ololon" (31.45, 63), while the wild thyme (a pun, probably) and the lark are Los's messengers, one "a mighty Demon" (35.54), the other "a

---

makes his structural bones palpable, so that we are quite sure where we are at every point, and we can see the structural necessity for each bit of description, or biography, or exposition. In Blake, the bones are so hidden that we often have to infer the progress of the narrative solely from the digressions.

mighty Angel" (36.12). Mortal eyes see only the hem of the garments of these Visions. Blake, having discovered to his surprise that natural objects by no means always deadened imagination in him, was seeing far more. This romance with nature was to be a brief one, for by the time he wrote *Jerusalem*, Blake had rediscovered the Whore of Babylon behind the pretty face.

Blake's imagistic passages use imitative prosodic techniques at a few points. The sun rising while stars remain in the sky would emerge joyously for some poets, but Blake makes this an image of effort and sullenness; note the long first line, the deep vowels, the repeated illustrative "drag":

When Lúvahs búlls êach mórning drág the súlphur Sún óut of the Déep
Harnessd with starry harness black & shining, kept by black slaves
That wórk áll níght at the starry harness. Strong and vigorous
They drag the unwilling Orb: (21.20–23)

Milton's musical demons reappear in Bowlahoola, "to ameliorate the sorrows of slavery":

The hard dentant Hammers are lulld by the flutes' lula lula
The bellowing Furnaces blare by the long sounding clarion,
The double drum drowns howls & groans, the shrill fife. shrieks & cries:
The crooked horn mellows the hoarse raving serpent, terrible but harmonious. (24.63–66)

Anticipating Shelley, Blake imitates the thrusting flight and song of birds:

Thou hearest the Nightingale begin the Song of Spring.
The Lark sitting upon his earthy bed: just as the morn
Appears: listens silent: then springing from the waving Cornfield! loud
He leads the Choir of Day: trill. trill. trill. trill. (31.28–31)

And with his messenger-larks' meeting, where he obtains the effect of duplication by the obvious and childlike device of repeating his words,

> When on the highest lift of his light pinions he arrives
> At that bright Gate another Lark meets him, & back to back
> They touch their pinions tip tip: (36.1–3)

the *l*'s and the delicate *t*'s and *p*'s, with the keen vowels of h*i*ghest, l*i*ght, arr*i*ves, br*i*ght, combined with the lighter *i*'s of l*i*ft, p*i*nions, t*i*p, are all working to imitate the birds' flight.

Yet these imitative passages are exceptions, for *Milton* is already a far more intellectual work than *The Four Zoas*, and its chief technical feature is the use of rhythms that vary, but by their own laws, not necessarily in obvious illustration of the text. This approach suits the general spirit of the poem, even if it does not follow the parts. *The Four Zoas* recorded Man's fall from vision, and his tremendous efforts to regain his former state. *Milton* records the experience of vision itself. It is therefore more stable. The poem was written, moreover, during a period in Blake's life when he was preaching patience to himself in his dealings with Hayley and in his feelings about international affairs, just as Los (23–24) preaches patience to his sons.[8] The calm of the verse reflects this.

Partly because Blake is not striving impatiently for special effects, the narrative of *Milton* is tighter, more sinewy, than the narrative of either *The Four Zoas* or *Jerusalem.* It resembles his best prose, the prose of *The Marriage of Heaven and Hell.* The dialogue and declamations also have greater firmness. And, in places, seemingly without effort, *Milton* rises to eloquence.

The first such point is Blake's opening invocation. Another is the brief outcry beginning "O how can I with my gross tongue" (20.15), which by its situation recalls Milton's invocation to Light; Blake had not Milton's poetic advantage of blindness, but he satisfied himself with a "gross tongue" and a "cold hand of

[8] See David V. Erdman, *Blake, Prophet Against Empire* (Princeton, 1954), p. 350, on the Felpham period: "What scholars have neglected is the peculiarly *un*revolutionary quality of this brief transitional period, and its relation to the peace and rumors of peace that hovered over Blake's seashore cottage." See ch. 24, *passim*, on Blake's doctrine of making do with the sorry state of society while awaiting the hoped-for millennium.

clay." The lament on the limited senses, beginning "Ah weak & wide astray" (5.19), which recalls the close of *Thel,* but with pathos rather than bitterness, is another high point. Blake liked these lines so well that he repeated them in *Jerusalem.* But the climax of *Milton* is its hero's final pronouncement:

To bathe in the Waters of Life: to wash off the Not Human
I come in Self-annihilation & the grandeur of Inspiration
To cast off Rational Demonstration by Faith in the Saviour
To cast off the rotten rags of Memory by Inspiration
To cast off Bacon. Locke & Newton from Albions covering
To take off his filthy garments. & clothe him with Imagination
To cast aside from Poetry. all that is not Inspiration
That it no longer shall dare to mock with the aspersion of Madness
Cast on the Inspired, by the tame high finisher of paltry Blots,
Indefinite. or paltry Rhymes, or paltry Harmonies.
Who creeps into State Government like a catterpiller to destroy;
To cast off the idiot Questioner who is always questioning,
But never capable of answering: who sits with a sly grin
Silent plotting when to question, like a thief in a cave:
Who publishes doubt & calls it knowledge: whose Science is Despair . . .
He smiles with condescension: he talks of Benevolence & Virtue,
And those who act with Benevolence & Virtue, they murder time on time. (41.1–20)

The bad syntax of this is irrelevant, since the rhetoric proceeds by another logic than that of grammar. It is the logic of the repeated "to cast off . . . cast off . . . cast off . . . take off . . . cast aside . . . cast off," the repeated "Inspiration" at the ends of lines, the repeated "paltry," the ironic "Questioner . . . questioning . . . question," the angry "Benevolence & Virtue . . . Benevolence & Virtue." It is the logic of "bathe" turning to the negative "wash *off*"; the logic of strong figures like "*r*otten *r*ags" and "filthy garments," "catterpiller" and "thief in a cave." Except in the repeated phrases, Blake has scarcely any sound-echoes here, for he is casting about him with a broad arm and aiming for magnitude rather than intensity. The parallel cadences of the first lines vary just enough to avoid monotony while gathering energy. A central break divides these lines into approximately equal halves, each the equivalent of three very free metrical feet, which makes for a rough symmetry. Rhetoric breaks into anger with the strong stresses of "nó lóngĕr shâll dáre," where the line extends to a full seven feet, and a peak is hit with the passionate briefer parallels of "the tame high finisher of paltry Blóts Indefinite. / or paltry Rhýmes,/or paltry Hármonies." The remaining lines, combining long and broken phrases, decline to a plateau, ultimately rounded off by the final, metrically balanced cadences. Here Blake assumes the robes of a "true Orator."

But this functional style, which fails to offer a texture delectable in itself and therefore depends on the poet's moments of oratorical inspiration, also has its disadvantages. These appear when inspiration departs, and intellect remains alone on the stage, bare-faced, with no painted mask to project its image.

In many places, the sheer conciseness and originality of Blake's thought saves the poetry:

> Time is the mercy of Eternity: without Times swiftness
> Which is the swiftest of all things: all were eternal torment.
>
> (24.72–73)

In other places, nothing can save it:

> So they are born on Earth, & every Class is determinate
> But not by Natural but by Spiritual power alone. Because
> The Natural power continually seeks & tends to Destruction
> Ending in Death: which would of itself be Eternal Death
>
> (26.39–42)

> Retaining only Satans Mathematic Holiness Length: Bredth & Highth
> Calling the Human Imagination: which is the Divine Vision & Fruition
> In which Man liveth eternally: madness & blasphemy. against
> Its own Qualities. which are Servants of Humanity. not Gods or Lords.
>
> (32.18–21)

These passages are poor, not because they cannot be scanned; the first is fairly straight hexameter, disrupted only by the odd pause pattern; the second has two lines of eight feet followed by two septenaries. The irregularities are no stronger than in many effective passages, and less severe than those in the long declaration just quoted, which much more nearly approaches our earlier definition of prose. It is only that these lines have no particular reason for being as they are. Blake is so occupied with what he wants to say that he lets the how of it trail along any which way. It is significant that the relatively technical terms Blake needs to employ in such passages do not of themselves tend to interesting sound patterns, and so we lose the alliteration and vowel harmony which redeem the work where Blake permits himself free rein in diction.

I have suggested that the technical, explanatory, didactic sections of *Milton* paralleled those of the *Paradiso*. But unlike the traditional poets of intellect, Lucretius or Dante, Blake made no effort to sweeten the spoon of doctrine with the honey of fair form. He respected vision more than he respected art. Indeed, he believed that the imposition of art, which he called artifice, would blur and damage the strict lineaments of vision. In *Milton*, where the theme of effectual self-renewal creates an ebullience independent of form, we need not mind the taste of bare metal. In *Jerusalem*, where the dominant theme is despair, the lack of a formal sweetener leaves our tongues coated with acid.

Foster Damon, in a rather playful comparison of Blake's and Milton's careers, finds parallels everywhere between their major works. Blake's *Songs* extend *L'Allegro* and *Il Penseroso*, *Thel* attacks *Comus*, *Visions of the Daughters of Albion* stands on the shoulders of the divorce tracts, *The Four Zoas* corrects *Paradise Lost*. But *Jerusalem*, says Damon, was Blake's *History of Britain*.[9]

This is hardly an invitation to the poetic delights of *Jerusalem*, which seems generally acknowledged to be an uninviting poem.

[9] "Blake and Milton," in *The Divine Vision, Studies in the Poetry and Art of William Blake*, ed. Vivian de Sola Pinto (London, 1957), pp. 92–95.

Even Frye, Blake's most ardent defender, admits its harshness, defending it on grounds of expressiveness, and comparing it to Goya's *Disasters of War*, where truth, not beauty or ugliness, is the relevant thing.[10] Between *Jerusalem* and a Goya etching, however, is the difference between an image and an idea. Blake's system, which began to proliferate in *Milton*, has in his last great prophetic work almost entirely gobbled up his poetry. "Putting on intellect" to Blake meant pursuing the ramifications of his thought down every crooked alley and lane to the last minute particular, leaving nothing unexplained, personifying the Sons and Daughters of Albion with the exactness of Biblical genealogies, declaring the dimensions of Golgonooza as precisely as Solomon's temple was measured, establishing the jurisdiction of the Twelve Tribes of Israel over "the Fifty-two Counties of England & Wales / The Thirty-six of Scotland & the Thirty-four of Ireland" (16.28–29) as faithfully as Homer gave his catalogue of ships, and filling every vacancy in the epic with wads of dialectic. The dwelling on natural objects in *The Four Zoas* and *Milton* has vanished, since Blake now renounces Nature as the source of any good. Analysis of human emotion has become analysis of geographical and numerological symbolism. Individual history has turned collective. Characters have become diagrammatic, and their dramatic interchanges, their clashes of wills, their triumphs and lamentations, have become doctrinal debates.

Another difference between Goya and the Blake of *Jerusalem* is the difference between outrage and despair. Goya's lurid portraits of the human wolf and serpent are inflammatory; they cry out for rebellion against the vicious, the ugly, the stupid. But Blake has gone beyond faith in rebellion. Where the dominant mood of *The Four Zoas* was struggle, and that of *Milton* visionary surety, the dominant mood of *Jerusalem* is a grim determination to let evil and error have their way, to let them express themselves unarrested, even to give them "a body," in the faith that only when it is fully grown, fully drunk with the blood of nations, and thus fully

[10] *Fearful Symmetry*, pp. 358–59.

recognized, may Falsehood "be cast off for ever" (12.13). Blake's rule for this poem seems to be that of Conrad's Stein: "In the destructive element immerse." *Jerusalem* is an incantation to raise the Devil on the presumption that when he is raised he will vanish. This is in fact what happens at the poem's close, when things have gotten so bad they cannot possibly get any worse: Antichrist appears, overshadowing and dividing Albion and Jesus; Albion to save Jesus "threw himself into the Furnaces of affliction," and in the very next line, without any of the tumult of Night IX in *The Four Zoas*, we discover that

> All was a Vision. all a Dream: the Furnaces became
> Fountains of Living Waters flowing from the Humanity Divine
> And all the Cities of Albion rose from their Slumbers. and All
> The Sons & Daughters of Albion on soft clouds waking from Sleep.
> (*J*, 96.36–39)

The impulse of Mankind to sacrifice himself for his friend, Jesus, has itself destroyed Antichrist. But up until this point, the dream has been a nightmare.

What happens to the verse in *Jerusalem* is that it shifts still further than before into the camp of irregularity, and is flayed of ornament so that the blood and muscle of Blake's thought can be seen unveiled. In the bulk of the poem, Blake hardly seems to be on civil speaking terms with his meter; he is far too occupied with the content of what he is saying to worry about the technique, which perforce must take care of itself. The effect of Blake's new preoccupations on his verse is at times painfully direct. *The Four Zoas* had recorded the crucifixion of Luvah in Blake's cruel lyric manner:

> They give the Oath of blood, they cast the lots into the helmet,
> They vote the death of Luvah & they naild him to the tree. . . .
> Then left the Sons of Urizen the plow & harrow the loom
> The hammer & the Chisel & the rule & compasses
> They forgd the sword the chariot of war the battle ax
> The trumpet fitted to the battle & the flute of summer,

> And all the arts of life they changd into the arts of death. . . .
> O Melancholy Magdalen, behold the morning breaks
> Gird on the flaming Zone. descend into the Sepulcher. . . .
> Remember all thy feigned terrors on the secret Couch
> When the sun rose in glowing morn with arms of mighty hosts
> Marching to battle who was wont to rise with Urizens harps
> Girt as a Sower with his seed to scatter life abroad.
> (*FZ*, VIIb.165–66, 170–74, 192–93, 196–99)

In *Jerusalem*, to ensure that the British people would not miss the relevance of the crucifixion to them—to make them see that they were the crucifiers—he simply added place names (italics mine):

> They cast the lots into the helmet: they give the oath of blood *in Lambeth*
> They vote the death of Luvah, & they nail'd him to *Albions* Tree *in Bath* . . .
> Then left the Sons of Urizen the plow & harrow, the Loom
> The hammer & the chisel. & the rule & compasses: *from London fleeing*
> They forg'd the sword *on Cheviot*, the chariot of War & the battle-ax,
> The trumpet fitted to mortal battle, & the Flute of Summer *in Annandale*
> And all the Arts of Life. they chang'd into the Arts of Death *in Albion*. . . .
> O melancholy Magdalen behold the morning *over Malden* break:
> Gird on thy flaming zone, descend into the sepulcher *of Canterbury*. . . .
> Remember all thy feigned terrors on the secret couch *of Lambeth's Vale*
> When the sun rose in glowing morn. with arms of mighty hosts
> Marching to battle who was wont to rise with Urizens harps
> Girt as a sower with his seed to scatter life abroad *over Albion*.[11]
> (*J*, 65.7–8, 12–16, 38–39, 42–45)

By good fortune or fortunate instinct, most of these additions simply change septenaries into passable, if rather overcrowded,

[11] This transformation has been noted as evidence of Blake's unconcern with technique by Bentley, "The Failure of Blake's *Four Zoas*," pp. 111–12.

eight-stress lines; and the lines "They forg'd the sword on Cheviot, the chariot of War & the battle-ax, / The trumpet fitted to mortal battle, & the Flute of Summer in Annandale," may even be considered a metrical enrichment. But the poet certainly has broken the back of his general movement, changing a flowing narrative to something much heavier. And it cannot be supposed that Blake was thinking consciously about his technique when he composed a line like "The hammer & the chisel. & the rule & compasses: from London fleeing." Although this line would be satisfactory in a prose context, its length is awkward here precisely because the rest of the passage still retains a degree of rhythmical uniformity.

The tendency toward a single unified style in *Milton* continues in *Jerusalem*, for despite the epic's exploded scope, passages which in earlier books might have had quite varied textures here seem often to have gone through the same grinder. Compare two descriptions of the Tree of Mystery springing up around Urizen in *The Four Zoas*, around Albion in *Jerusalem:*

> His book of iron on his knees he tracd the dreadful letters...
> Age after Age till underneath his heel a deadly root
> Struck thro the rock the root of Mystery accursed shooting up
> Branches into the heaven of Los they pipe formd bending down
> Take root again where ever they touch again branching forth
> In intricate labyrinths oerspreading many a grizly deep
> (*FZ*, VII.29–35)

> He sat by Tyburns brook, and underneath his heel shot up
> A deadly Tree, he nam'd it Moral Virtue. and the Law
> Of God who dwells in Chaos hidden from the human sight.
> The Tree spread over him its cold shadows, (Albion groand)
> They bent down, they felt the earth and again enrooting
> Shot into many a Tree: an endless labyrinth of woe! (*J*, 28.14–19)

In *The Four Zoas*, the passage is devoted to picturing the banyan's growth, in *Jerusalem* to explaining it. In *The Four Zoas* there are clusters of sound like "*r*oot... St*r*uck... *r*ock," "r*o*ot... thr*o*'

. . . r*oo*t . . . sh*oo*ting," "*B*ranches . . . *b*ending . . . *b*ranching." Its cumulative rhythms make use of little touches like "pípe fórm'd" and the enjambments "deadly root / Struck" and "shooting up / Branches." But in the *Jerusalem* passage the sound-echoes go no further than "*h*idd*en* . . . *h*um*an*," "c*o*ld shad*ow*s . . . gr*oa*nd"; and the rhythm is diffuse, headed nowhere, with the spondees "shót úp" and "bént dówn" wasted in it.

Again, compare two speeches by the Eternals:

Then the Divine Family said. Six Thousand Years are now
Accomplish'd in this World of Sorrow: Miltons Angel knew
The Universal Dictate: and you also feel this Dictate.
And now you know this World of Sorrow, and feel Pity. Obey
The Dictate! Watch over this World, and with your brooding wings.
Renew it to Eternal Life: Lo! I am with you alway. (*M*, 21.51–56)

Then those in Great Eternity who contemplate on Death
Said thus, What seems to Be: Is: To those to whom
It seems to Be. & is productive of the most dreadful
Consequences to those to whom it seems to Be: even of
Torments. Despair. Eternal Death; but the Divine Mercy
Steps beyond and Redeems Man in the Body of Jesus Amen.
(*J*, 36.50–55)

The *Milton* speech is merely pedestrian; the one from *Jerusalem*, until it wakes up in the last two lines, is absurd. Or compare the following:

It is an easy thing to rejoice in the tents of prosperity
Thus could I sing & thus rejoice, but it is not so with me.
(*FZ*, II.417–18)

It is easy to acknowledge a man to be great & good while we
Derogate from him in the trifles & small articles of that goodness:
Those alone are his friends, who admire his minutest powers.
(*J*, 43.56–58)

Here again, in the *Jerusalem* passage we have two lines which might be either verse or prose, and one which is unmistakably verse; none of which, however, makes use of rhythm to heighten meaning. There is nothing especially wrong here, but nothing especially right. As all these passages show, the "inferior" parts of *Jerusalem* may or may not be irregular. Irregularity is not their defect; their defect is that they are typically lacking in a cumulative rhythm and in the reinforcements of sound.

Too much of *Jerusalem* is "inferior" in this sense. Yet the total impression given by the verse of this epic not only conforms to, but enhances, Blake's doctrines. Because Blake has renounced Nature, there is no imitative versification. Because he has embraced Freedom, he can use enjambed weak endings habitually, and often seems to go out of his way for them as if deliberately to flout conventional prosody:

> The silent broodings of deadly revenge springing from the
> All powerful parental affection. (54.9–10)

> Such is the Forgiveness of the Gods, the Moral Virtues of the
> Heathen, (61.20–21)

This is disconcerting, but it reminds us that "Jerusalem is nam'd Liberty among the Sons of Albion."

Again, because he has decided to give Falsehood a body, he can have lines as ugly as:

> Calling the Rocks Atomic Origins of Existence: denying Eternity
> By the Atheistical Epicurean Philosophy of Albions Tree.
> (67.13–14)

Ugliness has been produced here by sound as well as sense, by the turkey-gobble of "Calling the R*o*c*k*s At*o*mic *O*rigins," and by the setting of the sedate Greek-derived words "Atheistical Epicurean Philosophy" to a burlesque jog as if they were so many camels.

Finally, because he has embraced Intellect, he can turn aside the rhythms of passion for the rhythms of idea. When Los speaks "swift as the shuttle of gold" to Enitharmon in the last moments before their mutual redemption, he makes no impassioned oration, but lectures her on how the sexes will vanish:

that we may Foresee & Avoid
The terrors of Creation & Redemption & Judgment. Beholding them
Displayd in the Emanative Visions of Canaan in Jerusalem & in Shiloh
And in the Shadows of Remembrance. & in the Chaos of the Spectre
Amalek. Edom. Egypt. Moab. Ammon. Ashur. Philistea. around Jerusalem. (92.19–23)

Moreover, it is almost uncanny how even in the midst of didactics, when a "poetic" figure appears, poetic rhythms appear also, as in the last line of:

For Art & Science cannot exist but in minutely organized Particulars
And not in generalizing Demonstrations of the Rational Power.
The Infinite alone resides in Definite & Determinate Identity
Establishment of Truth depends on destruction of Falshood continually
On Circumcision: not on Virginity, O Reasoners of Albion.
(55.62–66)

Yet it would be unfair to imply that *Jerusalem* lacks beauty even in the ordinary sense, for in its own odd, austere way, this poem has many effective passages. Los striving to master his Spectre emits power through his awkward, musclebound rhythms:

I knów thy decéit | & thy̆ | rĕvén|gĕs, ănd | ŭnléss thou desist
Ĭ wĭll cértăinly̆ crĕâte an eternal Hell for thee. Lísten: /
Be attént̀ive: / be obédient: / Lo the Furnaces are ready to receive thee. (8.7–9)

The balance is lopsided, yet every accent is like the crack of a whip. Or for a fuller sort of power, Blake can still manage a good exhortation:

Rúsh ón! Rúsh ón! Rúsh ón! ye vegetating Sons of Albion
Thĕ Sún shâll gó before you in Day: the Moon shall go
Before you in Night. Cóme ón! Cóme ón! Cóme ón! The Lord
Jehovah is before, behind, above, beneath, around. (49.50–53)

At times, too, the poem still approaches lyric, although Blake jealously guards his metrical irregularities even in his "mild &

gentle" sections; the description of Golgonooza has its septenaries and alexandrines, but also has lines of five and four feet:

The stones are pity, and the bricks, well wrought affections: (5)
Enameld with love & kindness, & the tiles engraven gold (6)
Labour of merciful hands: the beams & rafters are forgiveness . . . (7)
The cielings, devotion; the hearths, thanksgiving: (4)
(12.30–37)

The long lament of Jerusalem at her lowest ebb has bursts of despair framing a lyrical yet vigorous reminiscence of the past:

My ténts are fáll'n! my píllars are in rúins! my chíldren dásh'd
Upon Égypts íron flóors, & the márble pávemĕnts ŏf Ăssýria: . . .
Albion gave mĕ tŏ thĕ whóle Éarth to walk up & down; to pour
Jóy ŭpŏn évery̆ móuntăin, tŏ tèach sóngs to the shepherd & plowman
I táught the shíps of the séa to síng the sóngs of Zíon. . . .
I walk in affliction: I am a worm. ănd nó lívĭng sóul!
A wórm góing to eternal torment: ráisd úp in a night
To an eternal night of pain. lóst! lóst! lóst! for ever!
(79.1–2, 36–38; 80.3–5)

When *Jerusalem* has a rare song of joy, that too is dedicated to Freedom. At the close of the vision of Joseph and adulterous Mary, the forgiven Mary breaks forth like "a River of many Streams," and the verse also overflows its banks:

Then Mary burst forth into a Song! she flowed like a River of
Many Streams in the arms of Joseph & gave forth her tears of joy
Like many waters. and Emanating into gardens & palaces upon
Euphrates & to forests & floods & animals wild & tame from
Gihon to Hiddekel. & to corn fields & villages & inhabitants
Upon Pison & Arnon & Jordon. (61.28–33)

Finally, when *Jerusalem* reaches its denouement, when it is time for Albion to rise from his rock and rejoin Jesus, Blake wants a versification that will express the final vision of union and will erase all the horrors of the prior "dream" that mankind has lived until now. Yet he cannot return to the harmonic style which sufficed for *Milton*, since his vision is now a greater, a more inclusive and final one. He does not return; he extends his line of freedom once more, so that it reaches to eight feet instead of seven, and with this leavening eight-stress line he proceeds to march "forward forward irresistible from Eternity to Eternity" (98.27).

Plates 94 and 95, in which Albion awakes and "England who is Brittannia enterd Albion's bosom rejoicing" (95.22), both contain several eight-foot lines, as if in preparation for the coming movement. Plate 96, the colloquy between Albion and Jesus which culminates in Albion's self-sacrifice and the re-entry of the Four Zoas into Albion's bosom, reverts to septenary. In Plate 97, Albion draws his Bow and all the Four Zoas draw their Bows; Plate 98 gives the Fourfold shooting of the arrow of Love and the consequent humanizing of the universe; and Plate 99 is Blake's brief "consummatum est." All these are dominated by the eight-stress line, although Blake will not limit himself even now so much that he cannot still have some of his sevens and sixes, and a few lines in Plate 98 seem to be nine and ten feet long.

The final vision begins with the fourfold drawing of the Bow:

Só spáke the Vision of Albion & in him sò spáke in my hearing (6)
The Úniversal Fáther Then Álbion strétchd his hánd ínto Infínitude. (8)
And took his Bow. Fóurfŏld the Visĭon fŏr bríght béaming Urizen (7)
Láyd hĭs hánd ŏn the South & took a breathing Bow of carved Gold (8)
Lúvăh hĭs hánd strétch'd tŏ thĕ Éast & bore a Silver Bow bríght shíning (8)
Thármăs Wéstwărd a Bow of Brass púre fláming richly wrought (7)
Urthona Northward in thíck stórms a Bow of Iron, terrible thundering. (8)
(97.5–11)

One notes, at this point, the careful attention to sound; the repeated "So *s*pake . . . *s*o *s*pake," the triple alliteration "*b*right *b*eaming . . . *b*reathing *B*ow . . . *B*ow of *B*rass," and the key sound for the fourth, dark, laboring Zoa, "Ur*th*ona Nor*th*ward . . . *th*ick . . .*th*undering." The rhythm, too, once again performs a human task. There is a good distribution of trochees and spondees. The line openings vary, with three normal iambic openings (Thĕ Ŭnĭvérs-, Ănd tóok hĭs Bów, Ŭrthónă Nórth-), one spondee (Só spáke), two double trochees (Láyd hĭs hánd ŏn, Thármăs Wéstwărd), and one single trochee (Lúvăh) which then recurs internally to form a line with a lovely cadence, its first half moving with a swing, then straightening out to a steady beat, and concluding with a spondaic poise:

Lúvăh hĭs hánd / strétchd tŏ thĕ Éast / & bóre ă Sílvĕr Bów bríght shínĭng:

The effect of a double dactyl in "térrĭblĕ thúndĕrĭng" concludes this introduction to the "Human Fourfold."

The tenor of this passage and those which follow it is one of stately ceremony. There is a sense of decorum, surprising to find in Blake after all the contortions and ululations of *Jerusalem.* There is a feeling of alternating "expansion" of vision in such lines as:

Ănd thĕ dím Cháos brightend beneath, above, around: Éyed ăs the Peacock,
Accordĭng tŏ thĕ Húman Nerves of Sensatĭon, thĕ Fóur Rívĕrs ŏf thĕ Wáter of Life. (98.14–15)

and "contraction," when the human creatures look back on what is past and momentarily re-create its ugliness:

Where are the Kingdoms of the World & all their glory that grew on Desolation
The Fruit of Albions Poverty Tree when the Triple Headed Gog-Magog Giant
Of Albion Taxed the Nations into Desolation & then gave the Spectrous Oath (98.51–53)

But the final statement is that of harmony:

All Human Forms identified even Tree Metal Earth & Stone, all
Human Forms identified. living going forth & returning wearied
Into the Planetary lives of Years Months Days & Hours reposing,
And then Awaking into his Bosom in the Life of Immortality.

And I heard the Name of their Emanations they are named Jerusalem.
(99.1–5)

It is reasonable to ask, of *Jerusalem* and of the other Prophetic Books, whether the offspring justify the long travail. Do the many fine passages of poetry in *The Four Zoas* justify its disunity and the hectic, tortured tone of the whole? Does the firm oratory of *Milton* compensate for its tedious explanatory sections? Is the pilgrimage through *Jerusalem*, in whose dark caverns we hear almost nothing but the horrid clang of the Blake-Los hammer, made worthwhile by the ultimate emergence into daylight and the music of the spheres? Remember Johnson's remark about Milton's magnum opus, which seems even truer here: that it was admirable, but nobody ever wished it longer.

According to any conventional definition of a work of art, these would be flawed, uneven monsters whose defects greatly outweigh their virtues. Art must have its rules; Art must transform life's chaos to order; Art must create beauty from all things; Art must exhibit wholeness, harmony, radiance. But Blake, even in his metrics, deliberately breaks every rule he makes, refuses to impose order in art where there is no order in his visions, and insists, in his perverse honesty, on preserving every jot and tittle of man's foulness just as it stands, keeping beauty afar until he is ready for her. According to Blake's own expressive definition of art, he could have done no other.

The difficulty with expressivist poetry is that, by its nature, it refuses external standards of judgment. It insists that criteria of beauty, lucidity, wholeness, do not apply to it. If it is ugly, it was meant to express ugliness; if obscure, obscurity is its warp and woof; if fragmented, it will defend fragmentation as its necessary condition. You cannot declare that it is "good" or "bad" art, for it does not really care whether it is art or not. It would just as soon be something else, and if you require labels to your experiences, it does not care about you. All Blake's impulses—his didacticism, his passion for intellectual outline unblurred by sentiment, his obsession with liberty, his insistence on creating "a System" and setting it down in its entirety—converge to make the form of *Jerusalem*. Blake, like the parents of the Little Girl Lost, only

> Followed
> Where the vision led.

If the reader can enter into this form and find himself enlarged, so much the better. If not, so much the worse. This is a matter of taste and choice, as when two people go to a museum and look at some particularly grotesque Picasso. One says, "Ah, that man—he really has it. You just can't get around him." The other says, "Why didn't he just keep on doing more and more of those Blue Period things?"

For the reader who wants to give Blake the benefit of the doubt, the only possible help is repeated reading. One makes one's peace with the Prophetic Books, if at all, as the algebra student makes his peace with Imaginary Numbers. There is nothing in the real world to correspond to the square root of minus one; he is exasperated; but ambition, or his teacher, requires him to keep using the square root of minus one in equations until he grows to feel at home with it and becomes convinced that, real or unreal, the thing certainly is useful and probably makes sense. In the end, he is likely to feel that imaginary numbers are as true as anything else, and perhaps truer than most things.

Conclusion: The Place of Non-Artistic Art

Those men that in their writings are most wise
Own nothing but their blind, stupefied hearts.
(W. B. Yeats, "Ego Dominus Tuus")

We should not be surprised that Blake's Prophetic Books have not yet been popularly assimilated, considering the decades which passed before even his lyrics were taken seriously. The reactions of the great English Romantics to Blake's lyrics seem odd, now. Coleridge, perfunctorily responding to a Swedenborgian acquaintance who asked for comments on the *Songs*, shows a preference for *Innocence* over *Experience*, and for morally uplifting pieces like "A Divine Image," "Night," and "The Little Black Boy," over morally questionable ones like the "Chimney Sweeper," "Little Girl Lost," and "A Poison Tree" of *Experience*. He likes "The Tyger" quite well, but not among the best. His few and patronizing comments are either literal-minded or moralistic. He disapproves of the inaccurate line "Thou dost smile" of "Infant Joy," because a babe two days old does not smile. He thinks "A Little Girl Lost" should be omitted from the collection, "not for the want of innocence in the poem, but from the too probable want of it in many readers." Alas for Blake, who *in-*

tended the poem to reveal a want of innocence both in his heroine and in himself! And "The Little Vagabond," with its outspoken anticlericalism, Coleridge "cannot approve altogether," although he thinks it a good lesson to canting hypocrites. There is no indication that Coleridge found in these songs a religious sensibility as fierce as his own, or a symbolic gift as subtle.[1]

The recorded comments of other Romantics are even briefer than Coleridge's. Wordsworth, after reading a number of the *Songs*, remarks only: "There is no doubt this poor man was mad, but there is something in the madness of this man which interests me more than the sanity of Lord Byron and Walter Scott."[2] Nothing about the poetry. Lamb, having heard some of the poems recited, has "The Chimney Sweeper" of *Innocence* printed in *The Chimney Sweeper's Friend*, and reports that "The Tyger," which he misquotes, is "glorious." He too, however, seems most intrigued by the man, who he says in a letter is "flown, whither I know not—to Hades, or to a Mad House."[3] Southey in his *Doctor* (VI. 1847) prints the "Mad Song" as a piece of astonishing eccentricity. Landor is said to have been "strangely fascinated" by the writings of Blake, and gave his opinion in a notebook: "Blake: never did a braver or a better man carry the sword of justice."[4] He also "protested that Blake had been Wordsworth's prototype, and wished they could have divided his madness between them; for that some accession of it in the one case, and something of a diminution of it in the other, would have greatly improved both."[5]

One and all, the reactions are superficial. Time and propaganda,

[1] See Samuel Taylor Coleridge, *Letters*, ed. E. H. Coleridge (Boston and New York, 1895), II, 686–88; also B. R. McElderry, Jr., "Coleridge on Blake's Songs," *MLQ*, IX (1948), 298–302.

[2] Henry Crabb Robinson, *Reminiscences*, in Arthur Symons, *William Blake* (New York, 1907), p. 281.

[3] Charles and Mary Lamb, *Works*, ed. E. V. Lucas, 7 vols. (New York and London, 1903–5), VII, 642.

[4] Geoffrey Keynes, *A Bibliography of William Blake* (New York, 1921), p. 335.

[5] John Forster, *Walter Savage Landor, A Biography* (London, 1869), pp. 322–23.

evidently, were required to transform Blake's *Songs of Innocence and Experience* from curiosities to literature. Time and propaganda may yet perform the same task for his Prophetic Books. Rehabilitation has been and shall be required, because Blake is the Artist as Outlaw.

In the first part of "Notes from Underground," Dostoevsky's anti-hero imagines a Crystal Palace, the consummation of man's rationality, his sense of order and fitness, his ambitions for a happy society. The Crystal Palace attracts the Underground Man; he admires it. He also desires to thumb his nose at it; to smash it. Why? Because he feels that to suffer is to live; because he wishes to assert his one certain human quality, his free choice, his whim, and he cannot be sure that his choice is free unless it is to his own *dis*advantage; because, finally, "I admit that twice two makes four is an excellent thing, but if we are to give everything its due, twice two makes five is sometimes a very charming thing too." [6]

Both Dostoevsky and Blake insist on the sacredness of individual impulse as the only way to find out God. Dostoevsky has simply given the negative-thinking version of Blake's positive-thinking Proverbs: "If the fool would persist in his folly he would become wise." "No bird soars too high, if he soars with his own wings." "Sooner murder an infant in its cradle than nurse unacted desires." [7] In their effects, they are not too different. The Underground Man represents the perversity of utter hopelessness, Blake the perversity of utter idealism. One has the genius of disease, the other the genius of extreme health—which to the world looks like disease. Thus they share not only a common anti-rationality, but also a common alienation from all that is normal, expectable, suitable, all that embodies compromise. They share an impulse to smash.

Consider Blake's place, not only in the history of thought, but in

[6] Fyodor Dostoevsky, *The Short Novels of Dostoevsky*, trans. Constance Garnett (New York, 1945), p. 151.

[7] *MHH*, pp. 151, 152.

the history of art. Art, too, is a Crystal Palace perpetually under construction. It is both ornamental and useful, it both excites and consoles, it receives ideas, ideals, problems, paradoxes, yeas and nays, anger and joy, all things of any value, and cements them into its beautiful architecture. A William Blake happens by and tosses stones at it over his shoulder, partly from ignorance, a little from malice, with two results: he himself is sacrificed, he is not admitted into the palace; but the palace's inhabitants take his stones, polish them into jewels, make charming necklaces or little rock gardens of them, and are happier than before. Blake becomes aware of the palace, and decides he wants no part of it. He chooses larger stones, and begins to hurl them with deliberate aim. In the end, he is a small, solitary figure, feverishly deploying a complicated machine which catapults enormous, stupendous, mountainous boulders, one after another, through the shining walls. The palace remains as it was, and its inhabitants, when they encounter these boulders in their groves, can make nothing of them. The things are altogether too bulky, too monstrous, for any civilized use. They are also too difficult to remove. And so they stand, huge and undecorative, awaiting a craftsman.

Blake's two primary modes, the childlike lyric and the pounding prophetic, are both current today. But they appear in more civilized forms; that is, in forms more acceptable to the Crystal Palace.

Nobody in English literature has composed lyrics with quite the same extreme of a crude steady beat accented by very short lines, simple sentences, and repetitive language, modified by a roughened rhythm. Before him, no such verse existed. After him, there are many analogues.[8] Actually, the manner of *Innocence* and *Experience* is most nearly reproduced in nonliterary verse: in children's jingles, or in the sentimental, unsophisticated, amateur ditties of autograph albums, or school magazines, or daily newspapers. People who do not know how to write poetry write it like Blake.

[8] A good review article on Blake's influence is Kerker Quinn, "Blake and the New Age," *Virginia Quarterly*, XIII (1937), 271–85.

This mode, when practised by men who know how to write poetry, gives us polished stones, masterworks like Yeats' "Words for Music Perhaps" or Auden's series "Songs and Other Musical Pieces"; poems which are metrically quite similar to Blake's, with equivalent fluctuation of iambic, trochaic, and anapestic cadences, with similar short lines and frequent rhymes, the rhymes often careless like his, with emphatic basic beat and colloquial irregularity. In Yeats' case, the motive for simplicity resembles Blake's; Crazy Jane, the young girl, the young man, and Tom the Lunatic all are symbols of sensual or intellectual simplicity, figures stripped to bone, pure beings, as Blake's child was to Blake. In Auden there is a different kind of purity. His songs are songs of experience, ot evil in Blake's sense; their symbols are thus more diverse and more entwined with history and society, and their language more intellectual, more elaborate, more Latin. Still, the attempt to create an absolute harshness or hardness of surface, from which there should be no appeal, radically recalls Blake. A tiny gem like the second section of the "Song for St. Cecilia's Day" beginning "I cannot grow; / I have no shadow," in its economy, its repetition (especially of "I"), and its concreteness, is as much an inverted companion piece to Blake's "Infant Joy" as was his own "Infant Sorrow." Even the ironic fluency of pieces like "Lady, weeping at the crossroads" has its analogue in Blake's lyrics of smooth hypocrisy.

Yet Yeats and Auden, obviously, are professional poets in a way that Blake was not. The mode of simplicity is a chosen thing for them, one of many alternatives, where for Blake it was a necessity. Blake was primitive, they are primitivistic. When they don sackcloth, or go slumming in folk-forms of literature, they know what they are doing, and we know that they know, and in this mutual consciousness lies the subtlety of their gift to us. It is the dance, the ceremony, the game, the mask, not impulsive but learned and chosen, which distinguishes Art from Life, and which sometimes makes Art preferable to Life. But when Blake goes naked, we know that he has no choice, that he owns no clothing.

The prophetic mode, even more than the childlike or folk lyric, shuns the Crystal Palace of art. The prophet prides himself on being the lonely possessor of Truth in his time, and feels himself obliged to ram it down an unwilling public's throat. His isolation and his lust for combat lead him to espouse blatantly anti-traditional forms. His experiences of revelation, which, unlike the mystic's, are sudden and achieved without labor, make him scorn discipline and artifice. His impatience about changing the world expresses itself in the desire to overwhelm his readers, to hammer on their heads with words, until they surrender. He tries to convince not by persuasion, certainly not by reasons, but by the force of his images, by the persistent repetition of his ideas, by affecting a world-encompassing scope, and by the sheer bulk of his output.

When the prophet's gospel is one of freedom, as the message of the Hebrew prophets was not, his style often slides toward anarchy. If he writes prose, he may dabble in disordered syntax, catalogues and trains of images, heavy reliance on exclamation, anything that will bypass logic and orderly sequence. If he writes poetry, it is usually free verse. The nineteenth and twentieth centuries have fathered a brood of prophets, among whom, in America and England, may be counted such diverse characters as Carlyle, Whitman, D. H. Lawrence, Ezra Pound, and Henry Miller, all of whom except the first make liberty and spontaneity part of their creed. In today's anti-academic San Francisco movement, which encourages every man to hang out his prophet's shingle, we can see these ideals, pushed to extremes, exploding gorgeously and irresponsibly in prose and verse as consciously wanton in style as it is in thought.

Whitman, not Blake, is the spiritual sire of prophetic poetry today; and although Whitman read Blake in maturity, and D. H. Lawrence read him as a youth, and today's "hip" writers saturate themselves in him as in anything arcane, their mode is not quite his. Blake tried free verse on several occasions while he was developing his prophetic voice, but abandoned it. As an engraver, he was accustomed to a medium which resisted the craftsmen's hand, not one which yielded pliantly to it. Moreover, his libertarianism coexisted with a latent and then a realized Christianity which exacted an idea of order in the cosmos, in the individual, and in art. His last prophecies do not sidestep the issue of meter, but engage in mortal combat with it. This distinguishes his verse from the long-lined, evangelistic style of free verse, from Whitman to Allen Ginsberg, which most resembles his. The free verse is powerful, and creates a unified artistic effect, because it does not pretend to be anything but what it is: highly rhythmic language, not metered language. It is easy to read; we need only be receptive and let the waves of rhythm carry us. But in Blake's work there is a vicious wrestling between verse and prose, in which bones are broken and muscles horribly twisted, but neither side ever wins. This continual strain makes his prophetic books difficult, and often unpleasant, to read; and yet, in the teeth of artistic failure, Blake somehow seems larger, more inevitable, more a spiritual conqueror, than the others. He cannot be removed from the landscape.

APPENDIX A

Blake Versus Watts: Some Divine and Moral Rebuttals

Isaac Watts, one of that legion of pious people who read the Bible black where Blake read white, influenced the author of the *Songs of Innocence and Experience* in more than one way. His *Divine and Moral Songs*, "such as," he wrote, "I wish some happy and condescending genius would undertake for the use of children, and perform much better," were at once a model and a challenge to Blake.

In several cases, Watts' influence is fairly straightforward. His "Innocent Play," which informs children that they may learn much from the "cleanly and harmless" lambs, is a rudimentary version of one idea that Blake was trying to express in "The Lamb." In "The Sluggard," Watts has the line, "I pass'd by his garden and saw the wild brier." Blake took the image which Watts meant as a figure for spiritual idleness, and applied it to spiritual waste of a different kind in "The Garden of Love," where he finds the priests "binding with briars my joys and desires." Watts has poems on the fading of "The Rose," and the prudence of "The Ant, or Emmet," both designed to put children in mind of their latter ends. Blake also has poems on the rose and the emmet, although unlike Watts, he treats the plant and the insect as persons, not lessons. The parallel between Watts' "Cradle Hymn" and Blake's "Cradle Song" has already been discussed.

But a few of Watts' self-righteous effusions stung Blake to direct rebuttal. In "Praise for Mercies Spiritual and Temporal," Watts, or the child he speaks for, thanks his God that he is not like other men:

> Whene'er I take my walks abroad,
> How many poor I see!

It is, of course, the situation of "London." Watts continues:

> What shall I render to my God
> For all his gifts to me?
>
> No more than others I deserve,
> Yet God hath given me more;
> For I have food while others starve,
> Or beg from door to door. (p. 302)

He observes the hungry, unclothed, unhoused, and untaught "wretches," and humbly acknowledges that he does not deserve his own good food and clothing, warm bed, and firm moral training; but since God has seen fit to favor him, he will return the compliment:

> Then let me love thee more than they,
> And try to serve thee best.

Watts accepts both his own superiority, and the sufferings of the nonelect, with equanimity. All things are as they should be, as God has arranged. Blake, replying to Watts in "London," repeats the walk abroad, and the catalogue of wretches, but makes an opposite interpretation. He accepts nothing, least of all the God and King who symbolize the status quo. If, as I believe, Blake composed "London" with Watts' poem in mind, it is interesting to note one point of structural disparity. Watts rounds his poem off with a summary conclusion: since God has served him, he will serve God. His last stanza returns to his first. But "London" in effect has no last stanza. It stops in the air, with a ringing accusation, for Blake is saying that, unlike Watts, he not only is unable to reach a happy conclusion, but cannot reach any conclusion at all. The facts cry out for themselves, there is evil in the world, and he is speechless.

Another antagonizing poem was Watts' "Examples of Early Piety." Watts wrote:

> Jesus, who reigns above the sky,
> And keeps the world in awe,
> Was once a child as young as I,
> And kept his Father's law.
>
> At twelve years old he talk'd with men
> (The Jews all wondering stood)
> Yet he obey'd his mother then,
> And came at her command. (pp. 313–14)

Watts neatly suggests that the heavenly Father and the earthly parents had identical interests. Blake asserts otherwise, and makes Jesus a good example not for his obedience, but for his scorn:

> When twelve years old he ran away
> And left his Parents in dismay.
> When after three days' sorrow found,
> Loud as Sinai's trumpet sound:
> No Earthly Parents I confess—
> My Heavenly Father's business!
> Ye understand not what I say,
> And, angry, force me to obey.

"Obedience," Blake concludes ironically,

> is a duty then,
> And favor gains with God and Men. (*EG*, p. 748)

It gained favor with men like Watts, that is, and with Watts' God. The doctrine of obedience recurs in Watts' "Obedience to

Parents," where God and the earthly parents are once again identified. Watts is usually mild and abstract—Blake would say hypocritical—in his descriptions of punishment, but here he forgets himself:

> Have you not heard what dreadful plagues
> Are threaten'd by the Lord,
> To him that breaks his father's law,
> Or mocks his mother's word?
>
> What heavy guilt upon him lies!
> How cursed is his name!
> The ravens shall pick out his eyes,
> And eagles eat the same. (p. 324)

Blake was shocked, and vented his shock in "A Little Boy Lost" of *Experience*, whose title is at once a bitter play on the concept of "the lost soul," and a lament for the loss of life. Giving Watts the benefit of the doubt, he supposes that the "father's law" is the Law of Love, and that the rebellious little boy is a little rationalist. These are the two assumptions behind the poem's first stanza, which is the boy's speech:

> Nought loves another as itself
> Nor venerates another so.
> Nor is it possible to Thought
> A greater than itself to know.
> (*Experience*, p. 218)

Blake did not accept the little boy's premise that self is all-in-all, and he would have asserted that if "Thought" cannot discover anything greater than self, we must discover an alternative to Thought. But he does admire the boy's independence. Even Love cannot succeed as a law. It must be found independently by the casting-off of error and selfhood. If this little boy were left alone, he might in time discover Love.

Blake's second stanza draws the boy out of Watts' generalizing, and into individuality:

> And, Father, how can I love you
> Or any of my brothers more?
> I love you like the little bird
> That picks up crumbs around the door.

But then the Priest enters; and

> Lo! what a fiend is here! said he.

This corresponds to Watts' exclamation, "What heavy guilt upon him lies!" But because Blake's boy has already been made to seem alive and normal, instead of being merely a cipher labeled "Disobedience," the absurdity is evident. By a slight recasting of Watts' poem into dramatic form, Blake lets Watts convict himself.

This is still more apparent in Blake's conclusion. Watts implies that vengeance is impersonally meted out by God through natural agents, the raven and eagle. In effect, he is trying to escape personal responsibility. But Blake pins him down. Ravens and eagles will not do, even as figures of speech. It is not God, nor birds, but human beings—Priests, weeping but ineffectual parents, and "all" who "admir'd the Priestly care"—who cause little boys to be stripped to their little shirts, bound in iron chains, and burned in holy places where many have been burned before. If the implication is not clear enough, Blake confirms it in the last lines:

> The weeping parents wept in vain.
> Are such things done on Albion's shore?

They are done, says Blake, by sanctimonious moralists like Watts, who disguise intolerance and cruelty under the holy names of God and Love.

APPENDIX B

Incidence of False Rhymes

The table on the following page shows the frequency of false rhyme at several stages of Blake's lyric work. Eye-rhyme has words with like terminations in spelling, but the vowels pronounced differently (e.g., love-move), and is conventionally accepted throughout English poetry. Off-rhyme has the consonants alike but the vowels differing (e.g., shade-bed). Assonance has the vowels alike but the consonants differing (e.g., gold-rode). Proportions are given to the nearest 0.5%. For comparison, I have also taken the proportions in 100 lines each of Collins, Gray, Coleridge, and Shelley.

The comparison shows that Blake differs most from the other poets in his use of off-rhyme. But this is also the area in which his radicalism declines most sharply as he ages; although he begins with a higher incidence of off-rhyme than Shelley, who was noted for his carelessness, he ends with a considerably lower one. It is also noteworthy that, although the incidence of assonance in Blake is very slight, it is still higher than that of the other poets, who, except for Shelley, have none.

	Total No. Rhymes	Eye-Rhymes %	Off-Rhymes %	Asso-nance %	Total False Rhymes %
PS *1769–78*	164	6.5	15	2.5	24
Innocence *1789*	244	5	13.5	1.5	20
Experience *1789–94*	147	6	6	.5	12.5
Notebook *c. 1800–3*	113	8	2.5	—	10.5
Pickering MS *c. 1803*	201	4.5	5	.5	10
Notebook *c. 1808–11*	250	4.5	2.5	1.5	8.5
Collins	100	2	2	—	4
Gray	100	6	5	—	11
Coleridge	100	7	3	—	10
Shelley	100	10	10	1	21

Index